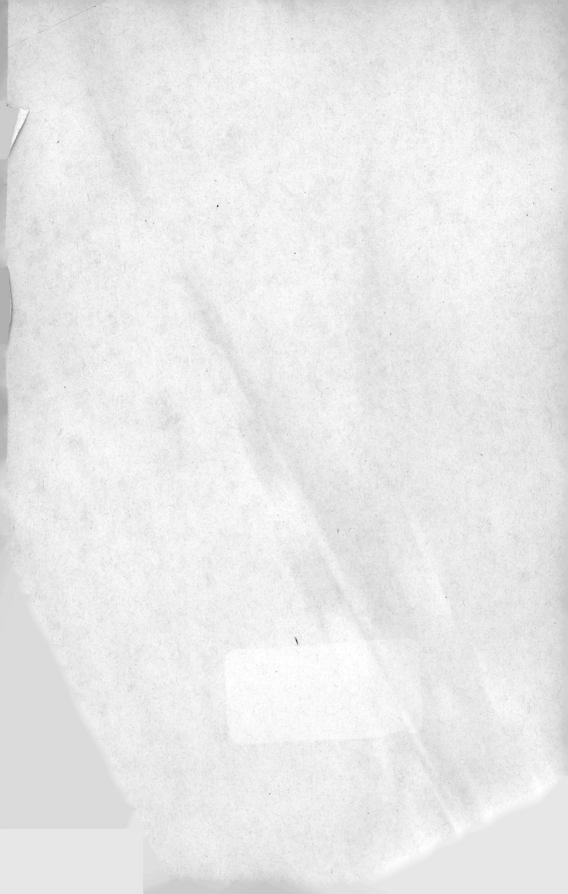

Lecture Notes of the Institute for Computer Sciences, Social Informatics and Telecommunications Engineering 496

The LNICST series publishes ICST's conferences, symposia and workshops.

LNICST reports state-of-the-art results in areas related to the scope of the Institute.
The type of material published includes

- Proceedings (published in time for the respective event)
- Other edited monographs (such as project reports or invited volumes)

LNICST topics span the following areas:

- General Computer Science
- E-Economy
- E-Medicine
- Knowledge Management
- Multimedia
- Operations, Management and Policy
- Social Informatics
- Systems

Qi Jiang · Xinghua Li · Ding Wang

Editors

Security and Privacy in New Computing Environments

5th EAI International Conference, SPNCE 2022
Xi'an, China, December 30–31, 2022
Proceedings

Springer

Editors
Qi Jiang (ID)
Xidian University
Xi'an, China

Xinghua Li
Xidian University
Xi'an, China

Ding Wang (ID)
Nankai University
Tianjin, China

ISSN 1867-8211 ISSN 1867-822X (electronic)
Lecture Notes of the Institute for Computer Sciences, Social Informatics
and Telecommunications Engineering
ISBN 978-3-031-30622-8 ISBN 978-3-031-30623-5 (eBook)
https://doi.org/10.1007/978-3-031-30623-5

This Springer imprint is published by the registered company Springer Nature Switzerland AG
The registered company address is: Gewerbestrasse 11, 6330 Cham, Switzerland

Preface

We are delighted to introduce the proceedings of the fifth edition of the European Alliance for Innovation (EAI) International Conference on Security and Privacy in New Computing Environments, SPNCE 2022. This conference, held December 30–31 in Xi'an, China, brought together researchers, developers, and practitioners around the world who are leveraging and developing security and privacy in new computing environments. The theme of SPNCE 2022 was "Data and network security: Authentication, Auditing, and Trust".

The technical program of SPNCE 2022 consisted of 12 full papers, comprising 10 papers accepted in the main tracks and 2 papers accepted in the fast track. Aside from the high-quality technical paper presentations, the technical program also featured one keynote speech. The keynote speaker was Weizhi Meng from Technical University of Denmark, Denmark.

Coordination with the steering chairs, Imrich Chlamtac and Ding Wang, was essential for the success of the conference. We sincerely appreciate their constant support and guidance. It was also a great pleasure to work with such an excellent organizing committee team for their hard work in organizing and supporting the conference. In particular, we are grateful to the Technical Program Committee, who completed the peer-review process from 38 submissions each paper secured at least three single-blind reviews for technical papers and helped to put together a high-quality technical program. We are also grateful to all the authors who submitted their papers to the SPNCE 2022 conference.

We strongly believe that the SPNCE conference provides a good forum for all researchers, developers, and practitioners to discuss all science and technology aspects that are relevant to new computing environments. We also expect that the future SPNCE conferences will be as successful and stimulating as this year's, as indicated by the contributions presented in this volume.

January 2023

Qi Jiang
Xinghua Li
Ding Wang
Debiao He
Joseph Liu
Shujun Li

Organization

Steering Committee

Chair

Imrich Chlamtac   University of Trento, Italy

Member

Ding Wang   Nankai University, China

Organizing Committee

General Co-chairs

Debiao He   Wuhan University, China
Joseph Liu   Monash University, Australia

Technical Program Committee Chairs

Xinghua Li   Xidian University, China
Ding Wang   Nankai University, China

Technical Program Committee Co-chair

Shujun Li   University of Kent, UK

Web Chairs

Qingxuan Wang   Nankai University, China
Guichuan Zhao   Xidian University, China

Publicity and Social Media Chairs

Hao Wang   Shandong Normal University, China
Jianbing Ni   Queen's University, Canada
Junwei Zhang   Xidian University, China

Workshops Chairs

Youliang Tian   Guizhou University, China
Ning Lu   Northeastern University at Qinhuangdao, China

Sponsorship and Exhibits Chairs

Wenbo Shi   Northeastern University at Qinhuangdao, China
Jian Shen   Nanjing University of Information Science &
                                     Technology, China

Publications Chairs

Jinbo Xiong   Fujian Normal University, China
Xiong Li   University of Electronic Science and Technology
                                     of China, China

Local Chair

Xindi Ma   Xidian University, China

Technical Program Committee

Xiaochun Cheng   Middlesex University, UK
Haipeng Cai   Washington State University, USA
Kai Chen   Institute of Information Engineering, Chinese
                                     Academy of Sciences, China
Kim-Kwang Raymond Choo   University of Texas at San Antonio, USA
Long Cheng   Clemson University, USA
Rongmao Chen   National University of Defense Technology,
                                     China
Xiaofeng Chen   Xidian University, China
Yi Deng   State Key Laboratory of Information Security,
                                     China
Ashok Kumar Das   Indian Institute of Technology Kharagpur, India

Longjiang Qu	National University of Defense Technology, China
Dimitrios Papadopoulos	HKUST, China
Bo Qin	Renming University, China
Michael Scott	MIRACL Labs, Ireland
Chao Shen	Xi'an Jiaotong University, China
Chunhua Su	University of Aizu, Japan
Jian Shen	Nanjing University of Information Science & Technology, China
Kun Sun	George Mason University, USA
Shifeng Sun	Monash University, Australia
Qingni Shen	Peking University, China
Salman Salamatian	MIT, USA
Ni Trieu	Oregon State University, USA
Yuan Tian	University of Virginia, USA
Junfeng Tian	Hebei University, China
Lei Wang	Shanghai Jiao Tong University, China
Qianhong Wu	Beihang University, China
Jianfeng Wang	Xidian University, China
Qian Wang	Wuhan University, China
Wei Wang	Beijing Jiaotong University, China
Zhe Xia	Wuhan University Of Technology, China
Liang Xiao	Xiameng University, China
Xiang Xie	PlatON, China
Peng Xu	Huazhong University of Science and Technology, China
Kuo-Hui Yeh	National Dong Hwa University, Taiwan
Min Yang	Fudan University, China
Kang Yang	State Key Laboratory of Cryptology, China
Hongyu Yang	Civil Aviation University of China, China
Xu Yang	Swinburne University of Technology, Australia
Danfeng (Daphne) Yao	Virginia Tech, USA
Heng Yin	University of California, Riverside, USA
Yu Yu	Shanghai Jiaotong University, China
Yong Yu	Shaanxi Normal University, China
Fangguo Zhang	Sun Yat-sen University, China
Jiang Zhang	State Key Laboratory of Cryptology, China
Mingwu Zhang	Hubei University of Technology, China
Yang Zhang	CISPA, Germany
Yunkai Zou	Nankai University, China
Yuexin Zhang	Deakin University, Australia
Rossi Kamal	Community Chain, Bangladesh

Qingfeng Cheng	PLA Information Engineering University, China
Xuexian Hu	PLA Information Engineering University, China
Fushan Wei	PLA Information Engineering University, China
Lei Wu	Shandong Normal University, China
Min Luo	Wuhan University, China
Cong Peng	Wuhan University, China
Fan Wu	Xiamen University Tan Kah Kee College, China
Yongjun Ren	Nanjing University of Information Science & Technology, China
Tao Wang	Shanxi Normal University, China
Zhuo Ma	Xidian University, China
Xuewen Dong	Xidian University, China
Liguo Zhang	Harbin Engineering University, China
Jinbo Xiong	Fujian Normal University, China
Ning Lu	Northeastern University at Qinhuangdao, China
Xindi Ma	Xidian University, China

Contents

Network Security

Authentication and Key Agreement

User Authentication Using Body Vibration Characteristics

Y. Zhang$^{(\boxtimes)}$ and Y. Ren

University of Electronic Science and Technology of China, No. 2006, Xiyuan Avenue, High tech Zone (West Zone), Chengdu, People's Republic of China
zhangyx_128@foxmail.com, renyanzhi05@uestc.edu.cn

Abstract. Traditional mobile phone authentication systems are based on knowledge or biological information. This paper shows an authentication system based on human vibration characteristics and implement it on smartphone. This kind of inspiration comes from signal transmitted based on solid conduction and is applied to the link between vibration motor and accelerometer. Therefore, we designed a system to extract user biometric features by active vibration. However, there is a great challenge for smartphone systems with low sampling rate and requiring real-time response. Therefore, we would realize the system through multiple signal processing stages rather than choose a high-performance neural network. Our system solves the problem of low sampling rate of mobile phone sensors through supersampling reconstruction method. Besides, we select appropriate statistical features and MFCC-based features through PCA algorithm, and finally complete the training through Gradient Boosting Tree. In order to avoid the threshold division problem of the multi-level classifier, we train each sample in two classifications at the time of registration, and store the parameters in the user profile. When the system performs user authentication, the user data is divided into five sections for testing, so as to increase the robustness of the system. Our approach could achieve short-time identity authentication, with an average accuracy rate of 85.3%.

Keywords: Vibration · Authentication · Mobile Sensing

1 Introduction

The convenience of mobile devices such as smartphones and smartwatches has greatly stimulated the development of the mobile industry in recent years. However, although users can enjoy the great convenience brought by mobile devices, the widespread use of mobile devices and mobile applications has caused major security problems [1]. For example, most applications need to obtain permissions such as user location and phone information. Therefore, identification and verification before using mobile devices has become the first barrier to protect data security.

© ICST Institute for Computer Sciences, Social Informatics and Telecommunications Engineering 2023
Published by Springer Nature Switzerland AG 2023. All Rights Reserved
Q. Jiang et al. (Eds.): SPNCE 2022, LNICST 496, pp. 3–14, 2023.
https://doi.org/10.1007/978-3-031-30623-5_1

Nowadays, the identity authentication process of smart phones mainly involves some traditional solutions, including PIN, fingerprint identification, face recognition, etc. In the U.S. consumer payment study, 66% of users set PINs and passwords as the first choice in smartphone authentication. Although PINs based authentication methods are easy to use and widely deployed, they also have the problem of password leakage. For example, people have been able to crack it through shoulder-surfing [2]. Besides, many studies show that attackers can infer your mobile phone's PIN through wifi signals [3]. Although the decryption cost of attackers will increase with the increase of PIN's complexity, it increases the burden of users' memory.

In addition, attackers can forge users' physiological and biometric information (such as fingerprints and faces) to deceive the system. If the user loses such information, authentication based on physiological biometrics will be permanently insecure. For example, researchers found that fingerprint based authentication security may suffer from smudge attacks [4] and the attacker can spoof face recognition by 3D masks using micro-texture analysis [5,6]. Therefore, we need to design a new biometric-based identity authentication method.

Moreover, high accuracy means expensive sensor costs. For most smartphone manufacturers, the hardware cost of smartphones is also an important fact to be considered. High performance sensors not only increase the cost of mobile phones, but also take up a lot of internal space of mobile phones. For example, the iris reader [7] of Samsung smartphones and the depth camera [8] of iPhone are expensive and vulnerable, so it is particularly critical to find an alternative authentication method.

Based on the existing research results, this paper focuses on the biological characteristics of the human body stimulated by vibration signals, and completes the training of the identity verification system by filtering and feature extraction of vibration signals. The main contributions of this work are summarized as follows: (1) Exploring the feasibility of smart phone authentication through the accelerometer and the vibration motor. (2) We analyze the signals with different vibration frequencies, study their influence on feature selection, and provide solutions to meet the needs of most existing mobile phone hardware devices. (3) For different environmental conditions, we propose an optimization algorithm to reduce the interference of noise to the system, so as to improve the stability of the system.

2   Background

We think that the vibration motor and accelerometer of the mobile phone work together as a system. The vibration wave generated by the vibration motor propagates through the surface of the mobile phone and is received by the accelerometer [9]. When propagating, when the vibration wave meets two different media boundaries, the vibration wave will form energy attenuation and multipath interference. Figure 1 shows reflection and diffraction of a vibration signal propagating on a solid surface. Since the transmitted vibration signal reaches the accelerometer through reflection and diffraction, the accelerometer will have unique vibration characteristics (such as wave attenuation and multipath interference), so it can be used to identify intelligent devices [10].

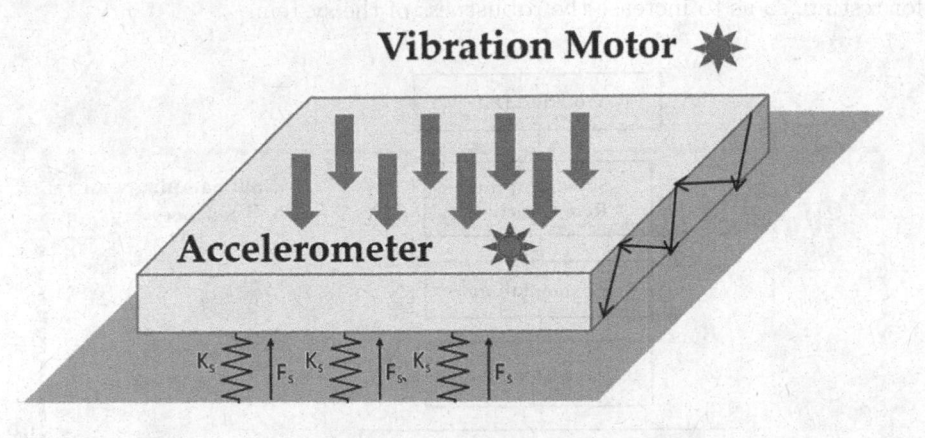

Fig. 1. Vibration signal propagation.

Figure 1 shows the force condition of the mobile phone screen when the vibration motor is working. When the user touches the mobile phone with his hand, a downforce shock wave is generated on the mobile phone screen, which affects the propagation path of the vibration signal. Where k_s is the effective spring constant and k_d is the damping coefficient. If the vertical displacement of the surface is x, we have

$$F_t = K_d \left(\frac{d}{dt} \right) x + K_s x + M \left(\frac{d}{dt} \right)^2 x \tag{1}$$

This indicates that the finger touching force could be captured by analyzing the received vibration signals and utilized as a biometric-associated feature in our system.

In addition, some experiment demonstrate that the vibration energy absorbed into the human finger-hand-arm system is different under different vibration frequencies [11]. Therefore, we will explore the impact of vibration frequency on the authentication system in the following sections.

3   System Overview

In this section, we introduce a verification method based on human biological characteristics corresponding to vibration. As shown in Fig. 2, our system solves the problem of low sampling rate of mobile phone sensors through supersampling reconstruction method. Besides, we select appropriate statistical features and

MFCC-based features through PCA algorithm, and finally complete the training through Gradient Boosting Tree. In order to avoid the threshold division problem of the multi-level classifier, we train each sample in two classifications at the time of registration, and store the parameters in the user profile. When the system performs user authentication, the user data is divided into five sections for testing, so as to increase the robustness of the system.

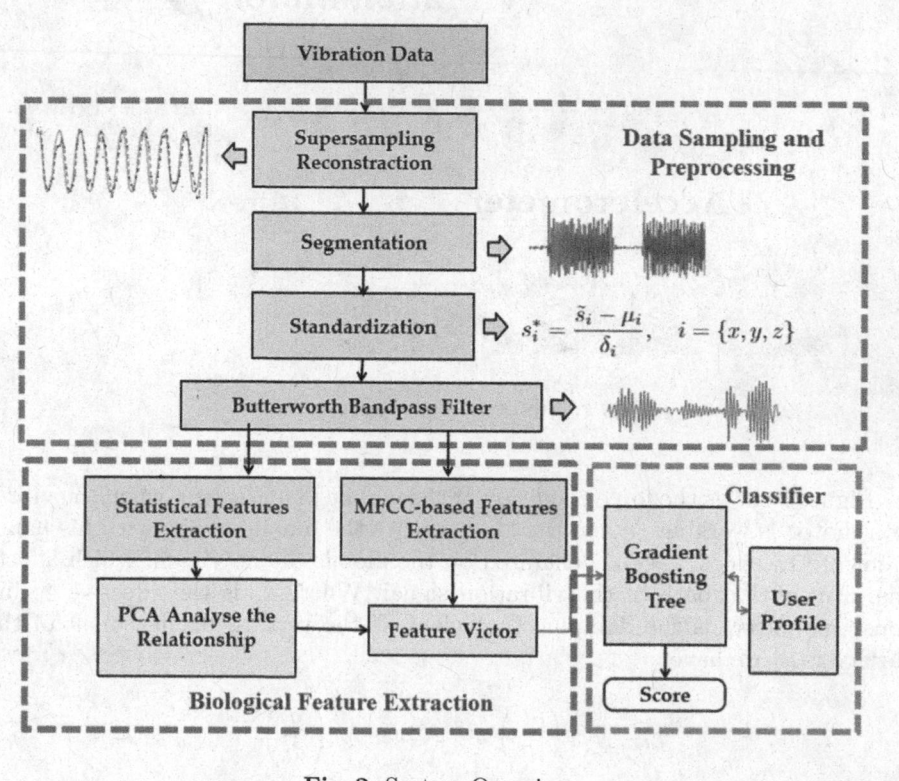

Fig. 2. System Overview.

3.1 Data Sampling and Preprocessing

Supersampling Reconstruction Method. According to the Nyquist Sampling Law, the low sampling rate results in the distortion of vibration waveform in the time-domain. Because we need to use the amplitude peak value as the signal characteristic in the subsequent work, this will lead to the increase of measurement error. The accelerometer in iPhone 7 supports the maximum sampling rate 100 Hz, which is much less than the frequency of vibro-motor at 167 Hz [12]. So we have to adopt the sampling rate up 400 Hz.

Due to realize this supersampling reconstruction method(SSR), the signal needs to have sufficient stability. For example, as shown in Fig. 3, put two signals with different resolutions on the same time axis, and find the sum of the minimized variances of the corresponding points. After calculation, the sum of the minimized variables of the corresponding points is extremely small. This means that we can obtain 400 Hz signal through the supersampling construction method

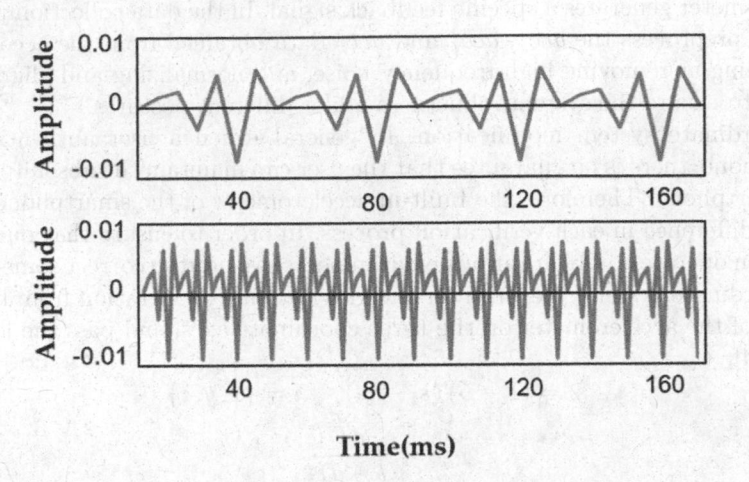

Fig. 3. Comparison of different frequency signals.

The specific method is that we can sample the same value instead of recording all signals for the current signal with too low sampling rate [13]. For example, if different sampling points are sampled in each cycle and timestamps are recorded, there will be a large number of labeled sampling points after several cycles. Next, we will combine them into a complete cycle and sort them.

But the more complicated problem is the determination of the sampling interval. It can be seen from the Fourier transform formula that,

$$X\left(e^{j\omega}\right) = \sum_{n=1}^{N} x\left[t_n\right] e^{-j\omega t_n} \tag{2}$$

When t_n is replaced by an arbitrary random number, the discrete fourier transform will introduce random noise in the frequency domain. Here we assume that the time t_n follows a uniform distribution, and the expectation of the spectrum can be obtained as follows:

$$
\begin{aligned}
E\left[X\left(e^{j\omega}\right)\right] &= \frac{1}{T_{\max}} \sum_{n=1}^{N} \int_0^{T_{\max}} x\left[t_n\right] e^{-j\omega t_n} dt_n \\
&= \frac{N}{T_{\max}} X(j\omega)
\end{aligned}
\tag{3}
$$

In our system, we set the cycle composition of 0.5 s active vibration and t_{gap} to 5 ms to apply SRR for four cycle reconstruction.

Standardization and Filtering. When the smartphone's motor vibrates, the accelerometer generates a specific feedback signal. In the data collection part, we need to preprocess the acc_x, acc_y and acc_z data obtained from the accelerometer, aiming at removing high-frequency noise, and normalizing and aligning the signals to ensure the system robustness under different postures.

Coordinate system modification. In general, when a user authenticates a smartphone, there is no guarantee that the user can maintain the absolute level of the smartphone. Therefore, the built-in accelerometer of the smartphone makes a huge difference in each verification process. In order to ensure that our equipment can operate stably in various environments, we need to correct some data of the coordinate system. We subtract the gravitational acceleration from the projection of the accelerometer on the three coordinate axes, and pass the low-pass filter [14].

$$\tilde{s}_i = (1 - \beta)(s_i - g_i), \quad i = \{x, y, z\} \tag{4}$$

$$\beta = \frac{dT}{t + dT} \tag{5}$$

where g_i and s_i are the projection of the gravitational acceleration and raw acceleration captured by the accelerometer along the i-th axis, respectively; $\tilde{s}_i$ is the associated acceleration after such an alignment; β is a filter factor determined by filter's time constant t and event delivery rate dT. In this work, we empirically choose β to be 0.2.

The accelerations and angular velocities collected by accelerometers and gyroscopes differ greatly among the three directions, even more among different device models. To ensure the numerical comparability and analysis stability, our system applies the Z_score standardization method [15] to the readings from each axis as follows:

$$s_i^* = \frac{\tilde{s}_i - \mu_i}{\delta_i}, \quad i = \{x, y, z\} \tag{6}$$

where $\tilde{s}$ is a single reading along the i-th axis after filtering, μ_i and δ_i are the mean and standard deviation of all $\tilde{s}$ along the same axis respectively. After the standardization, s_i^* is centered at 0 and scaled to have the standard deviation of 1. See Fig. 4 for the normalized signal.

For noise interference brought by the environment, such as music and thermal noise, and interference, such as arm movement and shaking, we choose a low-pass filter to reduce these effects. Through analysis, it can be found that the frequency of the built-in vibration motor of existing smartphones is generally between 150–250 Hz, while the motion frequency of humans is 10 Hz [16]. Therefore we develop a Butterworth bandpass using the cutting-off frequencies 10 Hz 250 Hz to filter the vibration noises and interferences outside this range. The filtered signal image is shown in Fig. 4.

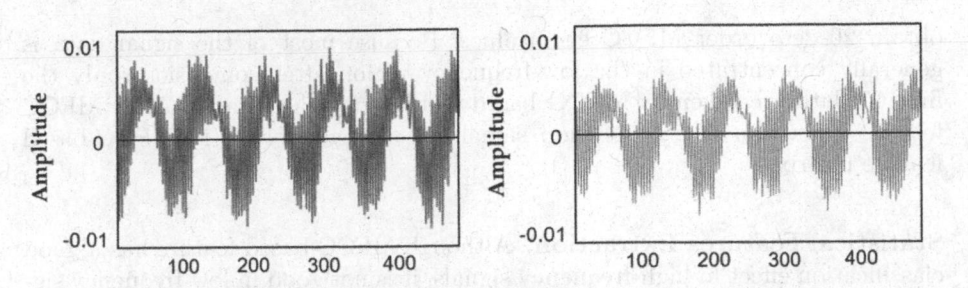

Fig. 4. Comparison before and after standardization and filtering.

3.2 Feature Extraction

MFCC-based Feature Extraction. The Mel-frequency cepstral coefficient (MFCC) is widely used to represent the short-term power spectrum of acoustic or vibration signals [17] and can represent the dynamic features of the signals with both linear and nonlinear properties. While the MFCCs are able to distinguish people's sound differences in speech and voice recognition, we find that they can also characterize the vibration signals transmitting via the medium of a solid surface on which the user's finger touches [18]. The MFCC feature extraction process is shown in the Fig. 5, mainly including pre emphasis, framing, windowing, fast Fourier transform (FFT), Mel filter bank, discrete cosine transform (DCT). Among them, FFT and Mel filter bank are the most important.

$$mfcc(i,n) = \sum_{m=1}^{M} \log[H(i,m)] \cdot \cos\left[\frac{\pi \cdot n \cdot (2m-1)}{2M}\right] \qquad (7)$$

$$K(i) = 1 + \left(\frac{L}{2}\right) \cdot \sin\left(\frac{\pi \cdot i}{L}\right) \quad i = 1, 2, 3 \ldots, 13 \qquad (8)$$

where M represents the number of Mel filters, i represents the data of the i-th frame, and n represents the n-th column of the i-th frame (the value range of n is 1–26). In our system, we calculate the MFCCs of each segment of signal. We set 26 Mayer filters and calculate in each 50 ms the Hamming window to

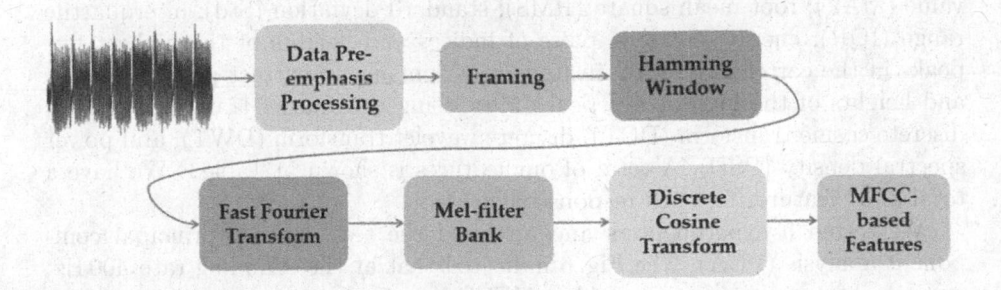

Fig. 5. MFCC Flowchart.

obtain 26 zero order MFCC eigenvalues. Because most of the signal data is generally concentrated in the low-frequency region after conversion, only the first 13 data are taken as MFCC based features for each frame. After MFCC feature extraction of 5S vibration signal, we can get a 11×13 MFCC-based feature matrix.

Statistical Features Extraction. Although MFCC-based feature has a good classification effect in high-frequency signals, it is not good in low-frequency signals. This makes it particularly difficult to classify different users simply through MFCC-based features. Therefore, we need to obtain more information of the low-frequency part from the time-domain and frequency-domain of the signal, considering of statistical features along with pairs of peak indicators and heights in the frequency domain and in the correlation of time domain.

Table 1. The total of 32 features for each response signal.

Abbreviation	Explaination
Var	variance
MAV	mean absolute value
RMS	root mean square
Std	standard deviation
IOR	interquartile range
Energy	Integral of square of signal amplitude
Entropy	Shannon entropy of continuous time series
Correlation	pairs of indices and heights of the highest five peaks
FFT	pairs of indices and heights of the highest five peaks
DCT	pairs of indices and heights of the highest five peaks
DWT	pairs of indices and heights of the highest five peaks
PSD	pairs of indices and heights of the highest five peaks

In the time domain, the statistical features are variance (Var); mean absolute value (MAV); root mean square (RMS); standard deviation (Std); interquartile range (IQR); energy; entropy; pairs of indices and heights of the highest five peaks in the correlation. Also, in frequency domain, we extract pairs of indices and heights of the highest five peaks after using fast fourier transform (FFT), discrete cosine transform (DCT), discrete wavelet transform (DWT), and power spectral density (PSD). A total of our features is shown in Table 1. We have a total of 32 features for each response signal.

We tested 5 experimenters and analyzed the test data by principal component analysis (PCA). The Fig. 6 indicated that at the sampling rate 400 Hz, statistical features are associated but MFCC-base features are loosely associated. Therefore, it is necessary to combine them as input features of classifier.

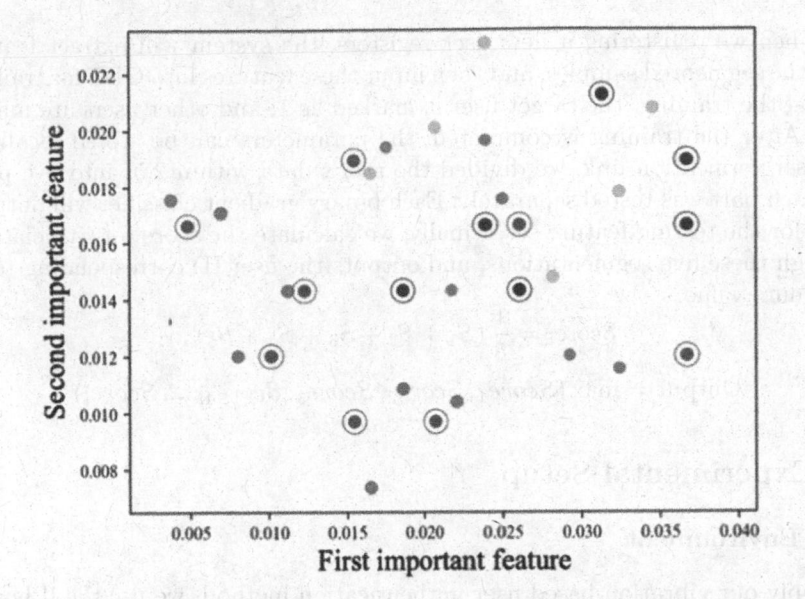

Fig. 6. User classification based on MFCC features and statistical features.

3.3   User Classification

We build a binary classifier for each user by using the Gradient Boosting Tree (GBT). We choose GBT mainly because (1) GBT is famous for its robustness to various types of features with different scales, which is the exact case in our project (e.g., the energy of the vibration signal is around 5, and the coefficients are the numbers fluctuated around 0 with value less than 1). Therefore, GBT would eliminate the efforts to normalize or whiten the feature data before classification. (2) GBT classifier is robust to the collinearity of feature data. Because our features are heterogeneous across different domains, it may result in unexpected correlation or unbalance ranges that possess the collinearity [19]. This means that we do not need to analyze the correlation of features, thus reducing the complexity of the algorithm.

Given N training samples (x_i, y_i), where x_i and y_i represent the feature vector (including statistical features and MFCC-based features) and corresponding user label (i.e., $y_i = 1$ or 0 represents whether x_i is from corresponding user), GBT seeks a function to iteratively select weak learners h_j and their weight ω_j to minimise the loss function [20].

$$\phi(x_i) = \sum_{m=1}^{M} \omega_m h_m(x_i) \tag{9}$$

We adopt the GBT implementation from the library of SQBlib, such as enough shrinkage (i.e., 0.1) and number of iterations (i.e., M = 2000). The above parameters adopted in GBT are optimized in terms of the speed and accuracy based on our empirical study.

When we registering a new user registers, the system will extract features from the segmented samples, and then input these features into GBT for training. During the training, the target user is marked as 1, and other users are marked as 0. After the training is completed, the parameters can be stored locally. In the user verification link, we divided the user's data within 2.5s into five parts, and each part was tested separately. Each binary gradient classifier will output a score for the testing feature set. Finally, we calculate the score for i-th classifier through these five segmentations, and outputs the user ID corresponding to the maximum value.

$$\text{Score}_i = \frac{1}{5}\left(S_1 + S_2 + S_3 + S_4 + S_5\right) \tag{10}$$

$$\text{Output} = \max\left(Score_1, Score_2, Score_3, Score_4, ..., Score_i\right) \tag{11}$$

4 Experimental Setup

4.1 Environment

To apply our vibration-based user authentication method, we use the iPhone 7, which can represent the basic performance of most mobile phones at present. The vibration frequency of vibro-motor was 167 Hz, and the accelerometer's sampling rate 100 Hz. The difference in waiting time was 50 ms, and we stopped sampling after the motor restarts five times.

4.2 System Performance

Here, we utilize the false rejection rate (FRR) and false acceptance rate (FAR) as metrics to evaluate the authentication accuracy of our system. FAR is the fraction of other users' data that are misclassified as the legitimate user's. FRR is the fraction of the legitimate user's data that are misclassified as other users' data. For security protection, a large FAR is more harmful than a large FRR. However, a large FRR would degrade the usage convenience.

To verify t effectiveness of our proposed model and techniques, we first collected 50 sets of data on a stationary desktop, and 50 sets of data during hand lifting from 3 experimenters, and the data time of each group was 2.5 s, forming a total of 800 samples. We utilized 10 fold cross validation for training and testing, and obtained the results shown in the Table 2.

Table 2. The FRR,FAR and accuracy of system.

State	FRR	FAR	Accuracy
Static	13.3%	8.5%	90.1%
Movement	17.5%	11.9%	85.3%

To explore the relationship between sample length and accuracy, we tested the changes of FRR and FAR under different sample lengths. The results are shown in the Fig. 7.

We found that with the increase of the sample length, the accuracy of the verification continued to rise. However, since the system needs to provide a better user experience, we believe that when the sample length is greater than 2.5 s, the small improvement in accuracy obtained by increasing the length is not cost-effective. In addition, with the increasing sampling rate of mobile phone sensors, the final accuracy of the system is also improving. This means that the technology has a higher upper limit in the future.

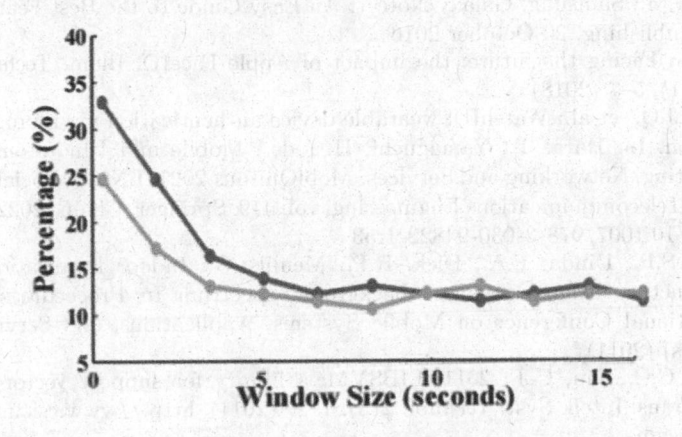

Fig. 7. FRR and FAR under different sample lengths.

5   Conclusion

In this paper, we proposed a vibration-based user authentication method for smartphone, which does not require user's personal information or privacy. We evaluated our method on a commercial smartphone, the iPhone 7, and default vibration types officially provided, which means no additional devices are required to authenticate users. In addition, our method produced a low EER of 0.147 for short-term signals. We expect our method to be suitable for a wide variety of smartphone on the market today.

References

1. Mayrhofer, R., Gellersen, H.: Shake well before use: intuitive and secure pairing of mobile devices. Mob. Comput. IEEE Trans. **8**(9), 729–806 (2009)
2. Chong, M.K., Mayrhofer, R., Gellersen, H.: A survey of user interaction for spontaneous device association. ACM Comput. Surv. (CSUR) **47**(1), 8:1–8:40 (2014)

3. Li, M., et al.: When CSI meets public WiFi: inferring your mobile phone password via WiFi signals. In: Proceedings of the 2016 ACM SIGSAC Conference on Computer and Communications Security, ACM, 2016, pp. 1068–1079 (2016)
4. Von Zezschwitz, E., Koslow, A., De Luca, A., Hussmann, H.: Making graphic-based authentication secure against smudge attacks. In: Proceedings of the 2013 International Conference on Intelligent User Interfaces, ACM, 2013, pp. 277–286 (2013)
5. Määttä, J., Hadid, A., Pietikäinen, M.: Face spoofing detection from single images using micro-texture analysis. In: Biometrics (IJCB), 2011 International Joint Conference on, IEEE, 2011, pp. 1–7 (2011)
6. Erdogmus, N., Marcel, S.: Spoofing face recognition with 3D masks. IEEE Trans. Inf. Forensics Secur. 9(7), 1084–1097 (2014)
7. Galleso, M.: Samsung, Galaxy Note 7: An Easy Guide to the Best Features, First Rank Publishing, 20 October 2016
8. Bud, A.: Facing the future: the impact of Apple FaceID. Biom. Technol. Today 12018(1), 5–7 (2018)
9. Cheng, J.Q., et al.: WatchID: wearable device authentication via reprogrammable vibration. In: Hara, T., Yamaguchi, H. (eds.) Mobile and Ubiquitous Systems: Computing, Networking and Services. MobiQuitous 2021. LNICS, Social Informatics and Telecommunications Engineering, vol. 419. Springer, Cham (2022). https://doi.org/10.1007/978-3-030-94822-1_53
10. Tarzia, S.P., Dinda, P.A., Dick, R.P., Memik, G.: Indoor localization without infrastructure using the acoustic background spectrum. In: Proceedings of the 9th International Conference on Mobile Systems, Applications, and Services (ACM MobiSys) (2011)
11. Chang, C.C., Lin, C.J.: 2011. LIBSVM: a library for support vector machines. ACM Trans. Intell. Syst. Technol. 2(3), 1–27 (2011). http://www.csie.ntu.edu.tw/cjlin/libsvm
12. Yu, Y., et al.: Initial validation of mobile-structural health monitoring method using smartphones. Int. J. Distrib. Sens. Netw. 11(2), 274391 (2015)
13. Huang, Y., et al.: Vi-liquid: unknown liquid identification with your smartphone vibration. In: Proceedings of the 27th Annual International Conference on Mobile Computing and Networking (2021)
14. AndroidDeveloper, Work with raw data, use the accelerometer. https://developer.android.com/studio
15. Kreyszig, E.: Advanced engineering mathematics, 10th edn. (2009)
16. Antonsson, E.K., Mann, R.W.: The frequency content of gait. J. Biomech. 18(1), 39–47 (1985)
17. Murty, K.S.R., Yegnanarayana, B.: Combining evidence from residual phase and MFCC features for speaker recognition. IEEE Signal Process. Lett. 13(1), 52–55 (2006)
18. Liu, J., et al.: Vibwrite: towards finger-input authentication on ubiquitous surfaces via physical vibration. In: Proceedings of the 2017 ACM SIGSAC Conference on Computer and Communications Security (2017)
19. Hastie, T., Tibshirani, R., Friedman, J.: The Elements of Statistical Learning, pp. 115–163. Springer, New York, NY (2001). https://doi.org/10.1007/978-0-387-84858-7
20. Galar, M., Fernández, A., Barrenechea, E., Bustince, H., Herrera, F.: An overview of ensemble methods for binary classifiers in multi-class problems: experimental study on one-vs-one and one-vs-all schemes. Pattern Recogn. 44(8), 1761–1776 (2011)

An Improved Authenticated Key Agreement Protocol for IoT and Cloud Server

Yongliu Ma[1,2], Yuqian Ma[1,2], and Qingfeng Cheng[1,2(✉)]

[1] State Key Laboratory of Mathematical Engineering and Advanced Computing,
Zhengzhou, China
qingfengc2008@sina.com
[2] Strategic Support Force Information Engineering University,
Zhengzhou 450001, China

Abstract. The internet of things (IoT) is a complex network system with applications in all walks of life. However, there are various risks in the process of information transmission between IoT devices and servers. Recently, research on the security of authenticated key agreement (AKA) protocols in the IoT environment has gradually increased. Iqbal et al. proposed an AKA protocol between IoT and cloud servers and proved that it was secure under the eCK model. This paper shows that the Iqbal et al.'s protocol has two security flaws, which are resisting ephemeral key leakage attack and key compromise impersonation attack, and proposes a new AKA protocol in the IoT environment. Through the security proof and formal analysis, it is proved that the new protocol is secure under the eCK model. Comparing the protocol proposed in this paper with other similar protocols, it is found that the protocol in this paper achieves a balance between security performance and communication consumption.

Keywords: IoT · AKA protocol · eCK model · Scyther formal tool

1 Introduction

1.1 Related Work

The internet of things (IoT) is a network that can realize the interconnection of any object anytime, anywhere. With the popularization of IoT smart devices, IoT plays an increasingly important role in life [1]. The IoT has a wide range of applications in infrastructure fields such as smart cities, smart malls, smart transportation, smart medical care, and smart logistics [2–4]. However, there may be attacks by malicious adversaries in the process of transmitting information between the devices and the servers [5]. Therefore, one of the foundations for building security services is authentication and session key agreement between IoT devices and servers. Many protocols for securing communication between IoT devices and cloud servers have been proposed.

© ICST Institute for Computer Sciences, Social Informatics and Telecommunications Engineering 2023
Published by Springer Nature Switzerland AG 2023. All Rights Reserved
Q. Jiang et al. (Eds.): SPNCE 2022, LNICST 496, pp. 15–31, 2023.
https://doi.org/10.1007/978-3-031-30623-5_2

Khelf et al. [6] proposed an IoT-oriented AKA micro-protocol to solve the security problem in wireless sensors, which could resist various types of attacks while reducing the computational cost. Qi et al. [7] proposed a two-factor AKA protocol based on elliptic curve cryptography for wireless sensor networks in the context IoT, and through heuristic security analysis showed that the protocol could resist various known attacks. Peng et al. [8] proposed an efficient protocol for IoT devices, which avoided the pairing operation of the client through an unbalanced computation method and proved the security of the protocol. Recently, Rostampour et al. [9] proposed an AKA protocol between IoT edge devices and cloud servers based on elliptic curve cryptography. Iqbal et al. [10] proved that the protocol proposed by Rostampour et al. was insecure under the eCK model, then they proposed a new AKA protocol called ITGR protocol below, at the same time, they used Scyther tool and BAN logic to prove that the protocol was secure under the eCK model. However, in this paper, we prove that the ITGR protocol cannot resist the ephemeral key leakage attack and key compromise impersonation attack, then we propose a new AKA protocol between IoT devices and cloud servers based on the ITGR protocol, called eITGR protocol. Finally, we prove that our protocol is secure under the eCK model.

1.2   Contribution

The contribution of this paper consists of the following four parts:

 (i) This paper analyzes the ITGR protocol between IoT devices and cloud servers based on elliptic curve cryptography, and points out that it cannot resist ephemeral key leakage attack and key compromise impersonation attack.
 (ii) A new AKA protocol between IoT devices and cloud servers is proposed, which makes up for the security defects of the ITGR protocol.
 (iii) Use the security proof to prove that the eITGR protocol is secure under the eCK model, and confirm it through the Scyther tool.
 (iv) By comparing the security properties and communication consumption of eITGR and similar protocols, the advantages of the eITGR protocol in terms of security and communication efficiency are shown.

1.3   Organization

The content of this paper is arranged as follows. Section 1 introduces the development status of the IoT, the research status of AKA protocol at home and abroad, and briefly introduces the research content and structure of this paper. Section 2 presents the basics of mathematics and cryptography applied during protocol design and analysis. A review of the ITGR protocol and analysis of security flaws are in Sect. 3. Section 4 proposes a new AKA protocol in the IoT environment, and its formal security proof, security analysis using Scyther tool and security properties analysis are shown in Sect. 5. The security properties, computation and communication cost of the protocol proposed in this paper and other similar protocols are compared in Sect. 6. Conclusion is given in Sect. 7.

2 Preliminaries and Security Model

The notations used in the paper are shown in Table 1.

Table 1. Notations used in the paper.

Notations	Description
U	User
S	Server
ID_u	Identity of U
t_u	Ephemeral private key of U
t_s	Ephemeral private key of S
x_s	Long-term private key of S
k	The security parameter
G	The cyclic additive group
p, q	The large prime
P	A generator of G
T	The timestamp
$H_i(i = 1, 2, 3)$	The hash functions

2.1 Computationally Difficult Problems

(i) *Elliptic Curve Discrete Logarithm Problem (ECDL)*: Let E be an elliptic curve on a finite field F. G is a cyclic subgroup of E with order q, and P is a generator of G. If the $P, Q \in G$ are known, it is hard to find $a \in Z_q^*$ satisfying $aP = Q$.

(ii) *Elliptic Curve Computational Diffie-Hellman Problem (ECCDH)*: Let the generator of prime order cyclic group G be P, and for $a_1, a_2 \in Z_q^*$, when $P, a_1 P, a_2 P$ are known, it is hard to calculate $a_1 a_2 P \in G$.

2.2 Security Model

In 2007, LaMacchia et al. [11] proposed a new security model, which gave the adversary stronger attack capabilities based on the CK model [12], referred to as the eCK model. Let $\{P_1, P_2, \cdots, P_n\}$ denote the set of all participants, $sid = (P_i, P_j, m_1, m_2, \cdots, m_l)$ is the symbol of the session, where participant P_i is the initiator of the session, and participant P_j is the responder of the session, $m_1, m_2, \cdots, m_l$ representing the message sent between the participants of the session. Let $\prod_{i,j}^{sid}$ be the sid session between participant P_i and P_j. The adversary's attack capabilities such as eavesdropping, tampering, and replay in the eCK model are reflected through the following query methods:

(i) StaticKeyReveal(P_i) query: The adversary can obtain the long-term private key of the participant P_i through this query.

(ii) EphemeralKeyReveal(P_i, sid) query: The adversary can obtain the ephemeral key of participant P_i in session sid through this query.

(iii) SessionKeyReveal(sid) query: The adversary obtains the session key generated in session sid through the query.

(iv) Send(sid, m) query: Through this query, the adversary can send message m to the session identified as sid, and get the corresponding reply according to the provisions of the protocol.

(v) Test(sid) query: The adversary can only interrogate the fresh session sid, which simulates a random coin tossing algorithm and makes corresponding answers according to the coin toss results. If the coin toss results $b = 1$, the oracle returns the real session key; if the coin toss results $b = 0$, the oracle returns a random value with the same distribution as the session key.

Definition 1. *If both sessions $\prod_{i,j}^{sid}$ and $\prod_{i,j}^{sid^*}$ are run successfully, the generated session keys are equal, and the session identifiers sid and sid* are the same, then the two sessions are called matching sessions.*

Definition 2. *Let the session run by users P_i and P_j be $\prod_{i,j}^{sid}$, and the session is called fresh if none of the following conditions hold:*

(i) *The adversary has interrogated session $\prod_{i,j}^{sid}$ or matching session $\prod_{j,i}^{sid}$ (if exists) for SessionKeyReveal(sid) query;*

(ii) *If the matching session $\prod_{j,i}^{sid}$ of session $\prod_{i,j}^{sid}$ exists, the adversary has performed EphemeralKeyReveal(P_i, sid) and StaticKeyReveal(P_i) queries at the same time, or performed both EphemeralKeyReveal(P_j, sid) and StaticKeyReveal(P_j) queries;*

(iii) *If there is no matching session for session $\prod_{i,j}^{sid}$, the adversary has performed EphemeralKeyReveal(P_i, sid) and StaticKeyReveal(P_i) queries at the same time, or performed a StaticKeyReveal(P_j) query.*

Definition 3. *Let k be a security parameter, if the probability of the adversary $\mathcal{A}$ winning the game is Pr, then the adversary's winning advantage can be defined as:*

$$Adv(k) = |Pr - \frac{1}{2}|. \tag{1}$$

If two honest participants complete the matching session and calculate the same key, and there is no adversary to win the security game with a non-negligible advantage, then the AKA protocol is secure under the eCK model.

3   Review and Security Analysis of ITGR Protocol

In this section, we review the ITGR protocol [10] and analyze the security properties of the protocol.

3.1   Review of ITGR Protocol

There are two types of participants in the ITGR protocol [10], namely IoT device U and server S. At the same time, the protocol consists of the following two phases: registration phase, and login and authentication phase.

Registration Phase. The registration steps are given as follows:

(i) Device U selects random number $x_u \in Z_q^*$ and its identity ID_u. Then U computes $R_u = x_u \cdot ID_u \cdot P$ and sends it to the server.

(ii) Server S receives the R_u and splits its private key x_s into two unequal parts x_s^1, x_s^2 such as $x_s^1 \neq x_s^2$, then server calculates $Y_u^1 = R_u x_s^1$, $Y_u^2 = R_u x_s^2$. The server sends $\{Y_u^1, Y_u^2\}$ to U and stores (R_u, Y_u^1, Y_u^2) in its database.

(iii) The device receives $\{Y_u^1, Y_u^2\}$ from server and stores (R_u, Y_u^1, Y_u^2) as its long-term private key securely.

Login and Authentication Phase. The steps of the login and authentication process between device U and server S are given as follows:

(i) Device U chooses its ephemeral key $t_u \in Z_q^*$ and computes $X_u = (Y_u^1 + Y_u^2) \cdot t_u \cdot H(R_u)$, $T_u = (Y_u^1 + Y_u^2) \cdot t_u$, then U sends $\{X_u, T_u\}$ to the server.

(ii) Server S receives $\{X_u, T_u\}$ and checks whether $T_u \overset{?}{=} X_u[H(R_u)]^{-1}$ to authenticate U. If true, the device U passes the identity authentication of server; else, login request from U is rejected.

(iii) The server S selects $t_s \in Z_q^*$ and computes $X_s = X_u t_s$, $T_s = (Y_u^1 + Y_u^2) \cdot t_s$, then S calculates its session key with U as $SK_{su} = T_u t_s$ and sends $\{X_s, T_s\}$ to the device U.

(iv) The device U receives $\{X_s, T_s\}$ from server S and checks whether $T_s \overset{?}{=} X_s[H(R_u)]^{-1} t_u^{-1}$ to authenticate S. If true, the server S passes the identity authentication of device; else, login response from S is rejected.

(v) The device U calculates its session key with S as $SK_{us} = T_s t_u$, then encrypts $E_{SK_{us}}[H(SK_{us})]$ and sends it to the server S.

(vi) The server S receives $E_{SK_{us}}[H(SK_{us})]$ and checks whether $H(SK_{su}) \overset{?}{=} D_{SK_{su}}[E_{SK_{us}}[H(SK_{us})]]$ to authenticate U and approve login request. If true, the session key exchange between U and S is over; else, the session key is invalid.

3.2   Security Analysis of ITGR Protocol

In this subsection, we prove that the ITGR protocol is susceptible to ephemeral key leakage attack and key compromise impersonation attack, and give specific attack methods.

Ephemeral Key Leakage Attack. If the ephemeral private key t_s of the server or the ephemeral private key t_u of the device is obtained by the adversary, then the adversary can calculate the session key by using the monitored transmission information. The specific steps are described as below:

If the adversary obtains the ephemeral private key t_s of the server S, and obtains T_u by monitoring the communication between the device and the server in public channel, then the adversary calculates $SK_{su} = T_u t_s$, and verify the session key by judging $H(SK_{su}) \overset{?}{=} D_{SK_{su}}[E_{SK_{us}}[H(SK_{us})]]$.

If the adversary obtains the ephemeral private key t_u of the device U, and obtains T_s by monitoring the communication between the device and the server in public channel, then the adversary calculate $SK_{us} = T_s t_u$, and verify the session key by judgment $H(SK_{us}) \overset{?}{=} D_{SK'_{us}}[E_{SK_{us}}[H(SK_{us})]]$.

Key Compromise Impersonation Attack. The registration information of each device is stored in the server, and the server is at risk of being attacked by an adversary, so (R_u, Y_u^1, Y_u^2) may be obtained by an adversary. If the adversary obtains the secret (R_u, Y_u^1, Y_u^2) of the device U, then the adversary can deceive the device by pretending to be a legitimate server in front of the device, and generate the session key with device through the AKA process. The specific attack steps are described as below:

(i) The adversary $\mathcal{A}$ receives $\{X_u, T_u\}$ from device U and checks whether $T_u \overset{?}{=} X_u[H(R_u)]^{-1}$ to authenticate U. If true, the device U passes the identity authentication of adversary $\mathcal{A}$; else, login request from U is rejected.

(ii) The adversary $\mathcal{A}$ selects $t'_s \in Z_q^*$ and computes $X'_s = X_u t'_s$, $T'_s = (Y_u^1 + Y_u^2) \cdot t'_s$, then $\mathcal{A}$ calculates its session key with U as $SK'_{su} = T_u t'_s$ and sends $\{X'_s, T'_s\}$ to the device U.

(iii) The device U receives $\{X'_s, T'_s\}$ from adversary $\mathcal{A}$ and checks whether $T'_s \overset{?}{=} X'_s \cdot [H(R_u)]^{-1} t_u^{-1}$. If true, the adversary $\mathcal{A}$ passes the identity authentication of device U; else, login response from $\mathcal{A}$ is rejected.

(iv) The device U calculates its session key as $SK'_{us} = T'_s t_u$, then encrypts $E_{SK'_{us}}[H(SK'_{us})]$ and sends it to the adversary $\mathcal{A}$.

(v) The adversary $\mathcal{A}$ receives $E_{SK'_{us}}[H(SK'_{us})]$ from U and checks whether $H(SK'_{su}) \overset{?}{=} D_{SK'_{su}}[E_{SK'_{us}}[H(SK'_{us})]]$ to authenticate U and approve login request. If true, the session key negotiation between U and $\mathcal{A}$ is over; else, the session key is invalid.

Since the session key calculated by adversary $\mathcal{A}$ and device U is equal, the session key negotiation is completed.

4   Proposed Scheme

The ITGR protocol cannot resist key compromise impersonation attack and ephemeral key leakage attack, so this paper proposes a new AKA protocol called eITGR protocol which makes up for the defects of ITGR protocol. The proposed protocol consists of three phases: system establishment phase, registration phase, and login and authentication phase.

4.1 System Establishment Phase

The server S establishes an elliptic curve $E(a,b) : y^2 = x^3 + ax + b$ on the finite field F, where G is a cyclic subgroup of E with order q, and P is a generator of G. Then the S selects three hash functions $H_1 : \{0,1\}^* \times G \to Z_q^*$, $H_2 : \{0,1\}^* \times G \times G \times \{0,1\}^* \to G$, $H_3 : \{0,1\}^* \times Z_q^* \to Z_q^*$.

4.2 Registration Phase

The registration phase is when the IoT device registers on the server in the secure communication environment, and generates a private key for communication between the two parties. The registration steps between device U and server S are as follows:

(i) Device U selects random number $x_u \in Z_q^*$ and its identity ID_u. Then U computes $X_u = x_u P, R_u = H_1(ID_u \| X_u) \cdot P$ and sends $\{ID_u, R_u\}$ to the server.

(ii) Server S receives the $\{ID_u, R_u\}$ from U and splits its private key x_s into two unequal parts x_s^1, x_s^2 such as $x_s^1 \neq x_s^2$, then server S calculates $y_u = x_s^1 + x_s^2 \cdot H_1(ID_u \| R_u)$, $Y_u = y_u P$. The server S sends Y_u to U and stores (ID_u, R_u, y_u) in its database.

(iii) The device receives Y_u from server and stores (x_u, R_u, Y_u) as its long-term private key securely.

4.3 Login and Authentication Phase

The login and authentication process between device U and server S is as follows:

(i) The device U chooses its ephemeral key $t_u \in Z_q^*$ and timestamp T, computes $T_u = t_u P, H_u = H_2(ID_u \| R_u \| T_u \| T)$, then U sends $\{ID_u, H_u, T_u, T\}$ to the server S.

(ii) After receiving the message $\{ID_u, H_u, T_u, T\}$, the server S first verifies the freshness of the timestamp T, then uses ID_u to find the corresponding entry (ID_u, R_u, y_u) in its database, After this server S uses the stored data to calculate $H_s = H_2(ID_u \| R_u \| T_u \| T)$, $X_u = H_u - H_s$ and checks whether $R_u \overset{?}{=} H_1(ID_u \| X_u) \cdot P$ to authenticate U. If true, the device U passes the identity authentication of server; else, login request from U is rejected.

(iii) The server S selects $t_s \in Z_q^*$ and computes $T_s = t_s P$, then S calculates $K_s = (t_s + y_u + H_1(ID_u \| X_u))(T_u + X_u)$ and its session key with U as $SK_{su} = H_1(ID_u \| K_s), Q_s = H_3(ID_u \| SK_{su})$, and sends $\{T_s, Q_s\}$ to the device U.

(iv) The device U receives $\{T_s, Q_s\}$ from S, calculates $K_u = (t_u + x_u)(T_s + Y_u + R_u)$ and its session key with S as $SK_{us} = H_1(ID_u \| K_u)$, then checks whether $Q_s \stackrel{?}{=} H_3(ID_u \| SK_{us})$ to authenticate S. If true, the server S passes the identity authentication of device and the session key exchange between U and S is over; else, the session key is invalid.

The login and authentication phase is given in Fig. 1.

Device: U	Server: S

$selects\ t_u \in Z_q^*$

$computes\ T_u = t_u P$

$\qquad H_u = H_2(ID_u \| R_u \| T_u \| T) + X_u$

$$\xrightarrow{\{ID_u, H_u, T_u, T\}}$$

$\qquad\qquad\qquad\qquad computes\ H_s = H_2(ID_u \| R_u \| T_u \| T)$

$\qquad\qquad\qquad\qquad\qquad X_u = H_u - H_s$

$\qquad\qquad\qquad\qquad verifies\ R_u \stackrel{?}{=} H_1(ID_u \| X_u) \cdot P$

$\qquad\qquad\qquad\qquad if\ true, selects\ t_s \in Z_q^*$

$\qquad\qquad\qquad\qquad computes$

$\qquad\qquad\qquad\qquad\qquad T_s = t_s P$

$\qquad\qquad\qquad\qquad\qquad K_s = (t_s + y_u + H_1(ID_u \| X_u))(T_u + X_u)$

$\qquad\qquad\qquad\qquad\qquad SK_{su} = H_1(ID_u \| K_s)$

$$\xleftarrow{\{T_s, Q_s\}} \qquad Q_s = H_3(ID_u \| SK_{su})$$

$computes$

$\qquad K_u = (t_u + x_u)(T_s + Y_u + R_u)$

$\qquad SK_{us} = H_1(ID_u \| K_u)$

$verifies\ Q_s \stackrel{?}{=} H_3(ID_u \| SK_{us})$

Fig. 1. Login and authentication phase of eITGR.

5   Security Analysis of eITGR Protocol

In this section, we present two proof methods for the eITGR protocol. First, we prove that the eITGR protocol is secure under the eCK model, then we use the Scyther tool to verify the security of the protocol.

5.1   Security Proof Under the eCK Model

We will prove that the protocol is secure under the eCK model [11] below.

Theorem 1. *The eITGR protocol satisfies eCK security if the ECCDH assumption holds on group G and H_1, H_2, H_3 are modeled by independent random oracles.*

Proof. Let the adversary $\mathcal{A}$ activates at most $n(k)$ honest parties and $s(k)$ sessions. The session key generated by the protocol is $SK = H_1(ID_u \| K)$ and H_1 is simulated as a random oracle, so the adversary has only three ways to distinguish the session key from the random value:

(i) Guessing attack: The adversary guesses the session key correctly.
(ii) Session key replication attack: The adversary establishes a session that does not match the test session but has the same session key. The adversary obtains the session key of the test session by querying the session key of the established session.
(iii) Forgery attack: The adversary $\mathcal{A}$ queries random oracle H_1 with the same secret value as that used to generate the test session key, and obtains the session key.

Since H_1 is a random oracle that obeys a uniform distribution, the probability $O(1/2^k)$ of the adversary guessing the correct key can be ignored. The two unmatched sessions cannot have the same session participant and ephemeral key, So the success probability of the session key replication attack is equivalent to find a collision of H_1, and the probability that two random oracles collide is $O(s(k)^2/2^k)$. Therefore, guessing attacks and session key replication attacks can be ignored, and only forgery attacks are considered below. Next, we show that if the adversary $\mathcal{A}$ wins the game by a non-negligible advantage, then the algorithm $\mathcal{S}$ can be constructed to solve the ECCDH problem with non-negligible probability. The algorithm $\mathcal{S}$ selects $A, B \in G$ where $A = aP$, $B = bP$, $a, b \in Z_q^*$, and sends the parameters (G, q, P, H_1, H_2, H_3) to $\mathcal{A}$. Then, algorithm $\mathcal{S}$ guesses that the adversary selects the session marked with *sid* as the test session, S_a and U_b are the owners of the test session and its matching session respectively with at least $1/n(k)^2 s(k)$ probability. Consider the following two cases according to the definition of session freshness:

(1) **Case 1:** The matching session of the test session exists, and the owner of the matching session is an honest participant;
(2) **Case 2:** No honest party owns a matching session for the test session.

Case 1 can be divided into the following four sub-cases:

(1) **Case 1.1:** The adversary performs the StaticKeyReveal(C) query on the test session and its matching session. Algorithm $\mathcal{S}$ sets A and B as the ephemeral public keys for participants S_a and U_b, and algorithm $\mathcal{S}$ assigns the long-time public-private key pair normally. Since algorithm $\mathcal{S}$ knows the long-term private keys of all participants, when queried by an adversary, algorithm $\mathcal{S}$ can answer truthfully according to the query ability in the model. When the adversary queries information about participants S_a and U_b, the algorithm $\mathcal{S}$ replies to the adversary as follows:

(i) StaticKeyReveal(C) query: The algorithm S provides the adversary with the long-term private key of participant C generated in the above simulation.

(ii) EphemeralKeyReveal(C, sid) query: If C is participant S_a or U_b, then algorithm S abandons the simulation, otherwise algorithm S returns the ephemeral key for party C in session sid.

(iii) Test(sid) query: If sid is not the test session, the simulation fails, otherwise, algorithm S returns a random value with the same distribution as the session key.

(iv) SessionKeyReveal(sid) query: If sid is a test session or its matching session, the simulation fails, otherwise set the session as $sid = (ID_s, ID_u, H_u, T_u, T_s, Q_s, T)$, then calculate the session key as $SK = H_1(ID_u \| K)$, where the input of K is as follows

$$K = ECCDH(T_u + X_u, T_s + Y_u + R_u). \tag{2}$$

Algorithm S queries whether the random oracle H_1 has been queried. If it has been queried, it outputs the correct session key; otherwise, it outputs a random value with the same distribution as the session key. Therefore, the algorithm S successfully simulates the environment in which the adversary A runs the protocol. If the adversary wins the forgery attack, then it must obtain the session key by querying, and the algorithm S must be able to solve the problem of ECCDH(A, B). In addition to, the only consideration is that the adversary solves the ECDL problem in time t while setting its advantage to be $Adv_G^{ECDL}(k, t)$. Let p_1 be the probability that the Case 1.1 occurs and the adversary succeeds through the forgery attack, so the advantages of simulating algorithm S to solve the ECCDH problem are as follows

$$Adv_G^{ECCDH}(k, t) \geq \frac{p_1}{n(k)^2 s(k)} - Adv_G^{ECDL}(k, t). \tag{3}$$

(2) **Case 1.2:** The adversary performs the StaticKeyReveal(C) query on the test session and EphemeralKeyReveal(C, sid) query on its matching session. Algorithm S sets A as the ephemeral public key of participant S_a, replaces X_u with B for participant U_b, and assigns a public-private key pair normally for the remaining participants. Then the algorithm S simulates the operating environment of the protocol, which is the same as in Case 1.1 except for the following query:

(i) StaticKeyReveal(C) query: If C is participant U_b, then algorithm S abandons the simulation; otherwise, algorithm S provides the adversary with the long-term private key of party C generated in the above simulation.

(ii) EphemeralKeyReveal(C, sid) query: If C is participant S_a, then algorithm S abandons the simulation; otherwise, algorithm S provides the adversary with the ephemeral key of participant C generated in the above simulation.

Let p_2 be the probability that the case 1.2 occurs and the adversary succeeds through the forgery attack, so the advantages of simulating algorithm $\mathcal{S}$ to solve the ECCDH problem are as follows

$$Adv_G^{ECCDH}(k,t) \geq \frac{p_2}{n(k)^2 s(k)} - Adv_G^{ECDL}(k,t). \tag{4}$$

(3) **Case 1.3:** The adversary performs the EphemeralKeyReveal(C, sid) query on the test session and StaticKeyReveal(C) query on its matching session. Algorithm $\mathcal{S}$ sets B as the ephemeral public key of participant U_b, replaces Y_u with A for participant S_a. Swap S_a and U_b, the rest is the same as case 1.2. Let p_3 be the probability that the case 1.3 occurs and the adversary succeeds through the forgery attack, so the advantages of simulating algorithm $\mathcal{S}$ to solve the ECCDH problem are as follows

$$Adv_G^{ECCDH}(k,t) \geq \frac{p_3}{n(k)^2 s(k)} - Adv_G^{ECDL}(k,t). \tag{5}$$

(4) **Case 1.4:** The adversary performs the EphemeralKeyReveal(C, sid) query on the test session and its matching session. Algorithm $\mathcal{S}$ replaces X_u with A and Y_u with B for participants S_a and U_b, computes $R_u = H_1(ID_u \| X_u) \cdot P$ and for the remaining $n(k) - 2$ participants, algorithm $\mathcal{S}$ assigns the public-private key pair normally. Then the algorithm $\mathcal{S}$ simulates the operating environment of the protocol, which is the same as in case 1.1 except for the following query:
(i) StaticKeyReveal(C) query: If C is participant S_a or U_b, then algorithm $\mathcal{S}$ abandons the simulation; otherwise, algorithm $\mathcal{S}$ returns the long-term private key for party C in session sid.
(ii) EphemeralKeyReveal(C, sid) query: The algorithm $\mathcal{S}$ provides the adversary with the ephemeral key of participant C generated in the above simulation.
Let p_4 be the probability that the case 1.4 occurs and the adversary succeeds through the forgery attack, so the advantages of simulating algorithm $\mathcal{S}$ to solve the ECCDH problem are as follows

$$Adv_G^{ECCDH}(k,t) \geq \frac{p_4}{n(k)^2 s(k)} - Adv_G^{ECDL}(k,t). \tag{6}$$

Case 2 can be divided into the following two sub-cases:

(1) **Case 2.1:** The adversary performs the EphemeralKeyReveal(C, sid) query on the test session. Since no honest participant participates in the matching session of the test session, it is equivalent that the adversary also obtains the ephemeral key of the intended communicating party, so it is similar with case 1.4.
(2) **Case 2.2:** The adversary performs the StaticKeyReveal(C) query on the test. Since no honest participant participates in the matching session of the test session, it is equivalent to the adversary also obtaining the ephemeral key of the intended communicating party, so it is similar with case 1.2.

In summary, if the adversary successfully distinguishes the session key from the random value with a non-negligible advantage, there is an algorithm $\mathcal{S}$ that solves the ECCDH problem with a non-negligible probability, which contradicts the ECCDH assumption. Therefore, the eITGR protocol given in this paper satisfies the security properties under the eCK model.   □

5.2 Security Analysis Using Scyther Tool

Cremers and his team [13] developed the Scyther tool in 2006 for formal analysis of protocols. This paper uses Scyther tool to formally analyze the eITGR protocol, and the setting used is presented in Fig. 2 to achieve highly strong security, including perfect forward security and resistance to ephemeral key leakage attack. According to the analysis result in Fig. 3, we point out that the eITGR protocol is secure under the eCK model, which is consistent with the security proof result in Sect. 5.1.

6 Comparison with Other Protocols

In this section, we compare the security properties, computation cost, and communication overhead of the eITGR protocol with several similar protocols. The protocols involved in the comparison include Rostampour et al.'s protocol [9], ITGR [10], Hassan et al.'s protocol [14], Zhang et al.'s protocol [15] and Zhou et al.'s protocol [16].

6.1 Comparison of Security Properties

Table 2. Comparison of security properties.

Scheme	SP1	SP2	SP3	SP4	SP5
Rostampour et al. [9]	Y	Y	N	N	N
ITGR [10]	Y	Y	N	Y	N
Hassan et al. [14]	Y	Y	Y	N	N
Zhang et al. [15]	Y	N	N	Y	Y
Zhou et al. [16]	Y	Y	Y	N	N
eITGR	Y	Y	Y	Y	Y

The security properties of several recently proposed protocols are shown in Table 2, where SP1 refers to known key security, SP2 refers to forward security, SP3 represents resistance to key compromise impersonation attack, SP4 represents resistance to ephemeral key compromise impersonation attack, and SP5 represents resistance to ephemeral key leakage attack, respectively. Simultaneously, Y refers to the scheme achieves this security property and N refers to

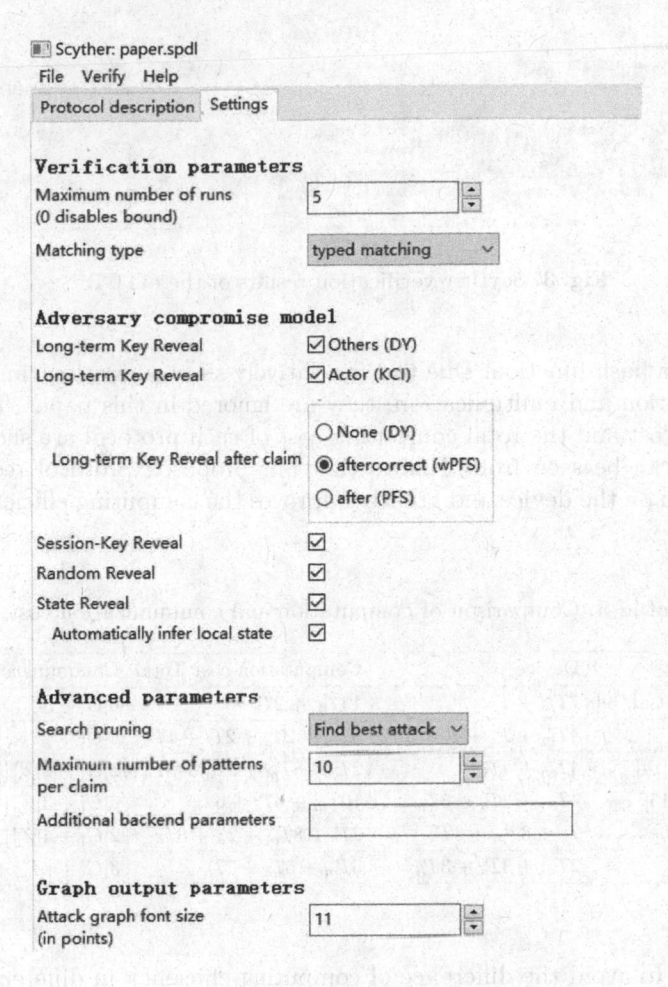

Fig. 2. The setting of Scyther.

the scheme does not achieve this security property. According to Table 2, the above-mentioned comparison protocols all have some security flaws. However, the protocol presented in this paper satisfies the above five security properties and is secure under the eCK model.

6.2 Computation and Communication Overhead Comparison

Computation efficiency and transmission consumption are important indicators to measure the communication performance of the protocol. In this section, we use T_b to denote the computation time of the bilinear map, T_m to represent the time of performing an scalar multiplication operation, T_a to represent the time of performing a point addition in elliptic curve group, T_i to represent the time of performing a multiplicative inverse operation and T_h to represent the time of

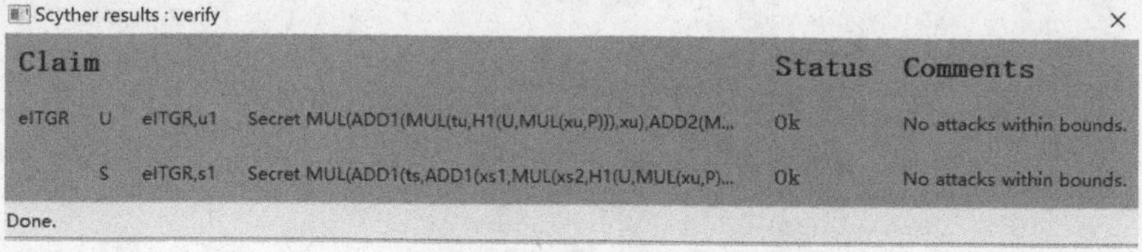

Fig. 3. Scyther verification results of the eITGR.

performing a hash function. Due to the relatively short operation time of XOR, integer addition and multiplication, they are ignored in this paper. The device computing cost and the total computing cost of each protocol are shown in the Table 3. It can be seen from Table 3 that our proposed protocol requires less computation on the device and greatly improves the computing efficiency on the device.

Table 3. Comparison of computation and communication cost.

Scheme	Device	Computation cost Total	Communication cost
Rostampour et al. [9]	$7T_m + T_a$	$13T_m + 2T_a$	$6|G|$
ITGR [10]	$4T_m + T_a + T_i + 2T_h$	$8T_m + 2T_a + 2T_i + 4T_h$	$4|G| + |E_{SK}[H(SK)]|$
Hassan et al. [14]	$4T_m + 4T_h$	$2T_b + 8T_m + 2T_a + 8T_h$	$2|G| + 2|Z_q^*| + |ID|$
Zhang et al. [15]	$4T_m + 3T_a + 3T_h$	$10T_m + 6T_a + 6T_h$	$6|G| + 3|Z_q^*|$
Zhou et al. [16]	$T_b + 3T_m + 3T_h$	$2T_b + 8T_m + T_a + 8T_h$	$2|G| + 4|Z_q^*| + 2|T|$
eITGR	$2T_m + 3T_a + 3T_h$	$5T_m + 5T_a + 7T_h$	$3|G| + |Z_q^*| + |ID| + |T|$

In order to avoid the difference of computing efficiency in different environments, this paper uses the Miracl function library in the C language environment [17]. According to the operation time in Table 4, the device running time and the total running time of the above protocols in the login and authentication phase are compared as shown in Fig. 4, where the abscissa is the protocol type, and the ordinate represents the time in milliseconds. It can be seen from Fig. 4 that the computing time on the device and total computing time of the eITGR protocol we propose is short, which greatly improves the practicability of the protocol in the IoT environment.

Table 4. Running time of various operations.

Operation	T_b	T_m	T_a	T_i	T_h
Computation time(ms)	7.8351	2.7580	0.0168	0.0147	0.0126

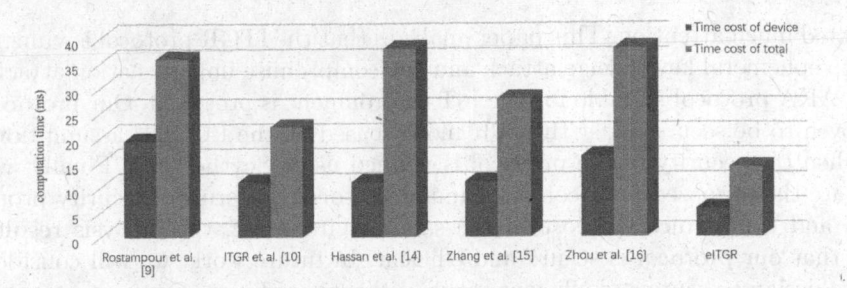

Fig. 4. Comparison of computation time.

The more data transmitted during the protocol operation, the more communication overhead. This paper compares the communication efficiency by comparing the amount of data that needs to be transmitted during the operation of different protocols. Table 3 shows the communication transmission data during the operation of each protocol. In order to compare the data transmission efficiency intuitively during the operation of the protocol, we set the parameter lengths as $|ID| = 10$ bytes, $|Z_q^*| = 20$ bytes, $|G| = 40$ bytes, timestamp $|T| = 8$ bytes and $|E_{SK}[H(SK)]| = 25$ bytes. The comparison of the amount of data transmitted by each protocol is shown in Fig. 5, where the abscissa represents the type of protocol, and the ordinate represents the amount of transmitted data in bytes.

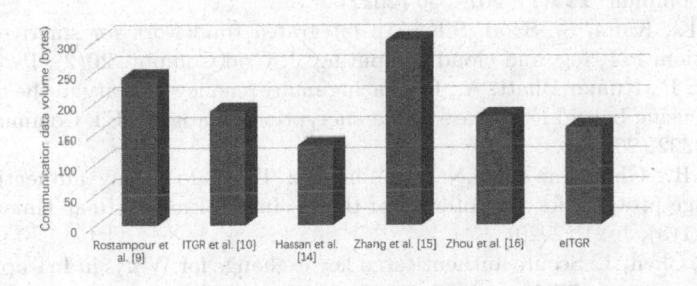

Fig. 5. Comparison of communication time.

In summary, in the case of more perfect security performance, the computation and communication overhead of the eITGR protocol proposed in this paper is relatively low, therefore, the eITGR protocol achieves a balance between security and communication efficiency.

7   Conclusion

With the wide application of IoT technology in life, the security of data transmission and identity authentication between devices and servers in the IoT has attracted much attention. This paper analyzes that the ITGR protocol is vulnerable to ephemeral key leakage attack and key compromise impersonation attack, so an AKA protocol suitable for the IoT environment is proposed. Our protocol is proven to be secure under the eCK model based on the ECCDH assumption, and then the security of the protocol is verified using Scyther tool. Finally, we compare the proposed protocol with similar protocols in terms of security properties and communication cost in the same environment, the analysis results show that our protocol is secure and efficient. In future work, we will consider how to design a secure and efficient group authenticated key agreement protocol for IoT and cloud server.

Acknowledgments. This work was supported in part by the National Natural Science Foundation of China (nos. 61872449 and 62172433).

References

1. Hassija, V., Chamola, V., Saxena, V., et al.: A survey on IoT security: application areas, security threats, and solution architectures. IEEE Access **7**, 82721–82743 (2019)
2. Al-Turjman, F., Zahmatkesh, H., Shahroze, R.: An overview of security and privacy in smart cities' IoT communications. Trans. Emerg. Telecommun. Technol. **33**(3), 1–19 (2022)
3. Lova Raju, K., Vijayaraghavan, V.: A self-powered, real-time, NRF24L01 IoT-based cloud-enabled service for smart agriculture decision-making system. Wirel. Pers. Commun. **124**(1), 207–236 (2022)
4. Saini, K., Kalra, S., Sood, S.K.: An integrated framework for smart earthquake prediction: IoT, fog, and cloud computing. J. Grid Comput. **20**(2), 1–20 (2022)
5. Kumar, P., Kumar Bhatt, A.: Enhancing multi-tenancy security in the cloud computing using hybrid ECC-based data encryption approach. IET Commun. **14**(18), 3212–3222 (2020)
6. Khelf, R., Ghoualmi-Zine, N., Ahmim, M.: TAKE-IoT: tiny authenticated key exchange protocol for the internet of things. Int. J. Embed. Real-Time Commun. Syst. **11**(3), 1–21 (2020)
7. Qi, M., Chen, J.: Secure authenticated key exchange for WSNs in IoT applications. J. Supercomput. **77**(12), 13897–13910 (2021)
8. Peng, A.L., Tseng, Y.M., Huang, S.S.: An efficient leakage-resilient authenticated key exchange protocol suitable for IoT devices. IEEE Syst. J. **15**(4), 5343–5354 (2020)
9. Rostampour, S., Safkhani, M., Bendavid, Y., et al.: ECCbAP: a secure ECC - based authentication protocol for IoT edge devices. Pervasive Mob. Comput. **67**, 1–36 (2020)
10. Iqbal, U., Tandon, A., Gupta, S., et al.: A novel secure authentication protocol for IoT and cloud servers. Wirel. Commun. Mob. Comput. **2022**(5), 1–17 (2022)
11. LaMacchia, B., Lauter, K., Mityagin, A.: Stronger security of authenticated key exchange. In: Susilo, W., Liu, J.K., Mu, Y. (eds.) ProvSec 2007. LNCS, vol. 4784, pp. 1–16. Springer, Heidelberg (2007). https://doi.org/10.1007/978-3-540-75670-5_1

12. Canetti, R., Krawczyk, H.: Analysis of key-exchange protocols and their use for building secure channels. In: Pfitzmann, B. (ed.) EUROCRYPT 2001. LNCS, vol. 2045, pp. 453–474. Springer, Heidelberg (2001). https://doi.org/10.1007/3-540-44987-6_28

13. Cremers, C.J.F.: Scyther: semantics and verification of security protocols. Eindhoven University of Technology, Eindhoven Netherlands (2006)

14. Hassan, A., Eltayieb, N., Elhabob, R., et al.: An efficient certificateless user authentication and key exchange protocol for client-server environment. J. Ambient. Intell. Humaniz. Comput. 9(6), 1713–1727 (2018)

15. Zhang, J., Huang, X., Wang, W., et al.: Unbalancing pairing-free identity-based authenticated key exchange protocols for disaster scenarios. IEEE Internet Things J. 6(1), 878–890 (2018)

16. Zhou, Y., Liu, T., Tang, F., et al.: An unlinkable authentication scheme for distributed IoT application. IEEE Access 7, 14757–14766 (2019)

17. Li, Y., Cheng, Q., Liu, X., et al.: A secure anonymous identity-based scheme in new authentication architecture for mobile edge computing. IEEE Syst. J. 15(1), 935–946 (2020)

Efficient Two-Party Authentication Key Agreement Protocol Using Reconciliation Mechanism from Lattice

Jinhua Wang[✉], Ting Chen, Yanyan Liu, Yu Zhou, and XinFeng Dong

Science and Technology on Communication Security Laboratory, Chengdu 610041, Sichuan, China
wjhcetc@163.com

Abstract. It is crucial and challenging to design a quantum-secure and efficient authentication key agreement scheme for IoT. The reasons are that not only there are various security requirements need to meet, but also communication party is resource-constrained. Recently, a large number of 2PAKA schemes for IoT have been presented, yet most of them are subject to quantum attack. In this paper, we put forward a quantum-secure 2PAKA protocol using lattice cryptography. The proposed LB-ID-2PAKA protocol makes use of identity-based signature to avoid the complicated certificate management of PKI-based protocol. At the same time, based on the Kyber.KE, we apply Peikert's reconciliation mechanism to save the communication cost. Our LB-ID-2PAKA protocol can be resistance against various attack and provide desired security property, especially support perfect forward secrecy. Moreover, the provable security analysis shows that our LB-ID-2PAKA protocol is provably secure under RO model and the hardness assumption of MLWE.

Keywords: Post-quantum · Key Agreement · Identity-based Signature · MLWE · Peikert's reconciliation mechanism

1 Introduction

Recently, with the breakthrough of 5G, the Internet of Things (IoT) has got rapid development. At the same time, due to the impact of the epidemic, the demand for telecommuting has increased, followed by a large number of devices connected to the Internet. It is estimated that 24.6 billion IoT devices will be connected globally by 2025 [1]. IoT has become the most developed way to share information among many resource-constrained devices that are connected to each other via the internet. While the IoT brings convenience, it also gives adversaries more options to attack. So, it is urgent to design a protocol for secure communication.

However, it is challenging to design an efficient authentication key agreement scheme for IoT. The reasons are that not only there are various security requirements need to meet, but also communication party is resource-constrained. With the advent of the DH

© ICST Institute for Computer Sciences, Social Informatics and Telecommunications Engineering 2023
Published by Springer Nature Switzerland AG 2023. All Rights Reserved
Q. Jiang et al. (Eds.): SPNCE 2022, LNICST 496, pp. 32–47, 2023.
https://doi.org/10.1007/978-3-031-30623-5_3

exchange in 1976 [2], two party authentication key agreement (2PAKA) protocols have got rapid development over the past few decades [3–7]. The existing 2PAKA protocols have been put forward based on the traditional cryptographic primitives (public-key cryptography [8], identity-based cryptography [9]), elliptic curve cryptography [10], bilinear mapping [11], Chinese Remainder Theorem [12] et.) and the hardness assumption of computational Diffie-Hellman (CDH), or integer factorization problem (IFP) or discrete logarithm problem (DLP).

However, Shor [13] pointed that there exists an adversary under the quantum computing environments can solve abovementioned computational hardness problem easily using polynomial-time algorithms. Thus, there is an urgent need to put forward a quantum-secure 2PAKA protocol for IoT. Due to the advantages of simple operations and less computational overheads, lattice-based cryptography attracts extensive attention from home and abroad.

With the proliferation of lattice-based cryptography, there are two designing ways of AKA protocol under quantum computing environments: one is using reconciliation mechanism and the other is using key encapsulation mechanism (KEM). Peikert [14] pointed that the learning with errors (LWE)-based KA protocol was technically feasible, but it did not design a protocol. After, Lindner et al. [15] presented the construction of DH-like key exchange based on LWE. In literature [16, 17], the author tries to extract the same secret from two approximations, so that the communication parties can obtain the same session key through calculation. Thus, based on LWE and its variants 2PAKA protocols are mostly designed through error reconciliation mechanism.

With its simplicity and modularity, 2PAKA protocol is designed using KEM becomes one of the research hotspots. However, using KEM will cause more communication overheads, it cannot applies to IoT directly. Moreover, most of them are based on public key infrastructure, which will lead to the complicated certificate management. To fill up the loophole, identity-based cryptography (IBC) is introduced to eliminate certificate management. Yet, most of existing identity-based 2PAKA protocols fail to provide quantum-secure. Therefore, it is crucial and challenging to devise a quantum-secure identity-based 2PAKA protocol for IoT.

1.1 Contributions

Although researchers have made considerable efforts to design an efficient and provably secure 2PAKA for IoT, most of them are subject to quantum attack. In this paper, we put forward a quantum-secure 2PAKA protocol using lattice cryptography(LB-ID-2PAKA) for IoT. The main contributions of LB-ID-2PAKA protocol are concluded as the following three dots:

- Combining IBC and lattice cryptography designs a LB-ID-2PAKA protocol. The protocol uses IBC to eliminate the cost of certificate management and uses lattice hard assumptions to confirm the quantum-secure.
- Based on the Kyber.KE, we apply Peikert's reconciliation mechanism to save the communication cost. Moreover, the probability of agreement failure is smaller.
- This paper provides the provable security of LB-ID-2PAKA protocol. The analysis result shows that the proposal is provably secure under RO model. Furthermore, the

LB-ID-2PAKA protocol can withstand various attacks and provide desired security property, especially support perfect forward secrecy.

1.2 Related Work

The communication between two parties in IoT could be performed to negotiate a session key. Since Diffie and Hellman [1] devised the first key agreement scheme, a large of 2PAKA protocols [6, 7] were proposed to provide stronger security and better performance. Most of these schemes are based on traditional PKI which need a certification authority to manage public-key certificates that binds the user to his public key. However, the storage, storage, and transmission of certificates require significant overheads. To remove the cost of certificate management, many identity-based 2PAKA (ID-2PAKA) were proposed. Using IBC, ECC and bilinear mapping, Gupta et al. [18] put forward a secure ID-2PAKA protocol for IIoT and claimed their scheme was efficient than other state-of-the-art competing protocols. Dang et al.[19] designed an ID-2PAKA and claimed their scheme was provably secure in eCK model. Unfortunately, Deng et al. [20] pointed that two specific attacks, put forward a novel ID-2PAKA protocol without pair operation and provided the security proofs in eCK model.

In 2012, DING [21] proposed the first provable security key exchange protocol based on LWE, which has high computational efficiency and can be extended to RLWE. The protocol solves the above error elimination problem by rounding the signal function and extracting the shared key from two very close values. In 2016, Zhao et al. [22] put forward an identity-based AKA protocol from the LWE, which applies DH ephemeral key to compute key materials, introduces error item, uses encoding bases of ideal lattice as the tool for analyzing error tolerance, and makes reasonable suggests for parameters setting. In 2019, Li et al. [23] using secure public-key encryption and ciphertext compression technology designs an implicit authentication key exchange protocol. After, combining a post-quantum DH like protocol with an identity-based signcryption scheme Chen et al. [24] put forward the AKA based on elliptic curve cryptography.

In 2020, Banerjee et al. [25] proposed a quantum-secure certificate-less AKA protocol for Transport Layer Security (TLS) handshakes which saves the communication overheads by using identity-based to replace traditional certificate-based cryptography. [26] uses standard Fujisaki-Okamoto transform [27] and ID-KEM generic constructions to convert post-quantum DLP-IBE [28] to CCA-secure IBE and IND-CCA2-secure ID-KEM. Then, combining IND-CCA2-secure ID-KEM and CPA-secure NewHope-KEM [29] designs a quantum-secure ID-AKA protocol based on the FSXY construction [30]. However, although [16] provides the quantum-secure, the AKE protocol constructed by KEM leads to more communication cost. At the same year, Islam et al. [31] proposed a post-quantum 2PAKA protocol using IBC. The scheme is provably security in RO model based on CBi-ISIS and Bi-ISIS.

Recently, Gupta et al. [32] proposed a lattice-based 2PAKA protocol using IBC for IoT. However, the communication overhead is huge.

1.3 Organization of the Paper

The paper of the remaining is organized as follows. In Sect. 2, the preliminaries used in presented protocol are presented. Section 3 describes the LB-ID-AKA protocol in detail. The correctness analysis is given in Sect. 4. Section 5 analyses the sufficient security strength of the proposed scheme. Lastly, Sect. 6 concludes the paper.

2   Preliminaries

In this section, for ease of understanding, we briefly describe the technology used in presented protocol.

2.1 Compression and Decompression

Suppose for $0 < d < \lceil \log(q) \rceil$ be an integer, and q is a modules. The compression technology [33] consists of two polynomial functions: $Compress_q(x, d)$ and $Decompress_q(x, d)$. These two functions are defines as:

- $Compress_q(x, d)$: It inputs $x \in Z_q$ and outputs an integer in $\{0, \ldots., 2^d - 1\}$ where $0 < d < \lceil \log(q) \rceil$. It can be represented as .

$$Compress_q(x, d) = \left\lceil (2^d/q) \cdot x \right\rfloor mod^+ 2^d, x \in Z_q. \tag{1}$$

- $Decompress_q(x, d)$: It inputs the result of $Compress_q$ function and outputs a value x' which is an approximate value of x. It can be described as follows:

$$Decompress_q(x, d) = \left\lceil (q/2^d) \cdot x \right\rfloor, x \in Z_q \tag{2}$$

These two functions satisfy $Decompress_q(Compress_q(x, d), d) = x + e_x$ where e_x is a much small value.

2.2 Peikert's Reconciliation Mechanism

Because of the efficiency, Peikert's reconciliation mechanism is widely used in the designing of AKA protocol based-LWE problem. We give a briefly introduction as follows. The details are in the [34].

Peikert's reconciliation mechanism consists of three functions, namely modular rounding function n $\lfloor \cdot \rceil_{q,2}$, cross-rounding function $\langle \cdot \rangle_{q,2}$ and reconciliation function $Rec()$. $\lfloor \cdot \rceil_{q,2}$.

Suppose for $x \in Z_q$, cross-rounding function $\langle x \rangle_{q,2}$ represents $Z_q \rightarrow Z_2$, which can be computed as $\langle x \rangle_{q,2} = \left\lfloor \frac{4}{q} x \right\rfloor mod\ 2$.

Given an integer q, modular rounding function $\lfloor \cdot \rceil_{q,2}$ represents $Z_q \rightarrow Z_2$, which can be computed as $\lfloor \cdot \rceil_{q,2} = \left\lfloor \frac{2}{q} x \right\rceil$.

If q is an odd, above-mentioned function needs to compute in Z_{2q} rather than Z_q to eliminate the error. Thus, the function used to realize $Z_q \rightarrow Z_{2q}$ is randomized doubling function $dbl()$, which can be computed as $dbl(v) = 2v + e$.

Error reconciliation mechanism represents $Z_{2q} \times Z_2 \rightarrow Z_2$, which can be computed as $Rec(w, \sigma) = \begin{cases} 0 \text{ if } w \in I_\sigma + E \bmod 2q \\ 1 \quad \text{otherwise} \end{cases}$.

Where $q \geq 2$ is an integer, $Z_q = \{-\frac{q}{2}, \ldots, 0, \ldots, \frac{q}{2} - 1\}$, two intervals $I_0 = \{0, 1, \ldots, \lfloor\frac{q}{2}\rfloor - 1\}$, $I_1 = \{-\lfloor\frac{q}{2}\rfloor, \ldots, -1\}$ and $E = [-\frac{q}{4}, \frac{q}{4})$.

2.3 MLWE

Module learning with errors (MLWE) was proposed by Langlois and stehle [35] in 2015 which is an extension of LWE and RLWE. Let k, m, η, n be positive integers, R_q denote $Z_q[x]/(x^n + 1)$, β_η is centered binomial distribution. MLWE is distinguishing uniform samples $(A_i, b_i = A_i s + e) \in (R_q^{m \times n} \times R_q^n)$ from sample $(A, b) \in (R_q^{m \times k} \times R_q^k)$ where $A_i \in R_q^{m \times k}$ is uniform and $b_i = A_i s + e$ with $s \leftarrow \beta_\eta^k$ common to all samples and $e \leftarrow \beta_\eta^m$ fresh for every sample. More precisely, for an algorithm $\mathcal{A}$, we define

$$\text{Adv}_{m,n,q,k,\eta}^{MLWE}(\mathcal{A}) = \left| \Pr\left[b' = 1 : \begin{array}{l} A \leftarrow R_q^{m \times k}, (s, e) \leftarrow (\beta_\eta^k, \beta_\eta^m) \\ b = As + e, b' \leftarrow \mathcal{A}(A, b) \end{array} \right] \right.$$

$$\left. - \Pr\left[b' = 1 : A \leftarrow R_q^{m \times k}, b \in R_q^m, b' \leftarrow \mathcal{A}(A, b) \right] \right|$$

3 The Proposed LB-ID-2PAKA Protocol

In this section, the system model is described firstly. Then, we designed a post-quantum AKA protocol based on the identity cryptography for two-party communication in IoT. The symbols and descriptions used in this paper are presented in Table 1.

The LB-ID-2PAKA protocol is made up of three phases, namely, system setup phase, registration phase and authentication key agreement phase. To illustrate this further, we describe the LB-ID-2PAKA in details.

3.1 System Setup Phase

The input of Setup phase is security parameter λ. At the end of Setup phase, KGC generates the system parameters and master private key and public key pair of KGC. The details are as follows:

a) KGC picks a random vector d_{KGC} as the private key and computes the corresponding public key $P_{KGC} = d_{KGC}^T A$.
b) It selects three one-way secure hash functions $H_i : \{0, 1\}^* \rightarrow Z_q^*$ for $i = \{1, 2, 3\}$.
c) It stores d_{KGC} secret and keeps the $pp = \{\lambda, q, m, A, P_{KGC}, H_i : i \in \{1, 2, 3\}\}$ public.

Table 1. Symbols and corresponding descriptions.

Symbol	Description
U_i/U_j	The user
KGC	Key generate center
λ	System security parameter
q	A positive integer
d_{KGC}	Private key of KGC
P_{KGC}	Public key of KGC
A	Matrix with rank n
ID_i/ID_j	The identity of user U_i/U_j
$r_i/x_i/y_i$	Random vector
D_i	Private key of user U_i
P_i	Public key of user U_i
T_i/T_j	The timestamp of user U_i/U_j
d_x/d_y	An integer in compress function
T	Transpose operations
H_i	One-way secure hash functions
$dbl()$	Randomized doubling function
$\lfloor \cdot \rceil_{p,q}$	Modular rounding function
$\langle \cdot \rangle_{p,q}$	Cross-rounding function
Rec	Reconciliation function

3.2 Registration Phase

Before the user U_i communicates with other entities in the IoT, U_i should initiate a registration request to the KGC through a secure channel. Then KGC computes and returns corresponding private key using identity-based cryptography. As shown in Fig. 1, the details are as follows:

a) U_i selects identifier ID_i and sends the registration request $\{ID_i\}$ to the KGC through a secure channel;

b) Receiving the registration request, KGC checks whether ID_i exists in the registry. If it exists, aborts session. Else, KGC performs the c) steps;

c) KGC firstly picks a vector $r_i \in z_q^m$ at random. Then, KGC calculates the private key $R_i = r_i^T A$ and $d_i = (r_i + h_i d_{KGC}) mod q$ where $h_i = H_1(ID_i, R_i)$, and returns U_i's private key $\{D_i = (d_i, R_i)\}$ to U_i;

d) After receiving D_i, U_i computes $h_i = H_1(ID_i, R_i)$ and verifies the validity of the private key by checking whether $d_i^T A? = R_i + h_i P_{KGC}$ is holds. At last, U_i calculates her/his public key $P_i = d_i^T A = R_i + h_i P_{KGC}$.

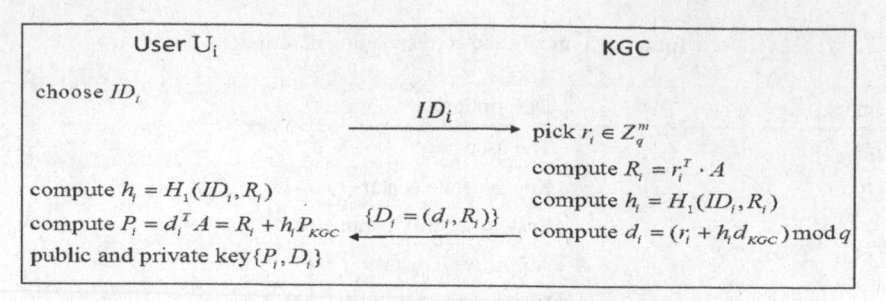

Fig. 1. The registration phase of LB-ID-2PAKA

3.3 Authentication Key Agreement Phase

Before U_i communicates with U_j, they should authenticate mutually and negotiate a common session key. The details are in Fig. 2.

a) U_i picks vectors $x_i, y_i \in z_q^m$ randomly, then calculates $Y_i = y_i^T A$, $X_i = Compress_q(Ax_i + e_1, d_x)$ and $l_i = H_2(X_i||Y_i||R_i||T_i)$, where T_i is the current timestamp. U_i computes the signature $\delta_i = y_i + l_i d_i \bmod q$ and sends the message $m_1 = \{ID_i, \delta_i, R_i, T_i, X_i, Y_i\}$ to U_j.

b) After the receipt m_1 from U_i, U_j checks whether $T_i' - T_i \leq \Delta T$ is holds. If not, the session is aborted. Else, U_j computes $l_i = H_2(X_i||Y_i||R_i||T_i)$ and U_i's public key $P_i = R_i + H_1(ID_i, R_i)P_{KGC}$. Then U_j checks the validity of signature δ_i by checking whether $\delta_i^T A? = Y_i + l_i P_i$ is holds. If it is equal, the user U_j authenticates U_i successfully. Else, the session aborts. After successful authentication, U_j computes $X'_i = Decompress_q(X_i, d_x)$ to obtain the key materials. Then, U_j selects random vectors $x_j, y_j \in z_q^m$, and calculates $Y_j = Compress_q(A^T x_j + e_2, d_y)$. After that, U_j executes Peikert's reconciliation mechanism to compute session key. U_j calculates $v = X_i'^T x_j + e$, $\bar{v} = dbl(v)$, $c = \langle \bar{v} \rangle_{2q,2}$ and $K_j = [\bar{v}]_{2q,2}$. Then, U_j computes $Y_j = y_j^T A$, $l_j = H_2(X_j||Y_j||R_j||T_j)$, the signature $\delta_j = y_j + l_j d_j \bmod q$ and sends $m_2 = \{ID_j, \delta_j, R_j, T_j, X_j, Y_j, c\}$ to U_i, where T_j is the current timestamp. After sending m_2, U_j computes the session key $SK_j = H(K_j||ID_i||ID_j||T_i||T_j)$.

c) After the receipt m_2 from U_j, U_i checks whether $T_j' - T_j \leq \Delta T$ is holds. If not, the session is aborted. Else, U_i computes $l_j = H_2(X_j||Y_j||R_j||T_j)$ and U_j's public key $P_j = R_j + H_1(ID_j, R_j)P_{KGC}$. Then U_i checks the validity of signature δ_j by checking whether $\delta_j^T A? = Y_j + l_j P_j$ is hold. If it is equal, the user U_i authenticates U_j successfully. Else, the session aborts. After successful authentication, U_i computes $X'_j = Decompress_q(X_j, d_y)$ to obtain the key materials. After that, the user U_i calculates $v' = 2x_i^T X'_j$ and $K_i = Rec(v', c)$ using reconciliation function. At last, U_i computes the session key $SK_i = H(K_i||ID_i||ID_j||T_i||T_j)$.

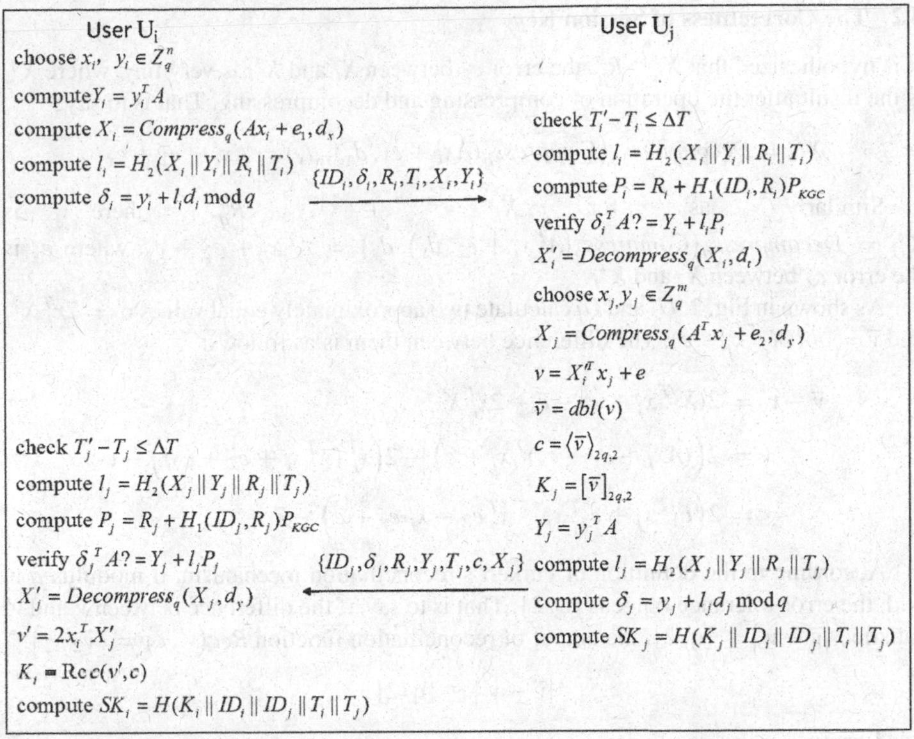

User U_i	User U_j
choose x_i, $y_i \in Z_q^n$	
compute $Y_i = y_i^T A$	
compute $X_i = Compress_q(Ax_i + e_1, d_x)$	check $T_i' - T_i \leq \Delta T$
compute $l_i = H_2(X_i \| Y_i \| R_i \| T_i)$	compute $l_i = H_2(X_i \| Y_i \| R_i \| T_i)$
compute $\delta_i = y_i + l_i d_i \bmod q$ $\quad \{ID_i, \delta_i, R_i, T_i, X_i, Y_i\} \longrightarrow$	compute $P_i = R_i + H_1(ID_i, R_i)P_{KGC}$
	verify $\delta_i^T A? = Y_i + l_i P_i$
	$X_i' = Decompress_q(X_i, d_t)$
	choose $x_j, y_j \in Z_q^m$
	$X_j = Compress_q(A^T x_j + e_2, d_y)$
	$v = X_i^\pi x_j + e$
	$\bar{v} = dbl(v)$
check $T_j' - T_j \leq \Delta T$	$c = \langle \bar{v} \rangle_{2q,2}$
compute $l_j = H_2(X_j \| Y_j \| R_j \| T_j)$	$K_j = [\bar{v}]_{2q,2}$
compute $P_j = R_j + H_1(ID_j, R_j)P_{KGC}$	$Y_j = y_j^T A$
verify $\delta_j^T A? = Y_j + l_j P_j$ $\quad \{ID_j, \delta_j, R_j, Y_j, T_j, c, X_j\} \longleftarrow$ compute $l_j = H_2(X_j \| Y_j \| R_j \| T_j)$	
$X_j' = Decompress_q(X_j, d_y)$	compute $\delta_j = y_j + l_j d_j \bmod q$
$v' = 2x_i^T X_j'$	compute $SK_j = H(K_j \| ID_i \| ID_j \| T_i \| T_j)$
$K_i = \mathrm{Rec}(v', c)$	
compute $SK_i = H(K_i \| ID_i \| ID_j \| T_i \| T_j)$	

Fig. 2. The authentication key agreement phase of LB-ID-2PAKA

4 Correctness Analysis

In this section, the correctness analysis is given in this section, which consist of signature's correctness and the correctness of session key.

4.1 The Correctness of Signature

The receiver verifies whether the equation $\delta_i^T A? = Y_i + l_i P_i$ is hold to check the authenticity of the message.

Proof:

$$
\begin{aligned}
\delta_i^T A &= (y_i + l_i d_i)^T A \\
&= (y_i + l_i d_i)^T A \\
&= (y_i + l_i(r_i + h_i d_{KGC}))^T A \\
&= y_i^T A + l_i r_i^T A + l_i h_i d_{KGC}^T A \\
&= Y_i + l_i R_i + l_i h_i P_{KGC} \\
&= Y_i + l_i(R_i + h_i P_{KGC}) \\
&= Y_i + l_i P_i
\end{aligned}
$$

The verification of $\delta_j^T A? = Y_j + l_j P_j$ is similar to above-mentioned proof.

4.2 The Correctness of Session Key

It is hypothesized that $X_i \in R_q^k$, the error e_x between X_i and X'_i is very tiny, where X'_i is the result after the operation of compressing and decompressing. That is to say:

$$X'_i = Decompress_q(Compress_q(Ax_i + e_1, d_x), d_x) = Ax_i + e_1 + e_x$$

Similarly,   as   for X_j $\in$ R_q^k,   there   is
$X'_j = Decompress_q(Compress_q(A^T x_j + e_2, d_y), d_y) = A^T x_j + e_2 + e_y$, where e_y is the error e_x between X_j and X'_j.

As shown in Fig. 2, U_i and U_j calculate two approximately equal values $v' = 2x_i^T X'_j$ and $\bar{v} = dbl(X'^T_i x_j + e)$. The difference between them is as follows:

$$\bar{v} - v' = 2(X'^T_i x_j + e) - \bar{e} - 2x_i^T X'_j$$
$$= 2\left((Ax_i + e_1 + e_x)^T x_j + e\right) - 2\left(x_i^T(A^T x_j + e_2 + e_y)\right) - \bar{e}$$
$$= 2\left(e_1^T x_j + e_x^T x_j - x_i^T e_2 - x_i^T e_y + e\right) - \bar{e}$$

According to the definition of Peikert's reconciliation mechanism, if modulus q is odd, the error-tolerance range is $\lfloor q/2 \rfloor$. That is to say, if the difference between $\bar{v}$ and v' satisfied $|\bar{v} - v'| \le \lfloor q/2 \rfloor$, the output of reconciliation function $Rec(v', c) = \lfloor \bar{v}_{2q,2} \rceil$.

$$|\bar{v} - v'| \le \lfloor q/2 \rfloor$$

Turn to

$$2\left(e_1^T x_j + e_x^T x_j - x_i^T e_2 - x_i^T e_y + e\right) - \bar{e} \le \left\lfloor \frac{q}{2} \right\rfloor$$

$$2\left(e_1^T x_j + e_x^T x_j - x_i^T e_2 - x_i^T e_y + e\right) - \bar{e} \le \left\lfloor \frac{q}{2} \right\rfloor$$

$$e_1^T x_j + e_x^T x_j - x_i^T e_2 - x_i^T e_y + e - \frac{1}{2}\bar{e} \le \left\lfloor \frac{q}{4} \right\rfloor$$

$$e_1^T x_j + e_x^T x_j - x_i^T e_2 - x_i^T e_y + e \le \left\lfloor \frac{q}{4} \right\rfloor \tag{3}$$

According to the definition, the $\bar{e}$ is tiny small, so $\frac{1}{2}\bar{e}$ is much smaller. Thus, the inequality can turn to (3). In contrast with the correctness proof of Kyber's public encryption scheme [36], the inequality (3) above is much the same. The inequality in Kyber's public encryption scheme is as follows (4)

$$e_1^T x_j + e_x^T x_j - x_i^T e_2 - x_i^T e_y + e + e_v < \left\lfloor \frac{q}{4} \right\rfloor \tag{4}$$

It is obvious that there is the slight difference between inequality (3) and (4). The inequality (4) increases an error vector e_v, which is much small. According to the analysis of Kyber, as long as selecting appropriate parameters, the probability that the inequality (4) is true is more than. That is to say, the probability that the inequality (3) fails is less than 2^{-128}. That is to say, the probability that our LB-ID-AKA protocol fails to negotiates the same session key is no more than 2^{-128}.

5   Security Analysis

5.1   Informal Security Analysis

In this section, the informal security analysis of the LB-ID-2PAKA is provided.

User Impersonation Attack. In the disguise of U_i, $\mathcal{A}$ must construct valid $\{ID_i, \delta_i, R_i, T_i, X_i, Y_i\}$ to pass authentication of the user U_j. However, $\mathcal{A}$ cannot acquired the correct signature δ_i without knowing d_i. Likewise, because $\mathcal{A}$ cannot construct valid authenticator δ_j, $\mathcal{A}$ fails to disguises U_j as a valid user. So the proposed LB-ID-AKA protocol can withstand user impersonation attack.

Man in the Middle Attack. As shown in Fig. 2, the user U_i and U_j achieve mutual authentication using identity-based signature. If an attacker $\mathcal{A}$ wants to launch man-in-the-middle attack, $\mathcal{A}$ needs to calculate the key materials $2x_i A^T x_j$ from messages $\{ID_i, \delta_i, R_i, T_i, X_i, Y_i\}$ and $\{ID_j, \delta_j, R_j, T_j, X_j, Y_j, c\}$ which are from the session $\mathcal{A}$ disguises as the user U_i/U_j communicated with U_j/U_i. However, the difficulty of calculating $2x_i A^T x_j$ is equivalent to the difficulty of solving LWE lattice hard problem, which is obviously not feasible. As a result, the proposed LB-ID-AKA protocol is immune to the man-in-the-middle attack.

Unknown Key-Share Attack. In our LB-ID-AKA protocol, the user U_i and U_j figure out the session key as $SK_i = H(K_i||ID_i||ID_j||T_i||T_j)$ and $SK_j = H(K_j||ID_i||ID_j||T_i||T_j)$ respectively, where $K_i = Rec(2x_i^T X'_j, c)$, $K_j = \left[dbl(X_i'^T x_j + e) \right]_{2q,2}$. The computation of session key consists of identity ID_i and ID_j, the key material K_i and K_j. The key material is verified by the identity-based signature δ_i and δ_j. Moreover, the adversary $\mathcal{A}$ has no knowledge of the private key d_i and d_j of the user U_i and U_j. Thus, $\mathcal{A}$ has no way to know the value of generated key SK. Therefore, our LB-ID-AKA protocol defends the unknown key-share attack.

Known-Key Attack. It is assumed that $\mathcal{A}$ obtains the current session key SK between U_i and U_j. In our LB-ID-AKA protocol, the user U_i and U_j figure out the session key as $SK_i = H(K_i||ID_i||ID_j||T_i||T_j)$ and $SK_j = H(K_j||ID_i||ID_j||T_i||T_j)$ respectively, where $K_i = Rec(2x_i^T X'_j, c)$, $K_j = \left[dbl(X_i'^T x_j + e) \right]_{2q,2}$. It is obvious that $\mathcal{A}$ has difficulty in calculating past session key, since $\mathcal{A}$ has no knowledge of ephemeral secret key x_i and x_j. Therefore, the designed LB-ID-AKA protocol is free of known-key attack.

Perfect Forward Secrecy. It is hypothesized that $\mathcal{A}$ obtains the perennial private key of communication parties U_i and U_j at T. If $\mathcal{A}$ wishes to calculate the session key before T, $\mathcal{A}$ needs to compute $SK_i = H(K_i||ID_i||ID_j||T_i||T_j)$. Because the value of K_i or K_j is calculated using Peikert's reconciliation mechanism, and the ephemeral secret key x_i and x_j are only public to itself, it's impossible for $\mathcal{A}$ to figure out past session key $SK_i = H(K_i||ID_i||ID_j||T_i||T_j)$. Therefore, our LB-ID-AKA protocol guarantees perfect forward secrecy.

No key Control. In our LB-ID-AKA protocol, the user U_i and U_j figure out the session key as $SK_i = H(K_i||ID_i||ID_j||T_i||T_j)$ and $SK_j = H(K_j||ID_i||ID_j||T_i||T_j)$ respectively, where $K_i = Rec(2x_i^T X'_j, c)$, $K_j = \left[dbl(X_i'^T x_j + e)\right]_{2q,2}$. Since the ephemeral secret key x_i and x_j are selected randomly by U_i and U_j respectively. As a result, the user $U_i(U_j)$ is incapable of making the negotiated SK_i be a pre-selected value. That is to say, a pre-selected value SK is only accepted by the party who selects. Thus, our LB-ID-AKA protocol satisfies no key control.

5.2 Security Proof

Based on the Dolev-Yao(DY) threat model [37] and random oracle model (ROM) [38], we present the adversary model for proposed LB-ID-2PAKA.

Threat Model

Participants. In a 2PAKA protocol, the participants consists of two categories: user(U_i) and key generation center(KGC). Both of them can run several instances Π. Π^t represents $t-th$ instance of an executing participant. Thus, Π_{KGC}^{t1} and $\Pi_{U_i}^{t2}$ represent of KGC and U_i respectively.

Queries. The interaction between the adversary $\mathcal{A}$ and challenger $\mathcal{C}$ is performed merely through the corresponding oracle query, which emulates the attack capability of the adversary in real world.

Setup(λ): The adversary $\mathcal{A}$ inputs parameter λ, challenger $\mathcal{C}$ performs all operations in the setup phase. At the end of the query, $\mathcal{A}$ can learn the major public and system parameter.

HashqueriestoH$_i$: The challenger $\mathcal{C}$ keeps a hash list L_{H_i}, which is empty initially. L_{H_i} is made up of several tuples (x, y), where x is the input of H_i, y is the output of H_i. In response to H_i asked by $\mathcal{A}$, $\mathcal{C}$ searchs the corresponding y to given x. If L_{H_i} exists tuple (x, y), $\mathcal{C}$ outputs y. Otherwise, $\mathcal{C}$ selects and returns a random $y \in Z_q^*$, and inserts the tuple (x, y) into the L_{H_i}.

Corrupt(ID_i): The challenger $\mathcal{C}$ plays the role of KGC in this query. At the end of this query, $\mathcal{A}$ registers successfully using the identity of ID_i and receives the private key of ID_i.

Unwrap_private_key(U_i): To response this query, challenger $\mathcal{C}$ returns the private key of the registered user U_i.

Execute$(\Pi_{i,j}^k)$: This query simulates the passive attack capability of $\mathcal{A}$. To reply this query, challenger $\mathcal{C}$ runs the LB-ID-2PAKA protocol Π_U^i with its partner. At the end of running LB-ID-AKA, $\mathcal{A}$ learns the message transmitting in the public channel.

Send$(\Pi_{i,j}^k, m)$: This query simulates the active attack capability of $\mathcal{A}$. To reply this query, challenger $\mathcal{C}$ plays the role of receiving the message m, he/she runs the LB-ID-AKA protocol Π_E^k with its partner. At the end of running LB-ID-2PAKA, $\mathcal{C}$ returns the message to $\mathcal{A}$. Especially, **Send**$(\Pi_{i,j}^k, start)$ can initiate protocol running, $\mathcal{A}$ will receive the login request.

Reveal$(\Pi_{i,j}^k)$: This query simulates the capability of $\mathcal{A}$ initiating known-key attack. Suppose for **Reveal**$(\Pi_{i,j}^k)$, $\mathcal{A}$ learns the past session key and uses it to perform attack. If $\mathcal{A}$ sends **Reveal**$(\Pi_{i,j}^k)$ query to $\mathcal{C}$, challenger $\mathcal{C}$ may reply as follows:

If Π_i^k and his partner Π_j^k has negotiated session key $SK_{i,j}$, and Π_i^k and his partner Π_j^k hasn't been performed $Test()$ query, $\mathcal{C}$ outputs the fresh session key $SK_{i,j}$.
Else, $\mathcal{C}$ outputs $\perp$ to $\mathcal{A}$.

Test$(\Pi_{i,j}^k)$: This query doesn't simulates the actual attack capability of $\mathcal{A}$, which is used for evaluating the semantic security of the session key. It is noted that the adversary $\mathcal{A}$ ask to $\mathcal{C}$ this query only once for each $\Pi_{i,j}^k$. As for $\Pi_{i,j}^k$, if this instance doesn't generate session key $SK_{i,j}$ at the end of protocol running, $\mathcal{C}$ outputs $\perp$ to $\mathcal{A}$ as a reply; Otherwise, $\mathcal{C}$ will perform coin toss experiment to generate random b. If $b = 0$, $\mathcal{C}$ outputs the actual session key $SK_{i,j}$; Else, $\mathcal{C}$ outputs a random string of the same length with the actual session key $SK_{i,j}$.

Corrupt$(\Pi_{i,j}^k)$: This query simulates the corrupt user capability of $\mathcal{A}$, which is used to evaluating the perfect forward security of the protocol. As a reply, $\mathcal{C}$ outputs the past session key $SK_{i,j}$ or $\perp$ to $\mathcal{A}$.

Definition (Semantic Security of Session Key): Suppose $\mathcal{A}$ is a probabilistic polynomial time (PPT) adversary, which $\mathcal{A}$ can distinguish the random number of the same size from session key. First, $\mathcal{A}$ executes above-mentioned queries any times and only once **Test**$(\Pi_{i,j}^k)$. Then, $\mathcal{A}$ output whether the result of **Test**$\left(\Pi_{i,j}^k\right)$ query is session key. $\mathcal{A}$ wins the tossing coin game if **Test**$\left(\Pi_{i,j}^k\right)$ query value b' is equal to the guessed value b of $\mathcal{A}$. The probability $\mathcal{A}$ successes in the game can be defined as

$$Adv_{\mathcal{P}}^{AKA}(\mathcal{A}) = |\Pr[\text{Succ}_0] - 1| \tag{5}$$

Provable Security Theorem 1: Suppose $\mathcal{A}$ is a PPT adversary who can execute above-mentioned queries any times and only once **Test**$(\Pi_{i,j}^k)$. The probability $\mathcal{A}$ breaks semantic security of session key can be defined as

$$Adv_{\mathcal{P}}^{AKA}(\mathcal{A}) = \frac{1}{q_{H_1}^2} + \frac{1}{q_{H_3}^2} + Adv_{p,q}^{MLWE}(\mathcal{A}_2) + Adv_{p,q}^{MLWE}(\mathcal{A}_1 \tag{6}$$

where $\mathcal{A}_1$ is an adversary who solves the decisional MLWE, q_s, q_{H_1} and q_{H_3} are the numbers of adversary executes $send()$ oracle, hash oracle, respectively.

It is proved that the negotiated session key is indistinguishable from the random bits through a series of game G_i $(i = 0, 1, 2, \ldots)$.

Game G_0: The initial game is to the real world.

$$\Pr[Succ_0] = 0 \tag{7}$$

Game G_1: In game G_1, $\mathcal{A}$ lunches **HashqueriestoH**$_1$. This game is similar to G_0, and the only difference is that the l_i and l_j are no longer generated using H_2, but is sampled in the hash list. The challenger $\mathcal{C}$ keeps the tuple of H_1^{list}. The adversary $\mathcal{A}$ who can distinguish between G_0 and G_1 can also distinguish the value computed through hash function from a value searched in the H_1^{list}. Moreover, according to birthday paradox, the probability of hash collision is $1/q_{H_1}^2$. Therefore, the advantage of $\mathcal{A}$ distinguishes G_1 from G_0 is

$$\Delta_0 = |\Pr[Succ_1] - \Pr[Succ_0]| = \frac{1}{q_{H_1}^2} \tag{8}$$

Game G_2: $\mathcal{A}$ lunches **Execute**$(\Pi_{i,j}^k)$ query, challenger $\mathcal{C}$ replies with $m_1 = \{ID_i, \delta_i, R_i, T_i, X_i, Y_i\}$ and $m_2 = \{ID_j, \delta_j, R_j, T_j, X_j, Y_j, c\}$ to $\mathcal{A}$ during LB-ID-AKA running. Then, $\mathcal{A}$ misuses m_1 and m_2 to learn session key $SK_j = H(K_j||ID_i||ID_j||T_i||T_j)$. The adversary $\mathcal{A}$ who can distinguish between G_2 and G_1 can also breaks MLWE. Due to the indistinguishability of G_2 and G_1, the advantage of $\mathcal{A}$ wins the game is

$$\Delta_1 = |\Pr[Succ_2] - \Pr[Succ_1]| = 0 \tag{9}$$

Game G_3: In game G_3, $\mathcal{A}$ lunches **Send**$(\Pi_{i,j}^k, m)$ query. $\mathcal{A}$ forges signature $\delta_i^* = Y_i^* + l_i^* P_i$ and c^* generated at random, then lunches **Send**$(\Pi_{i,j}^k, m)$ query using δ_i^* and c^* replace δ_i and c, respectively. Because the unforgeability of the signature, the probability $\mathcal{A}$ can distinguish between G_3 and G_2 is negligible. As a result, the advantage of $\mathcal{A}$ wins the game is

$$\Delta_2 = |\Pr[Succ_3] - \Pr[Succ_2]| = 0 \tag{10}$$

Game G_4: In game G_4, $\mathcal{A}$ lunches **HashqueriestoH**$_3$. This game is similar to G_3, and the only difference is that the l_i and l_j are no longer generated using H_3, but is sampled in the hash list. The challenger $\mathcal{C}$ keeps the tuple of H_3^{list}. The adversary $\mathcal{A}$ who can distinguish between G_4 and G_3 can also distinguish the value computed through hash function from a value searched in the H_3^{list}. Moreover, according to birthday paradox, the probability of hash collision is $1/q_3^2$. Therefore, the advantage of $\mathcal{A}$ distinguishes G_4 from G_3 is

$$\Delta_3 = |\Pr[Succ_4] - \Pr[Succ_3]| = \frac{1}{q_{H_3}^2} \tag{11}$$

Game G_5: In game G_5, the ephemeral public keys X_i and X_j of user U_i and U_j respectively, are no longer MLWE distribution samples, but are uniformly selected at random. In G_4, (A^T, X_j) and (A, X_i) are MLWE sample pairs generated using *Compress*(). Whereas in game G_5, (A^T, X_j) and (A, X_i) are selected from random distribution $U(R_q^{n \times n} \times R_q^n)$ uniformly. Adversary $\mathcal{A}$ who can distinguish between G_4 and G_5 can solve the decisional

MLWE hard problem based on lattice. Therefore, the advantage of $\mathcal{A}_1$ distinguishes G_5 from G_4 is

$$\Delta_4 = |\Pr[Succ_5] - \Pr[Succ_4]| = Adv_{n,q,\eta}^{MLWE}(\mathcal{A}_1) \tag{12}$$

Game G_6: Compared with G_5, (X_i', v) is no longer a sample pair from MLWE distribution in game G_6, which is a sample picked uniformly from random distribution $U(R_q^n \times R_q)$. Adversary $\mathcal{A}$ who can distinguish between G_6 and G_5 can solve the decisional MLWE hard problem based on lattice. Therefore, the advantage of $\mathcal{A}_1$ distinguishes G_6 from G_5 is

$$\Delta_5 = |\Pr[Succ_6] - \Pr[Succ_5]| = Adv_{n,q,\eta}^{MLWE}(\mathcal{A}_2) \tag{13}$$

As above, the probability $\mathcal{A}$ breaks semantic security of session key is

$$Adv_{\mathcal{P}}^{AKA}(\mathcal{A}) = \frac{1}{q_{H_1}^2} + \frac{1}{q_{H_3}^2} + Adv_{p,q}^{MLWE}(\mathcal{A}_2) + Adv_{p,q}^{MLWE}(\mathcal{A}_1)$$

6   Conclusion

With the proliferation of IoT, two-party communications attracts more and more attention, so how to secure negotiate session key in IoT has become one of the research hotspots. A large number of 2PAKA schemes have been presented recently, yet most of them are subject to quantum attack. In this article, we proposed a quantum-secure 2PAKA protocol using lattice cryptography for IoT. The proposed LB-ID-2PAKA protocol makes use of identity-based signature to avoid the complicated certificate management of PKI-based protocol. At the same time, the LB-ID-2PAKA protocol can provide desired security property and withstand various attacks, especially support perfect forward secrecy. Moreover, the provable security analysis shows that our LB-ID-2PAKA protocol is provably secure under the hardness assumption of MLWE.

Acknowledgments. This research was supported by Sichuan Science and Technology Program (no. 2022JDRC0061), the Stability Program of Science and Technology on Communication Security Laboratory (2022) and Foundation of Science and Technology On Communication Security Laboratory of China (No. 61421030107012102).

References

1. Karati, A., Islam, S.H., Karuppiah, M.: Provably secure and lightweight certificateless signature scheme for IIoT environments. IEEE Trans. Ind. Inform. **14**(8), 3701–3711 (2018)
2. Diffie, W., Hellman, M.: New directions in cryptography. IEEE Trans. Inf. Theory **22**(6), 644–654 (1976)
3. Hölbl, M., Welzer, T., Brumen, B.: An improved two-party identity-based authenticated key agreement protocol using pairings. J. Comput. Syst. Sci. **78**(1), 142–150 (2012)

4. Chen, L., Cheng, Z., Smart, N.P.: Identity-based key agreement protocols from pairings. Int. J. Inf. Secur. **6**(4), 213–241 (2007)
5. Ni, L., Chen, G., Li, J., Hao, Y.: Strongly secure identity-based authenticated key agreement protocols. Comput. Elect. Eng. **37**(2), 205–217 (2011)
6. Gupta, D.S., Biswas, G.P.: A novel and efficient lattice-based authenticated key exchange protocol in C-K model. Int. J. Commun. Syst. **31**(3), e3473 (2018)
7. Dierks, T., Rescorla, E.: The transport layer security (TLS) protocol version 1.2 (2008)
8. Cui, J., Wang, Y., Zhang, J., Xu, Y., Zhong, H.: Full session key agreement scheme based on chaotic map in vehicular ad hoc networks. IEEE Trans. Veh. Technol. **69**(8), 8914–8924 (2020)
9. Ouada, F.S., Omar, M., Bouabdallah, A., Tari, A.: Lightweight identity-based authentication protocol for wireless sensor networks. Int. J. Inf. Comput. Secur. **8**(2), 121–138 (2016)
10. Gupta, D.S., Biswas, G.: An ECC-based authenticated group key exchange protocol in IBE framework. Int. J. Commun. Syst. **30**(18), 3363 (2017)
11. Gupta, D.S., Biswas, G.: On securing bi-and tri-partite session key agreement protocol using IBE framework. Wirel. Pers. Commun. **96**(3), 4505–4524 (2017)
12. Guo, C., Chang, C.-C.: An authenticated group key distribution protocol based on the generalized Chinese remainder theorem. Int. J. Commun. Syst. **27**(1), 126–134 (2014)
13. Shor, P.W.: Polynomial-time algorithms for prime factorization and discrete logarithms on a quantum computer. SIAM Rev. **41**(2), 303–330 (1999)
14. Peikert, C.: Some recent progress in lattice-based cryptography. In: Reingold, O. (ed.) TCC 2009. LNCS, vol. 5444, p. 72. Springer, Heidelberg (2009). https://doi.org/10.1007/978-3-642-00457-5_5
15. Lindner, R., Peikert, C.: Better key sizes (and attacks) for LWE-based encryption. In: Kiayias, A. (ed.) CT-RSA 2011. LNCS, vol. 6558, pp. 319–339. Springer, Heidelberg (2011). https://doi.org/10.1007/978-3-642-19074-2_21
16. Alkim, E., Ducas, L., Pöppelmann, T., Schwabe, P.: Post-quantum key exchange -- a new hope. In: USENIX Security Symposium, pp.327–343. USENIX, Austin (2016)
17. Ding, J., Alsayigh, S., Lancrenon, J., Saraswathy, R.V., Snook, M.: Provably secure password authenticated key exchange based on RLWE for the post-quantum world. In: Handschuh, H. (ed.) CT-RSA 2017. LNCS, vol. 10159, pp. 183–204. Springer, Cham (2017). https://doi.org/10.1007/978-3-319-52153-4_11
18. Gupta, D.S., Islam, S.K.H., Obaidat, M.S., et al.: A provably secure and lightweight identity-based two-party authenticated key agreement protocol for IIoT environments. IEEE Syst. J. **PP**(99), 1–10 (2020)
19. Dang, L., et al.: Efficient identity-based authenticated key agreement protocol with provable security for vehicular ad hoc networks. Int. J. Distrib. Sens. Netw. **14**(4), 1–16 (2018)
20. Deng, L., Shao, J., Hu, Z.: Identity based two-party authenticated key agreement scheme for vehicular ad hoc networks. Peer-to-Peer Netw. Appl. **14**(4), 2236–2247 (2021). https://doi.org/10.1007/s12083-021-01181-8
21. Ding, J., Lin, X.: A simple provably secure key exchange scheme based on the learning with errors problem. IACR Cryptology Eprint Archive (2013)
22. Zhao, X., Gao, H., Wang, A.: An identity-based authenticated key exchange protocol from RLWE. J. Comput. Res. Dev. **53**(11), 2482–2490 (2016)
23. Li, Z., Xie, T., Zhang, J., Xu, R.: Post quantum authenticated key exchange protocol based on ring learning with errors problem. J. Comput. Res. Dev. **56**(12), 2694–2701 (2019)
24. Chen, M.: A composable authentication key exchange scheme with post-quantum forward secrecy. J. Comput. Res. Dev. **57**(10), 2157–2176 (2020)
25. Utsav, B., Chandrakasan, A.P.: Efficient post-quantum TLS handshakes using identity-based key exchange from lattices. In: 2020 IEEE International Conference on Communications (ICC) (2020)

26. Bos, J., Costello, C., Naehrig, M., et al.: Post-quantum key exchange for the TLS protocol from the ring learning with errors problem. In: IEEE. 2015 IEEE Symposium on Security and Privacy, pp. 553–570. IEEE, Piscataway (2015)
27. Hofheinz, D., Hövelmanns, K., Kiltz, E.: A modular analysis of the fujisaki-okamoto transformation. In: Kalai, Y., Reyzin, L. (eds.) TCC 2017. LNCS, vol. 10677, pp. 341–371. Springer, Cham (2017). https://doi.org/10.1007/978-3-319-70500-2_12
28. Ducas, L., Lyubashevsky, V., Prest, T.: Efficient identity-based encryption over NTRU lattices. In: Sarkar, P., Iwata, T. (eds.) ASIACRYPT 2014. LNCS, vol. 8874, pp. 22–41. Springer, Heidelberg (2014). https://doi.org/10.1007/978-3-662-45608-8_2
29. Poppelmann, T.: NewHope – algorithm specifications and supporting documentation. NIST Technical Report (2019)
30. Fujioka, A., Suzuki, K., Xagawa, K., Yoneyama, K.: Strongly secure authenticated key exchange from factoring, codes, and lattices. In: Fischlin, M., Buchmann, J., Manulis, M. (eds.) PKC 2012. LNCS, vol. 7293, pp. 467–484. Springer, Heidelberg (2012). https://doi.org/10.1007/978-3-642-30057-8_28
31. Islam, S.H., Zeadally, S.: Provably secure identity-based two-party authenticated key agreement protocol based on CBi-ISIS and Bi-ISIS problems on lattices. J. Inf. Secure Appl. **54** (2020)
32. Daya, S., Sangram, R., Tajinder, S., Madhu, K.: Post-quantum lightweight identity-based two-party authenticated key exchange protocol for internet of vehicles with probable security. Comput. Commun. **181**, 69–79 (2022)
33. Lyubashevsky, V., Peikert, C., Regev, O.: On Ideal lattices and learning with errors over rings. In: Gilbert, H. (ed.) EUROCRYPT 2010. LNCS, vol. 6110, pp. 1–23. Springer, Heidelberg (2010). https://doi.org/10.1007/978-3-642-13190-5_1
34. Peikert, C.: Lattice cryptography for the internet. International workshop on post-quantum cryptigraphy, pp. 197–219 (2014)
35. Langlois, A., Stehlé, D.: Worst-case to average-case reductions for module lattices. Des. Codes Cryptogr. **75**, 565–599 (2015). https://doi.org/10.1007/s10623-014-9938-4
36. Bos, J., Ducas, L., Kiltz, E.: CRYSTALS-Kyber: a CCA-secure module-lattice-based KEM. In: 2018 IEEE European Symposium on Security and Privacy (European S&P), pp. 353–367. IEEE (2018)
37. Dolev, D.A., Yao, A.: On the security of public key protocols. IEEE Trans. Inf. Theory **29**(2), 198–208 (1983)
38. Bellare, M., Rogaway, P.: Entity authentication and key distribution. In: Stinson, D.R. (ed.) CRYPTO 1993. LNCS, vol. 773, pp. 232–249. Springer, Heidelberg (1994). https://doi.org/10.1007/3-540-48329-2_21

Anonymous and Practical Multi-factor Authentication for Mobile Devices Using Two-Server Architecture

Haiyan Cao and Yong Xie[✉]

Department of Computer Technology and Application, Qinghai University,
Xining, China
mark.y.xie@qq.com

Abstract. At present, password authentication technology using single-server architecture has been widely used in practice. However, it cannot resist internal privilege attack, dictionary guessing attack, and other attacks. To solve the above problems, this paper proposes an anonymous and practical multi-factor authentication protocol for mobile devices using two-server architecture with honeywords. The protocol is more secure than the existing single-factor authentication protocols, and can solve serious security problems such as internal privilege attack and direct leakage of private data after the server is compromised using a single server architecture. The strict security analysis proves that the protocol is secure. Compared to similar protocols, our protocol needs lower computation and communication costs, and can better meet the practical application requirements.

Keywords: Mobile devices · Anonymous · Multi-factor authentication · Two-server architecture

1 Introduction

With the rise of mobile application, people are increasingly inseparable from mobile devices. Mobile devices are very useful in our life and become an indispensable part of people. According to the survey, the number of mobile device users in the world reached 6.8 billion in 2019 and is expected to rise to 7.33 billion by 2023 [1], which indicates that everyone in the world is using mobile devices on average. Users can use mobile devices for mobile office, cloud payment, video chat, e-commerce, mobile banking, etc. Mobile communication has penetrated into all aspects of social life.

However, due to the open characteristics of wireless network, although mobile devices bring people convenient and quick experience, there are serious security risks. For example, user privacy information leakage, mobile device loss or theft

Y. Xie—Supported by the National Natural Science Foundation of China under Grant 61862052.

Q. Jiang et al. (Eds.): SPNCE 2022, LNICST 496, pp. 48–61, 2023.
https://doi.org/10.1007/978-3-031-30623-5_4

exposed sensitive information, the hazard of man-in-the-middle attack, etc [2]. Therefore, reliable authentication between the mobile user and the server is essential. Moreover, anonymity in mobile communication and privacy protection of mobile users are indispensable. At present, security authentication protocols with privacy protection function have become the focus of many security researchers.

In [3], an anonymous authentication scheme has been proposed for wireless communication based on a smart card. However, as described in [4], this scheme failed to provide backward security and perfect anonymity. Later, Mun et al. [5] proposed a new global mobile network authentication scheme. Unfortunately, Reddy et al. [6] pointed out that the scheme in [5] was prone to impersonation attack, replay attack and internal privilege attack. To provide a location based service, Memon et al. [7] designed an anonymous communication scheme. But, Reddy et al. [8] found that the protocol still had some security flaws. In distributed systems, single-factor authentication and two-factor authentication are difficult to resist dictionary attack. In [9], a provably secure three-factor scheme has been proposed. Qiu et al. [10] found that the scheme in [9] cannot resist user impersonation attack of key leakage and offline password guessing attack. In addition, the current authentication schemes almost adopt the single-server authentication mode, which have serious security risks and are vulnerable to internal privilege attack and offline dictionary attack, and so on. This is one of the important elements causing the endless security events.

To solve the above problems, we propose an anonymous and practical multi-factor authentication protocol for mobile devices using two-server architecture with honeywords. The protocol uses password, smart card and biometric for identity authentication. Only when the password and biometric factor are correct, the smart card can be activated for identity authentication. It has higher security than single factor and two factors. At the same time, we use a two-server architecture to solve the serious security problems such as internal privilege attacks on a single server and direct leakage of private data after a single server is compromised. Our protocol is demonstrated to be secure under the random oracle model. The performance analysis proves that our proposed scheme is practical and efficient in mobile communication environment.

2   Related Work

Li et al. [11] proposed a user authentication scheme based on biometrics and smart cards. But, Das et al. [12] found that the scheme in [11] has defects in the login and authentication phase, password update phase, and the use of hash function to verify biometric technology. To address these defects, they designed a new scheme, which has good performances such as freely changeable password, low computation cost, and mutual authentication. But then An et al. [13] found that the scheme in [12] cannot resist some security attacks, including impersonation attack, dictionary guessing attack, insider attack, and designed a new scheme. Cao et al. [14] found that the scheme in [13] is prone to replay attack, user masquerading attack and does not guarantee anonymity. They added anonymity to the improved scheme and claimed that the scheme can resist many attacks. Park et al. [15] found that the scheme in [14] can not resist dictionary guessing attack and server impersonation attack. Then, they designed a new scheme. However, the scheme was later found to have many security problems.

Tan et al. [16] proposed a three-factor authentication scheme for user anonymity in the medical system. Unfortunately, Arshad et al. [17] found that the scheme in [16] could not resist replay attack, they designed a new scheme to solve this defect. Lu et al. [18] found that the scheme in [17] could not resist offline dictionary guessing attack and user impersonation attack. Then, they proposed a new scheme. Amin et al. [19] found that Arshad et al.'s scheme could not resist identity trace attack, impersonation attack and designed a new scheme. Wazid et al. [20] found that the scheme in [19] could not resist internal privilege attack, and proposed an efficient three-factor user authentication and key agreement scheme. However, it can be found that the scheme does not achieve true three-factor security.

3   Background

3.1   Fuzzy Extractor

In order to extract secure cryptographic key from biometric information, the fuzzy extractor is proposed [21]. The fuzzy extractor has generation algorithm and regeneration algorithm, described as follows: (1) $\langle \sigma, \theta \rangle = Gen(BIO)$. This is the generation algorithm, the fuzzy extractor inputs BIO based on biometric to generate a uniformly random string σ and an auxiliary string θ. (2) $\sigma = Rep(BIO', \theta)$. This is the regeneration algorithm because there are small deviations when sampling the same biometric BIO' (e.g., fingerprints) from the same person at different times. If $dis(BIO', BIO) \leq t$ (t is a parameter), that is, BIO' and BIO are fairly close to each other, the fuzzy extractor can recover σ by entering BIO' and the public auxiliary string θ.

4   System Model

Our system model is shown in Fig. 1, there are three types of entities involved in our system, namely the user (U_i), the primary server $(Server_A)$ and the secondary server $(Server_B)$ in the two-server model. In the registration stage, the user U_i divides his secret value into two parts, and sends his personal data and part of the secret value to the two servers respectively for registration. Each server has only part of the secret value, and $Server_A$ securely sends a smart card with some parameters to U_i. U_i inserts the smart card into the card reader. Then, U_i inputs identity ID_i, password PW_i and biometric BIO_i^* to authenticates with the two servers. Finally, $Server_A$ and U_i generate session key for subsequent secure communication.

User: U_i can send a login request to the system. After the system passes the authentication, the login is successful. Before logging in, U_i should register on the two servers respectively, which enables the server to verify the request sent by U_i.

Server: primary server $Server_A$ and secondary server $Server_B$. $Server_B$ performs the auxiliary calculation, and then $Server_A$ verifies whether the login request of U_i is legitimate. The servers cannot obtain any valid user information except the ciphertext.

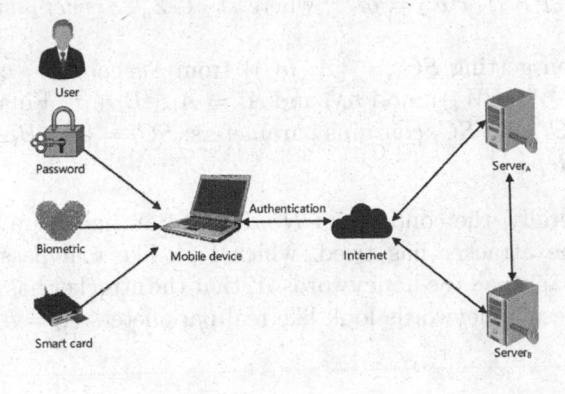

Fig. 1. System model.

5   Our Proposed Protocol

To simplify the following description, we give some notations: $\oplus$ indicates XOR and $\|$ indicates string concatenation.

5.1   System Initialization Phase

G represents a cyclic group whose generator is g, and q is prime order. $h(\cdot)$, $h_0(\cdot)$ are hash functions with ranges $\{0,1\}^l$ (l denotes output length of hash function).

5.2   Registration Phase

The U_i will register separately on two designated servers through a secure channel.

Step 1: U_i selects an identity ID_i and a password PW_i, U_i inputs biometric BIO_i and uses $Gen(\cdot)$ function to generate secret key σ_i and public parameter θ_i, where $\langle \sigma_i, \theta_i \rangle = Gen(BIO_i)$. U_i randomly generates an integer $2^4 \leq n_0 \leq 2^8$ and calculates $\alpha_i = h(h(ID_i \| \sigma_i) \bmod n_0)$. U_i generates random numbers

$x_1 \in Z_q^*$, $\beta_i \in Z_q^*$ and calculates x_2 to satisfy $\alpha_i \beta_i \leftarrow x_1 x_2 \,(\mathrm{mod}\,q)$. Then, U_i sends $\{ID_i, x_1\}$ to the $Server_A$ using a secure communication channel. Similarly, sending $\{ID_i, x_2\}$ to the $Server_B$ using a secure communication channel.

Step 2: After getting $\{ID_i, x_1\}$, $Server_A$ generates the private and public keys (sk_1, PK_1), $PK_1 = g^{sk_1}$, where $sk_1 \in Z_q^*$. $Server_A$ chooses a random integer $e_i \in Z_q^*$ and calculates $A_i = h(ID_i \| sk_1 \| e_i)$. $Server_A$ stores $\{ID_i, x_1, e_i, Honey\_List = 0\}$ in its database, issues a smart card SC_i to U_i, where $SC_i = \{A_i, h(\cdot)\}$.

Step 3: Upon getting $\{ID_i, x_2\}$ from U_i, $Server_B$ generates the private and public keys (sk_2, PK_2), $PK_2 = g^{sk_2}$, where $sk_2 \in Z_q^*$. $Server_B$ stores $\{ID_i, x_2\}$ in its database.

Step 4: Upon getting $SC_i = \{A_i, h(\cdot)\}$ from $Server_A$, U_i calculates $B_i = h((h(ID_i) \oplus \alpha_i \oplus h(PW_i)) \,\mathrm{mod}\, n_0)$ and $A_i^* = A_i \oplus B_i \oplus \sigma_i$. Finally, U_i replaces A_i with A_i^* in SC_i, and SC_i contains parameters: $SC_i = \{A_i^*, B_i, \theta_i, \beta_i, n_0, h(\cdot),$ $h_0(\cdot), Gen(\cdot), Rep(\cdot)\}$.

Remark 1. Generally, the contents of $Honey\_List$ are made up of all the honeywords that the attacker has tried, which look like real passwords but are not [22]. In our paper, all the honeywords A_i' that the attacker has tried are in the $Honey\_List$. These honeywords look like real parameters $A_i = h(ID_i \| sk_1 \| e_i)$ but are not.

5.3   Login and Authentication Phase

The registered U_i can make a login request, and the two server cooperate to verify whether the login request is valid.

Step 1: U_i inserts SC_i into the card reader. Then, U_i inputs identity ID_i, password PW_i and biometric BIO_i^*. SC_i computes $\sigma_i = Rep(BIO_i^*, \theta_i)$, $\alpha_i = h(h(ID_i \| \sigma_i) \,\mathrm{mod}\, n_0)$ and verifies $B_i \overset{?}{=} h((h(ID_i) \oplus \alpha_i \oplus h(PW_i)) \,\mathrm{mod}\, n_0)$. If verification fails, SC_i refuses the login request. If successful, SC_i calculates $A_i = A_i^* \oplus B_i \oplus \sigma_i$. Then, SC_i generates a random integer $r_i \in Z_q^*$ and current timestamp TS_1. SC_i calculates $R_0 = g^{r_i} \,(\mathrm{mod}\,q)$, $C_0 = ID_i \oplus h(PK_1^{r_i})$, $C_1 = A_i \oplus h(ID_i \| TS_1)$, $C_2 = h(ID_i \| A_i \| C_1 \| R_0 \| TS_1)$. Finally, SC_i sends $\{R_0, C_0, C_1, C_2, TS_1\}$ to $Server_A$.

Step 2: After obtaining the message $\{R_0, C_0, C_1, C_2, TS_1\}$, $Server_A$ judges $|TS_1 - TS_1^*| \le \Delta T$?, where TS_1^* indicates the time when the message was received and ΔT indicates the maximum transmission delay. If the verification is successful, $Server_A$ calculates $ID_i' = C_0 \oplus h\left(R_0^{sk_1}\right)$. Then, $Server_A$ searches $\{ID_i, x_1, e_i, Honey\_List\}$ in its database. If ID_i' (ID_i' is used to distinguish between the ID stored in the database and the ID' calculated by the server) is not found, the authentication process is stopped. Otherwise, $Server_A$ computes $A_i' = C_1 \oplus h(ID_i \| TS_1)$, $A_i = h(ID_i \| sk_1 \| e_i)$ and judges whether the derived A_i' equals the computed A_i. If not, $Server_A$ learns that the smart card of U_i has been corrupted and the real password was not obtained by the adversary. Therefore, $Server_A$ adds A_i' to $Honey\_List$ and ignores the login request. In addition, if $|Honey\_List| \geq S_0$, where S_0 represents a threshold, $Server_A$ pauses using the smart card. If they are equal, $Server_A$ checks whether $C_2 \overset{?}{=} h(ID_i \| A_i \| C_1 \| R_0 \| TS_1)$. If it does not match, the authentication process is stopped. Otherwise, $Server_A$ generates current timestamp TS_2 and computes $R_1 = R_0^{x_1} \pmod{q}$, $C_3 = R_1 \oplus h_0\left(PK_2^{sk_1}\right)$, $C_4 = ID_i \oplus h\left(PK_2^{sk_1} \| TS_2\right)$, $C_5 = h\left(ID_i \| C_4 \| R_1 \| TS_2\right)$. Finally, $Server_A$ sends $\{C_3, C_4, C_5, TS_2\}$ to $Server_B$.

Step 3: After receiving $\{C_3, C_4, C_5, TS_2\}$, $Server_B$ checks the condition $|TS_2 - TS_2^*| \leq \Delta T$?. If the verification is successful, $Server_B$ computes $ID_i' = C_4 \oplus h\left(PK_1^{sk_2} \| TS_2\right)$. Then, $Server_B$ searches $\{ID_i, x_2\}$ in its database. If ID_i' (ID_i' is used to distinguish between the ID stored in the database and the ID' calculated by the server) is not found, the authentication process is terminated. Otherwise, $Server_B$ computes $R_1 = C_3 \oplus h_0\left(PK_1^{sk_2}\right)$ and checks whether $C_5 \overset{?}{=} h\left(ID_i \| C_4 \| R_1 \| TS_2\right)$. If it does not match, the session is terminated. Otherwise, $Server_B$ generates current timestamp TS_3 and computes $R_2 = R_1^{x_2} \pmod{q}$, $C_6 = R_2 \oplus h_0\left(PK_1^{sk_2}\right)$, $C_7 = h\left(ID_i \| R_2 \| TS_3\right)$. Finally, $Server_B$ sends $\{C_6, C_7, TS_3\}$ to $Server_A$.

Step 4: After receiving the message $\{C_6, C_7, TS_3\}$, $Server_A$ checks the condition $|TS_3 - TS_3^*| \leq \Delta T$?. If the verification holds, $Server_A$ computes $R_2 = C_6 \oplus h_0\left(PK_2^{sk_1}\right)$ and judges whether $C_7 \overset{?}{=} h\left(ID_i \| R_2 \| TS_3\right)$. If the match fails, the session is terminated. Otherwise, $Server_A$ generates current timestamp TS_4 and calculates $SK_s = h(ID_i \| A_i \| R_0^{sk_1} \| R_2)$, $C_8 = h(ID_i \| A_i \| R_2 \| SK_s \| TS_4)$. Finally, $Server_A$ sends $\{C_8, TS_4\}$ to U_i.

Step 5: Upon getting the message $\{C_8, TS_4\}$, U_i judges $|TS_4 - TS_4^*| \leq \Delta T$?. If the verification is successful, SC_i continues to compute $R_2 = R_0^{\alpha_i \beta_i} \pmod{q}$, $SK_u = h(ID_i \| A_i \| PK_1^{r_i} \| R_2)$ and checks $C_8 \overset{?}{=} h(ID_i \| A_i \| R_2 \| SK_u \| TS_4)$. If it does not match, the session is terminated. Otherwise, both SC_i and $Server_A$ generate the common session key $SK = SK_u = SK_s$.

5.4 Password and Biometric Update Phase

This phase provides user password and biometric update functionality. This process is performed locally and does not require communication with the servers.

Step 1: U_i inserts SC_i into the card reader. Then, U_i provides ID_i, old PW_i and current biometric BIO_i^*. SC_i calculates $\sigma_i = Rep(BIO_i^*, \theta_i)$, $\alpha_i = h\left(h\left(ID_i \| \sigma_i\right) \bmod n_0\right)$ and judges $B_i \overset{?}{=} h((h(ID_i) \oplus \alpha_i \oplus h(PW_i)) \bmod n_0)$. SC_i refuses this update request if the match fails. Otherwise, SC_i requires U_i to supply new password and input new biometric.

Step 2: U_i inputs a new PW_i^{new} and a new BIO_i^{new}. Then, SC_i generates a random integer $2^4 \leq n_0' \leq 2^8$ and calculates $\langle \sigma_i^{new}, \theta_i^{new} \rangle = Gen(BIO_i^{new})$, $\alpha_i^{new} = h\left(h\left(ID_i \| \sigma_i^{new}\right) \bmod n_0'\right)$. SC_i computes $\beta_i^{new} \in Z_q^*$ to satisfy $\alpha_i^{new} \beta_i^{new} = \alpha_i \beta_i$, $B_i^{new} = h((h(ID_i) \oplus \alpha_i^{new} \oplus h(PW_i^{new})) \bmod n_0')$, $A_i^{*new} = A_i^* \oplus B_i \oplus \sigma_i \oplus B_i^{new} \oplus \sigma_i^{new}$.

Step 3: Finally, SC_i replaces $\{A_i^*, B_i, \theta_i, \beta_i, n_0\}$ with $\{A_i^{*new}, B_i^{new}, \theta_i^{new}, \beta_i^{new}, n_0'\}$.

5.5 Smart Card Revocation Phase

If a legitimate U_i lost SC_i, U_i can apply for a new smart card SC_i^{new}. The specific process is as follows:

Step 1: U_i uses the original ID_i, and selects a new PW_i'. U_i inputs biometric BIO_i' and computes $\langle \sigma_i', \theta_i' \rangle = Gen\,(BIO_i')$. U_i generates a random number $2^4 \leq n_0' \leq 2^8$ and computes $\alpha_i' = h\,(h\,(ID_i \| \sigma_i') \bmod n_0')$. U_i generates random numbers $x_1' \in Z_q^*$, $\beta_i' \in Z_q^*$ and computes x_2' to satisfy $\alpha_i' \beta_i' \leftarrow x_1' x_2' \,(\bmod q)$. Then, U_i sends $\{ID_i, x_1'\}$ to the $Server_A$ using a secure channel. Similarly, sending $\{ID_i, x_2'\}$ to the $Server_B$ using a secure channel.

Step 2: Upon getting $\{ID_i, x_1'\}$ from U_i, $Server_A$ generates the private and public keys (sk_1, PK_1), $PK_1 = g^{sk_1}$, where $sk_1 \in Z_q^*$. $Server_A$ chooses a random value $e_i' \in Z_q^*$ and calculates $A_i' = h\,(ID_i \| sk_1 \| e_i')$. $Server_A$ stores $\{ID_i, x_1', e_i', Honey\_List = 0\}$, issues a new $SC_i^{new} = \{A_i', h(\cdot)\}$ to U_i.

Step 3: Upon getting $\{ID_i, x_2'\}$ from U_i, $Server_B$ generates the private and public keys (sk_2, PK_2), $PK_2 = g^{sk_2}$, where $sk_2 \in Z_q^*$. $Server_B$ stores $\{ID_i, x_2'\}$ in its database.

Step 4: After receiving SC_i^{new} from $Server_A$, the user U_i computes $B_i' = h\,((h\,(ID_i) \oplus \alpha_i' \oplus h\,(PW_i')) \bmod n_0')$ and $A_i^{*'} = A_i' \oplus B_i' \oplus \sigma_i'$. Then, U_i replaces A_i' with $A_i^{*'}$ in SC_i^{new}. Finally, $SC_i^{new} = \{A_i^{*'}, B_i', \theta_i', \beta_i',\ n_0', h\,(\cdot),\ h_0\,(\cdot), Gen\,(\cdot), Rep\,(\cdot)\}$.

6 Security Analysis

6.1 Security Model

We propose a formal security model under the assumption of CDHP, which is mainly inspired by the model for AKE [23,24].

Participants and Initialization. Our scheme involves three participants: U_i, $Server_A$, $Server_B$. We define the i-th instance of U_i as U^i, the j-th instance of $Server_A$ as S_A^j, and the k-th instance of $Server_B$ as S_B^k. We define P^i as the i-th instance of a participant. Each user U_i selects a password PW_{U_i} from the dictionary $\mathcal{D}$.

Queries. Through oracle queries, the adversary $\mathcal{A}$ interacts with the simulator $\mathcal{C}$. Oracle queries simulate $\mathcal{A}$'s ability in true attacks. $\mathcal{A}$ can use the following query types:

- $Execute\left(U^i, S_A^j, S_B^k\right)$: We use the query to simulate $\mathcal{A}$'s passive eavesdropping attack. $\mathcal{A}$ can run this query to obtain the messages interchange among the three participants U^i, S_A^j and S_B^k.
- $Send\left(P^i, M\right)$: The active attack of $\mathcal{A}$ will be simulated by using the query. $\mathcal{A}$ simulates a participant sending message M to P^i and gets the response from P^i.

- *Reveal* (P^i): We use this query to simulate a known session key attack. If the instance P^i accepts the session, the session key SK held by P^i is returned. Otherwise, the response is NULL.
- *Corrupt* (U^i, a): We use this query to simulate the corruption ability of $\mathcal{A}$. If $a = 1$, then PW of U_i is displayed; if $a = 2$, then it reveals all parameters stored in the smart card.
- *Corrupt* $\left(S_A^j / S_B^k, a\right)$: The private key of server is displayed if $a = 1$. The account $\{ID_i, x_2\}$ is printed if $a = 2$.
- *DDHP*: The decision DHP oracle is to check $(g^a, g^b)? = g^{ab}$, only $\mathcal{C}$ can query the oracle once in one session.
- *Test* (P^i): This query will not simulate any actual functionality of $\mathcal{A}$. It can define semantic security. If P^i accepts, flip a coin b. If $b = 1$, the real SK is sent to $\mathcal{A}$. Otherwise, $\mathcal{A}$ will be given a random value (the length is the same as SK). Whether the key is real or random is something that $\mathcal{A}$ must determine.

Partner. Two instances U^i and S_A^j are partners of each other if they meet the following conditions: (1) U^i and S_A^j are accepted (this indicates that SK has been negotiated). (2) The same session identification sid is shared between U^i and S_A^j. (3) U^i's partner identifier pid is S_A^j and vice versa.

Freshness. If the instance is fresh, the following three conditions need to be met: (1) P has calculated an accepted SK. (2) The Reveal queries are not made by P and its partner. (3) P is asked the Corrupt queries at most only once.

Semantic security of session key. $\mathcal{A}$ needs to distinguish between a real SK and a random key. $\mathcal{A}$ can make several Test queries for some fresh instances. b' is the guessed bit for bit b selected for the Test query. If the condition $b' = b$ is met, $\mathcal{A}$ wins the game, which is expressed as $Succ$. For protocol P, the advantage of $\mathcal{A}$ for destroying its semantic security is:

$$Adv_P^{AKA}(\mathcal{A}) = |2Pr\left[Succ(\mathcal{A})\right] - 1| = |2Pr\left[b' = b\right] - 1|. \qquad (1)$$

6.2 Security Proof

Theorem 1. *For protocol P, it is assumed that $\mathcal{A}$ breaches the semantic security within a bounded time t in the random oracle, $\mathcal{D}$ is a uniformly distributed dictionary, and the size of $\mathcal{D}$ is $|\mathcal{D}|$. Suppose that $\mathcal{A}$ asks less than q_s times sessions, q_d times Send queries, q_e times Execute queries and q_h times Hash oracle queries. Then,*

$$Adv_P^{AKA}(\mathcal{A}) \leq \frac{q_h^2}{2^{l+2}} + \frac{(q_d + q_e)^2}{2q} + 4\frac{q_d}{2^l} + \frac{q_d}{|\mathcal{D}|} + \\ q_s^2 q_h Adv_G^{DLP}(t) + q_s q_h Adv_G^{CDH}(t + (q_d + q_e) t_e). \qquad (2)$$

where t_e represents the computation time of exponentiation in G.

Proof. Suppose that $\mathcal{A}$ breaches the semantic security of P, $\mathcal{C}$ can solve $CDHP$ problem. The proof consists of sequence of games. For each $Game_i$, we assume that $\mathcal{A}$ correctly guesses b is an event $Succ_i$. $AskPara_n$ represents $\mathcal{A}$ calculating A_i by Hash queries with $(ID_i \| sk_1 \| e_i)$. $AskH_n$ represents $\mathcal{A}$ calculating A_i by Hash queries with $(D_i \| A_i \| R_2 \| SK_s \| TS_4)$.

$Game_0$: This game corresponds to a true attack without any restrictions, where $Succ_0 = \{b' = b\}$. Thus,

$$Adv_P^{AKA}(\mathcal{A}) \le |2Pr[Succ_0] - 1|. \tag{3}$$

$Game_1$: $\mathcal{C}$ simulates a random oracle h in this game, a hash list $List_h = (i, j, k)$ is generated (it is empty at the beginning.). When $\mathcal{A}$ runs a query j, if the request has been asked before, it will give the answer k from the list $List_h$. Otherwise, $\mathcal{C}$ chooses $j \in_n (0, 1)^l$ and returns the answer j, while adding the new record (i, j, k) to $List_h$, where i stands for the query time, j stands for the content set, and k stands for the corresponding answer set.

Compared to $Game_0$, $\mathcal{C}$ sets a relevant record in $Game_1$, so this game is completely indistinguishable from the true game. Thus,

$$|Pr[Succ_1] - Pr[Succ_0]| = 0. \tag{4}$$

$Game_2$: This game simulates all queries, just like in the $Game_1$. If a collision occurs, all simulations will be aborted. The probability of collision on the output of hash queries is at most $\frac{q_h^2}{2^{l+1}}$. The probability of collision on the exchanged messages $\{R_0, C_0, C_1, C_2, TS_1\}$, $\{C_3, C_4, C_5, TS_2\}$, $\{C_6, C_7, TS_3\}$ and $\{C_8, TS_4\}$ is at most $\frac{(q_d + q_e)^2}{2q}$. On the basis of the birthday paradox, we can get,

$$|Pr[Succ_2] - Pr[Succ_1]| \le \frac{q_h^2}{2^{l+1}} + \frac{(q_d + q_e)^2}{2q}. \tag{5}$$

$Game_3$: Without random oracle query, the execution are halted if $\mathcal{A}$ correctly guesses the authentication elements C_2, C_5, C_7, C_8. The game is indistinguishable from $Game_2$, except that the instance refuses to use the correct authentication elements. Hence,

$$|Pr[Succ_3] - Pr[Succ_2]| \le \frac{q_d}{2^l}. \tag{6}$$

$Game_4$: If $\mathcal{A}$ guessed A_i without the Hash query and successfully spoofed U_i or servers, then execution will pause. Therefore, we can get,

$$|Pr[Succ_4] - Pr[Succ_3]| \le \frac{q_d}{2^l}. \tag{7}$$

$Game_5$: The executions are finished if $\mathcal{A}$ calculates the secret value A_i by Hash queries with $(ID_i \| sk_1 \| e_i)$. $Game_5$ and $Game_4$ are indistinguishable if $AskPara_5$ does not occur. Therefore,

$$|Pr[Succ_5] - Pr[Succ_4]| \le Pr[AskPara_5] \tag{8}$$

From security model, $\mathcal{A}$ can query both $Corrupt\,(U^i, a)$ and $Corrupt\left(S_A^j/S_B^k, a\right)$. Therefore, we obtain the following conclusions.

$$
\begin{aligned}
&Pr\,[AskPara_5] = \\
&Pr\,[AskPara_5WithCorrupt\,(U_i, 1)] \\
&+Pr\,[AskPara_5WithCorrupt\,(U_i, 2)] \\
&+Pr\left[AskPara_5WithCorrupt\left(S_A^j/S_B^k, 1\right)\right] \\
&+Pr\left[AskPara_5WithCorrupt\left(S_A^j/S_B^k, 2\right)\right] \\
&= Pr\,[*\,\|PW_i] + Pr\,[\sigma_i\,\|*_i] + Pr\,[ID_i\,\|*\,\|PW_i] + Pr\,[ID_i\,\|*\,\|sk_1] \\
&\leq \tfrac{q_d}{2^l} + \tfrac{q_d}{|\mathcal{D}|} + \tfrac{q_d}{2^l} + q_s^2 q_h Adv_G^{DLP}\,(t) = 2\tfrac{q_d}{2^l} + \tfrac{q_d}{|\mathcal{D}|} + q_s^2 q_h Adv_G^{DLP}\,(t)
\end{aligned} \tag{9}
$$

$Game_6$: The execution are halted if $\mathcal{A}$ calculates the values (C_2, C_5, C_7, C_8, SK). If $AskH_6$ occurs, $\mathcal{A}$ queries the hash function with $(ID_i\,\|A_i\,\left\|R_0^{sk_1}\right\|R_2\,)$, where $CDHP\,(R_0, PK_1) = R_0^{sk_1}$. $\mathcal{C}$ selects a session as the test session and adds the $CDHP$ parameter, $\mathcal{C}$ can solve the CDHP.

In a non-test session, $\mathcal{A}$ makes a Hash query with (C_2, C_5, C_7, C_8). $\mathcal{C}$ receives such a query will check the list $List_h$. If the request was asked before, it will give the same answer. DDHP oracle to check $(R_0, PK_1)? = R_0^{sk_1}$. If it is not equal, NULL is returned, otherwise a random value to $\mathcal{A}$ is returned, due to $\mathcal{C}$ does not know r_i and sk_1 in (C_2, C_5, C_7, C_8).

In a test session, $\mathcal{C}$ randomly selects g^x and g^y, lets $R_0 = g^x$, $PK_1 = g^y$. $\mathcal{A}$ makes a Hash query with $(ID_i\,\|A_i\,\|g^{xy}\,\|R_2\,)$, where $g^{xy} = CDHP(R_0, PK_1)$. This game is no different from the previous one if $AskH_6$ does not occur. Therefore,

$$
|Pr\,[Succ_6] - Pr\,[Succ_5]| \leq Pr\,[AskH_6]. \tag{10}
$$

where, $Pr\,[AskH_6] \leq q_s q_h Adv_G^{CDH}\,(t + (q_d + q_e)t_e)$, $Pr\,[Succ_6] = \tfrac{1}{2}$.

Finally, We can conclude that,

$$
\begin{aligned}
Adv_P^{AKA}\,(\mathcal{A}) &= 2Pr\,[Succ_0] - 1 \\
&= 2Pr\,[Succ_6] - 1 + 2\,(Pr\,[Succ_0] - Pr\,[Succ_6]) \\
&\leq 2\{|Pr\,[Succ_1] - Pr\,[Succ_0]| + |Pr\,[Succ_2] - Pr\,[Succ_1]| \\
&\quad + |Pr\,[Succ_3] - Pr\,[Succ_2]| + |Pr\,[Succ_4] - Pr\,[Succ_3]| \\
&\quad + |Pr\,[Succ_5] - Pr\,[Succ_4]| + |Pr\,[Succ_6] - Pr\,[Succ_5]|\} \\
&\leq \tfrac{q_h^2}{2^{l+1}} + \tfrac{(q_d + q_e)^2}{2q} + 4\tfrac{q_d}{2^l} + \tfrac{q_d}{|\mathcal{D}|} + q_s^2 q_h Adv_G^{DLP}\,(t) \\
&\quad + q_s q_h Adv_G^{CDH}\,(t + (q_d + q_e)\,t_e)\,.
\end{aligned} \tag{11}
$$

$\square$

7   Performance Analysis

We analyze the security features, computation costs and the communication costs of our scheme and several related schemes. For a fair comparison, we choose several authentication protocols with two-server architecture.

7.1 Security Feature

Table 1 shows the comparison between the security features of our scheme and the four related schemes [25–28]. We define $SF1$, $SF2$, $SF3$, $SF4$, $SF5$, $SF6$, $SF7$ and $SF8$ are user anonymity, forward secrecy, offline password guessing attack, freely password update, insider attack, key agreement, online password guessing attack and formal security proof, respectively. Where, ✓ indicates that the scheme meets relevant security requirements. × indicates that the scheme does not meet the security requirements. From Table 1, it can be see that our scheme meets all the security requirements.

Table 1. Security features comparison.

Schemes	$SF1$	$SF2$	$SF3$	$SF4$	$SF5$	$SF6$	$SF7$	$SF8$
Kumari et al. [25]	×	✓	✓	×	✓	✓	×	✓
Yi et al. [26]	×	×	✓	×	×	✓	✓	✓
Jin et al. [27]	×	×	✓	×	×	✓	×	×
Zhang et al. [28]	×	✓	×	×	✓	✓	×	✓
Our	✓	✓	✓	✓	✓	✓	✓	✓

7.2 Computation Cost

The various notations and the running times of the existing experiments [29, 30] are shown in Table 2. The experimental equipment is a four-core 3.2 GHz machine with 8 GB memory. We ignore lightweight operations. Table 3 shows the comparison of client and server computation costs between our scheme and other schemes in the login and authentication phase.

In our scheme, the computation cost is 295.1 millliseconds. In [25–28], the computation costs of their schemes are 390.88, 768.16, 473.14, 472.8 millliseconds, respectively. Through the above results, our computation cost is much lower compared to similar schemes, which proves the absolute computational advantage of our two-server scheme.

Table 2. The execution time of related operations..

Notation	Operations	Time(in seconds)
T_e	Exponentiation operation	0.0192
T_m	Modular multiplication operation	0.00088
T_h	Regular hash operation	0.00032
T_f	Biometric-fuzzy extractor operation	0.0171

Table 3. Computation costs comparison.

Protocols	Client	Server	Total cost
Kumari et al. [25]	$3T_e + 3T_h$	$17T_e + 2T_h + 6T_m$	$20T_e + 5T_h + 6T_m \approx 390.88ms$
Yi et al. [26]	$19T_e + 5T_h + 10T_m$	$20T_e + 6T_h + 8T_m$	$39T_e + 11T_h + 18T_m \approx 768.16ms$
Jin et al. [27]	$8T_e + 3T_h + 2T_m$	$16T_e + 5T_h + 9T_m$	$24T_e + 8T_h + 11T_m \approx 473.04ms$
Zhang et al. [28]	$8T_e + 5T_h + 2T_m$	$16T_e + 5T_h + 8T_m$	$24T_e + 10T_h + 10T_m \approx 472.8ms$
Our	$4T_e + 10T_h + T_f + T_m$	$10T_e + 16T_h$	$14T_e + 26T_h + T_f + T_m \approx 295.1ms$

7.3 Communication Cost

Table 4 compares the communication costs of different existing schemes and our scheme in the login and authentication phase. We make reasonable assumptions about the length of the security parameter: $l_u = 64$ bits (user identity), $l_r = 128$ bits (random number), $l_h = 256$ bits (SHA-256), $l_t = 32$ bits (timestamp) and $l_g = 1024$ bits (a group element in G).

In our protocol, the communication costs of messages $\{R_0, C_0, C_1, C_2, TS_1\}$, $\{C_3, C_4, C_5, TS_2\}$, $\{C_6, C_7, TS_3\}$ and $\{C_8, TS_4\}$ are 1824 bits, 1568 bits, 1312 bits and 288 bits. Thus, our communication cost is $(1824 + 1568 + 1312 + 288) = 4992$ bits. From Table 4, it can be seen that our scheme is much lower communication cost compared to similar schemes. On the premise of ensuring security, our protocol is more efficient, which is very suitable for mobile lightweight devices with limited resources.

Table 4. Communication costs comparison.

Protocols	Total messages	Total cost (bits)
Kumari et al. [25]	6	12928
Yi et al. [26]	6	22784
Jin et al. [27]	6	12224
Zhang et al. [28]	9	21184
Our	4	4992

8 Conclusion

In this paper, we propose an anonymous and practical multi-factor authentication protocol for mobile devices using two-server architecture with honeywords, which solves the security and privacy preserving problems of user data currently faced by mobile devices. Only when the password and biometric factors are correct, the protocol can activate the smart card for authentication, which has higher security than single factor and two factors. At the same time, we use a two-server architecture to avoid serious security problems such as internal privilege attack and direct leakage of private data after a single server is compromised. Through a strict security analysis, we demonstrate the security of the protocol. Our performance evaluation proves that our proposed protocol has obvious efficiency advantages compared with similar protocols. Although our protocol meets many security requirements, more functional features are necessary for authentication protocols. Our future work is to increase the functionality of the protocol while keeping it secure and efficient.

References

1. Statista: Forecast number of mobile users worldwide from 2019 to 2023 (2020)
2. Koved, L., Trewin, S., Swart, C., Singh, K., Cheng, P.C., Chari, S.: Perceived security risks in mobile interaction. In: Symposium on usable privacy and security (SOUPS), pp. 24–26 (2013)
3. Zhu, J., Ma, J.: A new authentication scheme with anonymity for wireless environments. IEEE Trans. Consum. Electron. 50(1), 231–235 (2004)
4. Lee, C.C., Hwang, M.S., Liao, I.E.: Security enhancement on a new authentication scheme with anonymity for wireless environments. IEEE Trans. Industr. Electron. 53(5), 1683–1687 (2006)
5. Mun, H., Han, K., Lee, Y.S., Yeun, C.Y., Choi, H.H.: Enhanced secure anonymous authentication scheme for roaming service in global mobility networks. Math. Comput. Model. 55(1–2), 214–222 (2012)
6. Goutham Reddy, A., Yoon, E.J., Das, A.K., Yoo, K.Y.: Lightweight authentication with key-agreement protocol for mobile network environment using smart cards. IET Inf. Secur. 10(5), 272–282 (2016)
7. Memon, I., Hussain, I., Akhtar, R., Chen, G.: Enhanced privacy and authentication: an efficient and secure anonymous communication for location based service using asymmetric cryptography scheme. Wireless Pers. Commun. 84(2), 1487–1508 (2015)
8. Reddy, A.G., Das, A.K., Yoon, E.J., Yoo, K.Y.: A secure anonymous authentication protocol for mobile services on elliptic curve cryptography. IEEE Access 4, 4394–4407 (2016)
9. Islam, S.H., Vijayakumar, P., Bhuiyan, M.Z.A., Amin, R., Balusamy, B., et al.: A provably secure three-factor session initiation protocol for multimedia big data communications. IEEE Internet Things J. 5(5), 3408–3418 (2017)
10. Qiu, S., Wang, D., Xu, G., Kumari, S.: Practical and provably secure three-factor authentication protocol based on extended chaotic-maps for mobile lightweight devices. IEEE Trans. Dependable Secure Comput. 19(2), 1338–1351 (2020)
11. Li, C.T., Hwang, M.S.: An efficient biometrics-based remote user authentication scheme using smart cards. J. Netw. Comput. Appl. 33(1), 1–5 (2010)
12. Das, A.K.: Analysis and improvement on an efficient biometric-based remote user authentication scheme using smart cards. IET Inf. Secur. 5(3), 145–151 (2011)
13. An, Y.: Security analysis and enhancements of an effective biometric-based remote user authentication scheme using smart cards. J. Biomed. Biotechnol. 2012 (2012)
14. Cao, L., Ge, W.: Analysis and improvement of a multi-factor biometric authentication scheme. Secur. Commun. Netw. 8(4), 617–625 (2015)

15. Park, Y., Park, K., Lee, K., Song, H., Park, Y.: Security analysis and enhancements of an improved multi-factor biometric authentication scheme. Int. J. Distrib. Sens. Netw. **13**(8), 1550147717724308 (2017)
16. Tan, Z.: A user anonymity preserving three-factor authentication scheme for telecare medicine information systems. J. Med. Syst. **38**(3), 1–9 (2014)
17. Arshad, H., Nikooghadam, M.: Three-factor anonymous authentication and key agreement scheme for telecare medicine information systems. J. Med. Syst. **38**(12), 1–12 (2014)
18. Lu, Y., Li, L., Peng, H., Yang, Y.: An enhanced biometric-based authentication scheme for telecare medicine information systems using elliptic curve cryptosystem. J. Med. Syst. **39**(3), 1–8 (2015)
19. Amin, R., Islam, S., Biswas, G., Khan, M.K., Obaidat, M.S.: Design and analysis of an enhanced patient-server mutual authentication protocol for telecare medical information system. J. Med. Syst. **39**(11), 1–20 (2015)
20. Wazid, M., Das, A.K., Kumari, S., Li, X., Wu, F.: Design of an efficient and provably secure anonymity preserving three-factor user authentication and key agreement scheme for tmis. Secur. Commun. Netw. **9**(13), 1983–2001 (2016)
21. Dodis, Y., Reyzin, L., Smith, A.: Fuzzy extractors: how to generate strong keys from biometrics and other noisy data. In: Cachin, C., Camenisch, J.L. (eds.) EUROCRYPT 2004. LNCS, vol. 3027, pp. 523–540. Springer, Heidelberg (2004). https://doi.org/10.1007/978-3-540-24676-3_31
22. Juels, A., Rivest, R.L.: Honeywords: Making password-cracking detectable. In: Proceedings of the 2013 ACM SIGSAC Conference on Computer & Communications Security, pp. 145–160 (2013)
23. Bellare, M., Pointcheval, D., Rogaway, P.: Authenticated key exchange secure against dictionary attacks. In: Preneel, B. (ed.) EUROCRYPT 2000. LNCS, vol. 1807, pp. 139–155. Springer, Heidelberg (2000). https://doi.org/10.1007/3-540-45539-6_11
24. Liu, X., Li, Y., Qu, J., Jiang, Q.: Maka: provably secure multi-factor authenticated key agreement protocol. J. Internet Technol. **19**(3), 669–677 (2018)
25. Anitha Kumari, K., Sudha Sadasivam, G.: Two-server 3d elgamal diffie hellman password authenticated and key exchange protocol using geometrical properties. Mobile Netw. Appl. **24**(3), 1104–1119 (2019)
26. Yi, X., Hao, F., Bertino, E.: ID-based two-server password-authenticated key exchange. In: Kutyłowski, M., Vaidya, J. (eds.) ESORICS 2014. LNCS, vol. 8713, pp. 257–276. Springer, Cham (2014). https://doi.org/10.1007/978-3-319-11212-1_15
27. Jin, H., Wong, D.S., Xu, Y.: An efficient password-only two-server authenticated key exchange system. In: Qing, S., Imai, H., Wang, G. (eds.) ICICS 2007. LNCS, vol. 4861, pp. 44–56. Springer, Heidelberg (2007). https://doi.org/10.1007/978-3-540-77048-0_4
28. Zhang, H., Kumari, S., Obaidat, M.S., Wei, F.S.: Gateway-oriented two-server password authenticated key exchange protocol for unmanned aerial vehicles in mobile edge computing. IET Commun. **14**(15), 2427–2433 (2020)
29. Srinivas, J., Das, A.K., Kumar, N., Rodrigues, J.J.: Cloud centric authentication for wearable healthcare monitoring system. IEEE Trans. Dependable Secure Comput. **17**(5), 942–956 (2018)
30. Srinivas, J., Das, A.K., Wazid, M., Kumar, N.: Anonymous lightweight chaotic map-based authenticated key agreement protocol for industrial internet of things. IEEE Trans. Dependable Secure Comput. **17**(6), 1133–1146 (2018)

Data Security

Cross-Chain Data Auditing for Medical IoT Data Sharing

Kuan Fan[1], Zhuoxuan Liu[1], Mingxi Liu[1], Yihong Wen[3], Ning Lu[1,2(✉)], and Wenbo Shi[1(✉)]

[1] School of Computer Science and Engineering, Northeastern University, Shenyang, China
{luning,shiwb}@neuq.edu.cn
[2] School of Computer Science and Technology, Xidian University, Xi'an, China
[3] The 54th Research Institute of China Electronics Technology Group Corporation, Shijiazhuang, China

Abstract. Secure medical IoT data sharing significantly improves medical collaboration and facilitates patients' medical treatment. Since block chain provides integrity and traceability management for medical data, many IoT medical data choose block chain as a storage medium. However, the isolation of block chain hinders data sharing between heterogeneous chains, so how to realize the secure sharing of medical IoT data in heterogeneous block chains and allow users to obtain correct and credible shared data is still a challenge. Existing data integrity verification techniques ensure the correctness of shared data by comparing off-chain data with metadata stored on-chain. However, these schemes ignore the consistency of shared data and the correctness of cross-chain data. This paper builds a cross-chain medical IoT data-sharing framework, introduces a relay chain, and verifies the consistency between data requests and actual storage through registration, auditing, and other methods. Based on this framework, this paper uses homomorphic signature technology and batch auditing to design a cross-chain audit protocol to verify the consistency of registered data attributes and the correctness of shared data. Security analysis and simulation experiments based on security reduction demonstrate the security and effectiveness of the proposed scheme.

Keywords: Cross-chain · Data sharing · Consistency verification · Data auditing

1 Introduction

Medical IoT data collection is becoming more extensive with the widespread use of medical sensor devices. For the data management of the Medical Internet of Things, most health systems establish data storage and query platforms based on block chain and share desensitization data with authorized users to carry out medical research or regional pathological statistics [1]. However, data users are unsatisfied with pulling data from a single block chain based shared platform because of the more comprehensive data usage needs. Considering the user's tolerance for data retrieval, if the data is retrieved

Q. Jiang et al. (Eds.): SPNCE 2022, LNICST 496, pp. 65–81, 2023.
https://doi.org/10.1007/978-3-031-30623-5_5

from different platforms, the serial time is high, and the data usage fee may be wasted due to data redundancy [2]. Cross-chain data sharing will be one of the feasible solutions.

At present, many scholars use attributes to represent medical data [3, 4]. Some medical organizations also publish various types of medical data, usually composed of attribute data [5]. Therefore, we use attributes to describe the medical Internet of Things data, as shown in Table 1. Each record contains an identification code, age, gender, blood pressure, heart rate, blood sugar, and other information. A relay chain is regarded as a data-sharing center in a cross- chain scenario to realize data sharing among heterogeneous chains [6]. After the resource chain registers the data size and attributes (age, sex, etc.) on the relay chain, the data demander sends a request to the relay chain, and the relay chain matches the registration data. The matched resource chain sends data to the data demander. The above process can realize cross-chain data sharing, but the following problems need to be solved to improve the quality of shared:

1. Data consistency: The size of the shared data provided by the resource chain is related to the revenue obtained, so the resource chain may exaggerate the data size when releasing the transmitted data. The resource chain may also provide data that is not related to the required data [7].
2. Data integrity: Due to the limited storage space of the resource chain, the resource chain may delete some data. When a user requests to delete data, the resource chain may return irrelevant data to the user as the requested attribute data [8].

Table 1. Multi-attribute medical IoT data

ID	Age	Sex	Blood pressure	Heart rate	Blood sugar
0001	35	0	120/80	70	5.0
0002	58	0	145/90	90	10.9
0003	67	1	120/80	70	5.5

Many scholars have studied data-sharing audits, which can be divided into two categories. The first type focuses on sharing data. These articles address privacy protection, integrity audit, dynamic modification of data, and other issues [9–12]. The second is about the data owner, including such issues as identity auditing, identity tracing, and key distribution [13]. The above research ensures the security and efficiency of data sharing in many aspects. However, they can not be applied to the cross-chain sharing scenario. It can not solve the problem mentioned in this paper.

This paper proposes a cross-chain audit scheme for medical multi-attribute data (CCDAS), which focuses on the data consistency and integrity problems encountered in cross-chain sharing. We introduce a relay chain to build the cross- chain data-sharing framework. We use the off-chain oracle to obtain the shared data information and audit data proof. The protocol includes registration, which ensures that the registered data scale is consistent with the actual data scale. After the audit, the data information is written into the relay chain. In the data- sharing stage, the protocol uses different keys to encrypt the data's attributes and adopts the batch audit to ensure data integrity. Our main contributions are as follows:

1. This paper proposes a cross-chain data-sharing architecture based on the relay chain. The relay chain acts as a data-sharing center, handling data requests and sharing. The off-chain oracle is responsible for obtaining data on heterogeneous resource chains and auditing data proof.
2. This paper analyzes the data consistency and integrity in the cross-chain sharing scenario. Based on the Challenge-Response method and batch auditing, we designed the auditing protocol to ensure data consistency and integrity.
3. We provide the security analysis of the proposed protocols and demonstrate that the desired security requirements are satisfied. Performance evaluation shows that the scheme is practical.

2   Related Work

Existing cross-chain sharing architectures need to give more consideration to data security. Many scholars have studied this issue. Jiang et al. proposed a cross- chain solution to integrate multiple block chains for IoT data management. They built a consortium block chain to integrate multiple block chains for efficient and secure IoT data management [14]. Li et al. proposed a multi-domain authentication framework for cross-chain data sharing. They designed smart contracts to protect the confidentiality of the authentication data [15]. Qiao et al. proposed a dynamic autonomous cross-consortium chain mechanism in e-Healthcare. They developed a mechanism of cross-chain consensus to simplify heterogeneous node communication topology and improve node identity trustworthiness [2]. Zhao et al. proposed a secure and scalable access control model for cross-chain data sharing, which includes an access control strategy written by smart contracts and a storage system adopted by IPFS to reduce the cost of storage on the block chain [16]. Chang et al. proposed an epidemic data-sharing model based on a cross-chain mechanism. To improve the availability of sharing system, they constructed a model of epidemic data sharing between multiple consortium block chains based on a cross-chain mechanism to guarantee security [17]. Although the above solutions achieve security and efficient cross-chain data sharing, they need to conduct effective data integrity protection.

Existing data auditing schemes provide data integrity verification, but they are rarely able to verify data consistency. Zhou et al. propose an efficient certificates multi-copy integrity auditing scheme named MDSS, which entails massive overhead of certificate computation and management [18]. They improve the classic Merkle Hash Tree to achieve batch updates for multi-copy storage, which allows the communication overhead incurred for dynamics to be independent of the replica number. Xu et al. propose a block chain enabled deduplicate data auditing mechanism [19]. They first designed a client-side data deduplication scheme based on bilinear pairing technology to reduce the burden on users and service providers. They realized a reliable and efficient data auditing mechanism using block chain technology and a bilinear pairing cryptosystem. Hahn et al. propose a fast public auditing mechanism supporting dynamic verification [20]. They study a new challenge-response protocol that significantly reduces the computational cost of TPA and increases the speed of verification of audit results. Zhang et al. propose a block chain based multi-cloud storage data auditing scheme with locating faults [21]. They present an arbitration mechanism to detect service disputes and effectively identify malicious service providers. Gao et al. propose an auditing scheme to verify the integrity of ciphertext keyword search data [22]. They study a relational authentication label (RAL) for verifying the relation in documents containing query keywords without exposing sensitive information in audit proofs. Although these protocols can realize efficient and secure data integrity auditing, they cannot verify the consistency between the requested data and the obtained data. These protocols are also not applicable to data auditing in cross-chain data sharing.

In summary, there needs to be a solution to achieve efficient auditing under cross-chain data sharing. Therefore, based on the homomorphic signature, we design an auditing protocol for cross-chain data-sharing consistency and integrity.

3   Problem Statement

In this section, we introduce system model, threat model, and Design goals.

Table 2 summarizes the notations in this paper.

Table 2. Notations described in the CCDAS.

Notation	Description
RC	Relay chain
DC	Demand chain
RSC	Resource chain
OCO	Off-chain oracle
OC	Oracle contract
HZp	Hash function in Zp
H_G	Hash function in G
M_G	Multiply function in G
P_G	Bilinear pairing operation
E_G	power operation in G

3.1   System Model

Multi-party healthcare data sharing provides health assessment services for the public. Currently, medical data from different institutions are often stored on various block chains. To improve the availability and correctness of heterogeneous chain shared data, a CCDAS system model is proposed in this paper.

In the CCDAS model, there are multiple entities: Demand Chain (DC), Resource Chain (RSC), Relay Chain (RC), Oracle contract(OC), and Off-chain Oracle(OCO).

- Demand Chain: requests the RSC for data that meets specific attributes and quantities.
- Resource Chain: owns a portion of medical data and shares this data with DC.
- Relay Chain: assists in cross-chain transactions.
- Oracle contract: includes user contracts and oracle contracts. User contracts are mainly used to receive DC requirements. The oracle contract can manage data according to the scheme's requirements and is primarily responsible for uploading the data sent by the oracle node to the chain and passing it to the user contract.
- Off-chain Oracle: runs the middle-ware of the oracle protocol, forming a distributed network outside the block chain nodes, which is responsible for collecting and verifying the data provided by the resource chain and passing it to the contract on the relay chain.

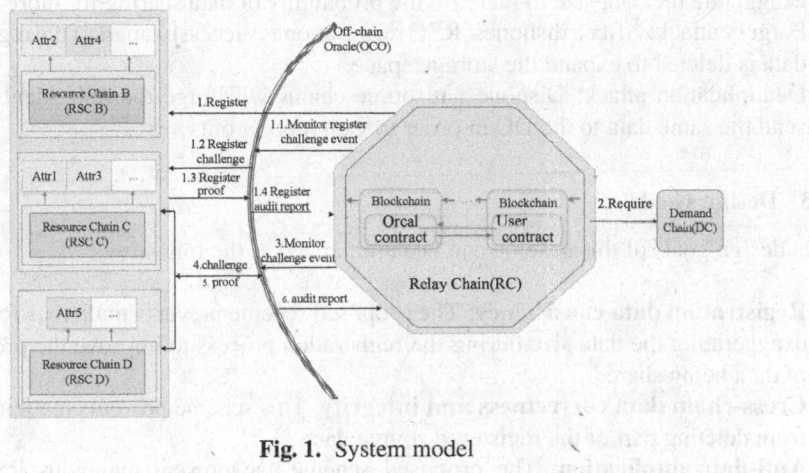

Fig. 1. System model

Combined with Fig. 1, we provide a detailed overview of the CCDAS protocol. The program is divided into two parts. The first section ensures that RSC registration data is consistent with actual data. The RSC sends registration information (data attributes, scale, and hash values) to the RC. Then, OCO monitors this event and sends a challenge message to the RSC. The RSC generates evidence and returns it to the OCO node. When the OCO node successfully verifies the registration evidence, the RC writes the registration information to the block chain. The second part ensures data integrity, preventing RSC from deleting registered source data and providing irrelevant data to DC. When the DC needs data, it sends the requirements (data attributes and size) to the RC. When the RC receives the request, it checks the registration information, finds the appropriate RSC, and generates a challenge. The requirements and challenges are then written into the user contract and the oracle contract is invoked to authorize OCO to audit the integrity of the data, including the registration attributes and data content. The OCO monitors the

OC in real time and sends requirements and challenges to the RSC under the contract. Upon receipt, the RSC generates data evidence and returns it to the OCO. OCO reviews the evidence and provides feedback to OC. If the audit is successful, RC calls OC to fetch the resource chain data and return it to the demand chain

3.2   Threat Model

We define the resource chain as a semi-honest entity. It will forge its data scale or attribute information during registration to improve the probability of sharing. At the same time, It also fakes multiple identities, using different identities to provide the same data. In addition, due to the consensus mechanism of other chains, it is necessary to ensure the consistency of cross-chain information. Therefore, the proposed CCDAS scheme should ensure data consistency and integrity and defend against the following attacks:

– Consistency attack: When dishonest RSCS register data with the relay chain, they will exaggerate the data size to increase the probability of data sharing for more benefit.
– Forgery attack: After a dishonest RSC registration is successful, part of the registration data is deleted to expand the storage space.
– Deduplication attack: Dishonest resource chains will forge multiple identities and send the same data to the DC in order to gain more profits.

3.3   Design Goals

The design goals of this scheme can be summarized as the following.

– **Registration data consistency**: The proposed scheme prevents malicious RSC from exaggerating the data size during the registration process to improve the probability of data being shared
– **Cross-chain data correctness and integrity**: This scheme prevents malicious RSC from deleting part of the registered source data.
– **Anti-data duplication**: The proposed scheme can prevent malicious RSC from forging multiple identities, providing the same data to the demand chain for more revenue.

3.4   Security Model

According to the threat model, RSC is a "semi-honest" entity. Therefore, according to the security requirements of CCDAS, the following security model is given to analyze the security of CCDAS.

Definition 3. During the audit process, it is not feasible to use forged proof to pass the integrity audit of the CCDAS protocol.

– **Initialization**: The proof unforgeable game between challenger C and adversary A is constructed. C constructs the algorithm B_A, and simulates the CCDAS environment for A. A generates proof by inquiring B_A, and B_A verifies the proof. B_A and A are the verifier and the prover respectively.

– **Query**: In this phase, A can make the hash queries and signature queries.

   (a) Hash queries: A queries B_A for the hash value of some data blocks (a_i, j, m_{ij}), and B_A calculates and sends it to A.

   (b) Signature queries: A queries the signature of the data block (a_i, j, m_{ij}), C runs the SigGen algorithm to calculate the signature of (a_i, j, m_{ij}), and sends to A.

– **Challenge**: B_A checks A with a random challenge $Chal_t$ consisting of some blocks that have not been queried. Aording to $Chal_t$, A generates the corresponding signatures σ_t and $proof_t$, and then returns them to C.

– **Forged output**: If A can forge proof based on the challenge and pass the verification of C, then A wins the game.

Definition 4. The CCDAS protocol is resistant to consistency attacks if a dishonest RSC can not pass the audit on registration.

Definition 5. The CCDAS protocol is resistant to data duplication attacks, if a dishonest RSC cannot pass the verification using the same data.

4   The Proposed CCDAS Scheme

4.1   Main Idea

The CCDAS protocol is divided into two parts. The first part mainly solves the consistency of RSC data and its registration information, which is realized by bilinear pairing and hash function [23]. After the successful audit, write the data attribute, data scale, and hash value to the RC to complete the registration. Data attributes and data scales are used for data-sharing queries. The hash value is used to assist the second part of the protocol in implementing attribute consistency audit and data content integrity audit. The second part ensures attribute consistency, data integrity, and correctness of cross-chain data through bilinear pairing and BLS signatures. But different from traditional auditing, this scheme assigns a public-private key pair to each attribute. It adopted batch auditing to complete the consistency of data attributes, registered attributes, and data content integrity. In addition, the CCDAS protocol can resist traditional audit attacks and resist the attack behavior of resource chain forging identities to provide the same data multiple times.

4.2   Construction of CCDAS

Setup: Given a security parameter λ, and a prime k, it outputs the system public parameters $params = (p, g, G, G1, H, h, e)$, where p is the large prime order of multiplicative cyclic groups G and G_1, g is the random generator of G and G_1, $e : G \times G \leftarrow G_1$ is a bilinear pairing, $H^* : 0, 1 \leftarrow G$ and $h : 0, 1^* \leftarrow Z_p^*$ are collision-resistant hash function.

KeyGen: As shown in Fig. 2, the RSC divides data into blocks according to attributes $F = \{a_1 : A_1, a_2 : A_2, \ldots, a_n : A_n\}$, where a_i is the attribute name, $A_i = \{m_{i1}, m_{i2}, \ldots, m_{ik}\}$ is the data set of a_i and n is the number of attribute. The RC randomly generates n signing key pair $(ssk_i, spk_i)_{1 \le i \le n}$, and chooses random values $a_i \leftarrow Z_p$, calculate $v_i \leftarrow g_i^\alpha$. The private key for attribute a_i is (a_i, ssk_i), and the public key v_i for a_i is (g_i^α, spk_i).

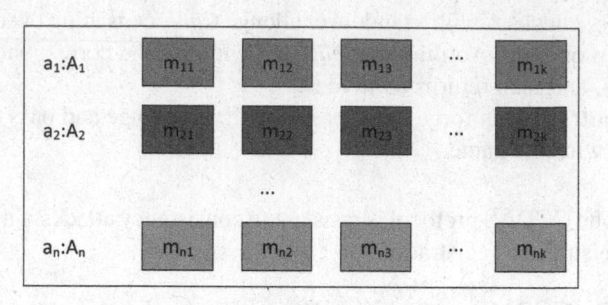

Fig. 2. Attribute data

SigGen: The RSC choose n random values $\{u_i \leftarrow G\}_{1 \le i \le n}$, and calculate the signature $\sigma_{ij} = \left(H\left(m_{ij}\right) \cdot u^{m_{ij}}\right)^{\alpha_i}$ of each data block in the A_i. The data attribute signature set is $\phi = \{\sigma_i\}_{1 \le i \le n}$, where $\sigma_i = \sum_{j=1}^{k} \sigma_{ij}$, the RSC choose random value $r \leftarrow Z_p$, calculate the lable $\tau = \left(g^r, g^{r \cdot h(F)}\right)$ of F.

RegisterChal: The RSC sends registration information $\left\{attr_i, H\left(\sum_{j=1}^{k} m_{ij}\right), size\right\}_{1 \le i \le n}$ to the RC, where $attr_i$ represents an attribute of RSC, $H\left(\sum_{j=1}^{k} m_{ij}\right)$ is the hash value of the accumulated data from $attr_i$, and k is the number of $attr_i$. After the RC receives the information, it generates $n*k$ random number $\{r_{ij}\}$ to form registration challenge $ReChal$, where n is the number of attribute from RSC. RC writes $ReChal$ into the oracle contract to register "Register Challenge event". The off-chain oracle node listens to the "Register Challenge event" and sends challenge information $ReChal$ to the RSC.

RegisterProof: The RSC is calculated according to the following formula:

$$H_{attr_i} = \sum_{j=1}^{k} H\left(m_{ij}\right)^{r_{ij}} \tag{1}$$

RegisterProof is $RePoof = \{H_{attr_i}\}_{1 \le i \le n}$. The RSC returns $RePoof$ to the off-chain oracle node.

RegisterAudit: The off-chain oracle node calculates the verification equation according to the following formula:

$$e\left(\prod_{i=1}^{n}\left(\prod_{j=1}^{k} H\left(m_{ij}\right)^{r_{ij}}\right), g\right) \stackrel{?}{=} e\left(\prod_{i=1}^{n}\left(\prod_{j=1}^{k} H\left(m_{ij}\right),\right), \prod_{i=1}^{n}\left(\prod_{j=1}^{k} g^{r_{ij}}\right)\right) \tag{2}$$

If the equation is equal, it means that the RSC does have the number of data shown in the registration information.

ChalGen: The RC receives the data request information $Reinfor = \{attr_i, k\}_{1 \leq i \leq y}$ sent by the DC, where $attr_i$ represents attribute name, k is the number of the data for $attr_i$, and y is the number of required attribute. RC randomly extracts t pieces of data from each attribute data, and generates $y * t$ random value w_{ij} to generate challenge $Chal = (t, w_{ij})_{1 \leq i \leq y, 1 \leq j \leq t}$. The RC writes the challenge into the user contract and registers it as"Challenge Event" on the oracle contract. The off-chain oracle node listens to the challenge event and sends data requirements $Reinfor$ and challenge information $Chal$ to the RSC according to the event requirements.

DataProofGen: The RSC receives challenge and requirement, calculates proof according to the following formula:

$$\mu_i = \sum_{j=1}^{t} w_{ij} \cdot m_{ij} \tag{3}$$

$$\xi_i = \prod_{j=1}^{t} \sigma_{ij}^{w_{ij}} \tag{4}$$

The attribute proof is $DataProof = (\mu_i, \xi_i)$.

DataVerify: The off-chain oracle node calculates the verification equation according to the following formula:

$$Pr_1 = e\left(\prod_{i=1}^{y} \xi_i, g\right) \tag{5}$$

$$Pr_2 = e\left(\prod_{i=1}^{y} \left(\prod_{j=1}^{k} H(m_{ij})^{w_{ij}} \cdot u_i^{\mu_i}\right), \prod_{i=1}^{y} v_i\right) \tag{6}$$

If $Pr1 == Pr2$, it means that the attributes owned by RSC are the same as the registered attributes, and it also means that the content of the registration data has not changed; otherwise, the transaction is terminated.

In order to prevent data conflict, the off-chain oracle node randomly selects the data labels of two RSCs $\tau_1 = (g^{r_1}, g^{r_2 \cdot h(F_1)})$ and $\tau_2 = (g^{r_2}, g^{r_1 \cdot h(F_2)})$, verify according to the following equation

$$e((g^{r_1}, g^{r_2.h(F_1)})) \overset{?}{=} e(g^{r_2}, g^{r_1.h(F_2)}) \tag{7}$$

If the verification passes, it means that F_1 and F_2 are different from datasets, otherwise, terminate the transaction. Off-chain oracle nodes repeat verification until all RSC verification are completed. The off-chain oracle will send two audit success messages to RC.

5 Security Analysis

Theorem 1: Under the computational CDH problem, CCDAS is resistant to forgery attacks.

Proof: Suppose A can successfully forge some data blocks proofs ξ with non-negligible probability $\in$, and the forgery-proof game is won by verification. In that case, BA can solve the CDH hard problem with negligible probability [24].

Initialization: Given $\alpha \in Z_p$, $\beta \in Z_p$, g is generator of group G, α_i is the private key of attribute a_i in the RSC, g^{α_i} is the public key of α_i. Let $u = g^{\theta}$, where $\theta \in Z_p$ be the random value chosen by B_A. The input value of B_A are g^{α_i}, and g^{β}, and then B_A can solve the CDH problem with a non-negligible probability and output $g^{\alpha_i \beta}$.

Hash-Oracle: A queries B_A for the hash value $H(m_{ij})$ of data block m_{ij}:

If m_{ij} is in the hash list $H = \{m_{ij}, H(m_{ij})\}$, B_A obtains data $\{k_0, i, j, m_{ij}, h_{m_{ij}}\}$ from the list, and then reply A $H(m_{ij}) = h_{m_{ij}}$.

If m_{ij} is not in the hash list, B_A randomly selects a number from $k_0 = \{0, 1\}$, where $P_r[k_0 = 0] = \Theta$, random value $r_{ij} \leftarrow Z_p$. When $k_0 = 0$, B_A calculates $h_{m_{ij}} = g^{r_{ij}}$ When $k_0 = 1$, B_A calculates $h_{m_{ij}} = (g^{\beta})^{r_{ij}}$. B_A store $\{k_0, i, j, m_{ij}, h_{m_{ij}}\}$ into the hash list, and reply A $H(m_{ij}) = h_{m_{ij}}$.

Signature-Oracle: In order to ensure that the interaction between B_A and A is the same as the actual attack, the B_A maintains the signature list $sig = \{i, j, m_{ij}, \sigma_{ij}\}$, and responds to the request of the data block m_{ij} signature according to the signature list.

1. If the signature of m_{ij} is in the signature list, B_A obtains signature σ_{ij} from the list, and then reply A the signature.
2. If the signature of σ_{ij} is not in the signature list, B_A finds the hash list corresponding to $H(m_{ij})$. When the target entry does not exist in the hash table, the B_A queries the oracle again.

    (a) If the corresponding record is in the hash list and $k_0 = 0$, then B_A selects $H(m_{ij}) = g^{r_{ij}}$ according to the Hash-Oracle, and generates the signature as follows:

    $$\sigma_{ij} = (H(m_{ij}) \cdot u^{m_{ij}})^{\alpha_i}$$
    $$= (g^{\alpha_i})^{r_{ij}} \cdot g^{\alpha_i})^{\theta(m_{ij})} \tag{8}$$

    B_A adds the data $\{i, j, m_{ij}, \theta_{ij}\}$ to the signature list, and sends σ_{ij} to A.
    (b) When $k_0 = 1$, the B_A refuses to respond to corresponding signature to A.

Challenge: Suppose the B_A generation challenge $chal = \{(i, j, w_{ij}), 1 \le i \le n, 1 \le j \le k\}$. There is a tuple in the $chal$ that is not in the signature list.

Forged Output: A generates a legal proof $\{\mu', \xi'\}$ depend on the *chal*. According to the formula (5) and formula (6), it can be known that:

$$e\left(\prod_{i=1}^{n} \xi', g\right) = e\left(\prod_{i=1}^{n}\left(\prod_{j=1}^{k} H\left(m_{ij}\right)^{w_{ij}} \cdot u_i^{u'}\right), \prod_{i=1}^{n} g^{\alpha_i}\right) \tag{9}$$

At the same time, A cannot request the Signature Oracle for the data $\left(i^*, j^*, w_{ij}^*\right)$ from the *chal*. This means that the hash value $h_{m_{ij}}$ of $\left(i^*, j^*, w_{ij}^*\right)$ can be found in the Hash list, and the signature list has no record for the data $\left(i^*, j^*, w_{ij}^*\right)$. B_A queries the signature list to obtain signatures for other challenge values. If the target records does not exist, then the BA queries the Hash-Oracle or Signature- Oracle. If $\left(i^*, j^*, w_{ij}^*\right)$, $k_0 = 0$, B_A rejects the hash value $H\left(m_{ij}\right)$, otherwise, B_A can solve the CDH problem.

In the Hash list, $k = 0$ for the challenge value $\left(i^*, j^*, w_{ij}^*\right)$, and $k = 1$ for other challenge values, so the right side of formula (9) can be expressed as:

$$e\left(\left(\prod_{i,j\in chal, i,j\neq i^*, j^*} \left(g^{r_{ij}}\right)^{w_{ij}}\right) \cdot \prod_{i,j\in chal} u_i^{\mu'} \cdot \left(g^{\beta r_{i^*j^*}}\right)^{g^{w_{i^*j^*}}}, \prod_{i,j\in chal} g^{\alpha_i}\right)$$

$$= e\left(\left(g^{\beta \alpha^* r_{i^*j^*}}\right)^{w_{i^*j^*}}, g\right) \cdot e\left(g^{\sum_{i,j\in chal, i,j\neq i^*, j^*} r_{ij}\cdot w_{ij}\cdot \alpha_i}, g^{\sum_{i,j\in chal, i,j\neq i^*, j^*} \theta_i\cdot \alpha_i\cdot \mu'}, g\right) \tag{10}$$

The solution to the computational CDH hard problem is:

$$g^{\alpha_i^*\beta} = \left(\xi'(g^{\sum_{i,j\in chal, i,j\neq i^*, j^*} r_{ij}\cdot w_{ij}\cdot \alpha_i} \cdot (g^{\sum_{i,j\in chal, i,j\neq i^*, j^*} \theta_i\cdot \alpha_i\cdot \mu'} \cdot g)^{-1})^{-1}\right)^{\frac{1}{w_{i^*j^*}\cdot r_{i^*j^*}}} \tag{11}$$

Probabilistic Analysis of Reduction: Analyze the probability that B_A uses A forged proof to solve a computational CDH problem, for three things:

- E_1: B_A does not reject all of A's inquiries to the signature oracle.
- E_2: A generates a legal proof according to the *chal*.
- E_3: After the E_2 event, $k_0 = 1$ for i^* in the Hash list.

If A can succeed in all of the above events, then the probability that B_A successfully solves the computational CDH problem is:

$$Pr[E_1 \cap E_2 \cap E_3]$$
$$= Pr[E_1]\cdot Pr[E_2|E_1]\cdot Pr[E_3|E_2 \cap E_1] \tag{12}$$
$$= \Theta^{n_s}\epsilon_1(1 - \Theta)$$

$\Theta = n_s/(n_s + 1)\sqrt{a^2 + b^2}$, where n_s is the number of signatures, then the probability $Pr[E_1 \cap E_2 \cap E_3]$ is at least $\epsilon_1/\hat{e}(n_s + 1)$ where $\hat{e}$ is a natural logarithm. Since ϵ_1 is nonnegligible, B_A can solve the CDH problem with a non-negligible probability, but this contradicts the CDH difficulty problem, so CCSA can resist the forged proof attack initiated by A.

Theorem 2. In the CCDAS scheme, the data registered by the RSC to the RC must be real data.

Proof: In the registration phase, RSC sends data $(attr_i, H\left(\sum_{j=1}^{k} m_{ij}\right))_{1\leq i\leq n}$ to the RC. RC generates $n*k$ random numbers r_{ij} based on the received data and returns it to the RSC as a challenge. After the RSC receives the challenge, it calculates the proof $H_{attr_i} = \prod_{j=1}^{k} H(m_{ij})^{r_{ij}}$ and sends it to the RC. The RC inputs the generated challenge and the proof into the audit formula as parameters and uses the bilinear pairing property to verify the data scale. In the verification phase, the random value r_{ij} and the hash value $\prod_{j=1}^{k} H(m_{ij})$ generated by RC are input into the audit equation as parameters, so RSC cannot exaggerate the data size during the verification process. Even if a malicious RSC passes audit verification by falsifying data, RC retains the data hash value, which requires RSC to share the registered data.

Theorem 3. In the CCDAS protocol, RSC can not pass the verification with the same data.

Proof: The RSC generates tags $\tau = \left(g^r, g^{r.h(F)}\right)$ for file F in the SigGen algorithm. In the DataVerify algorithm, OCO randomly selects the tags $\tau_1 = \left(g_1^r, g^{r_2.h(F_1)}\right)$ and $\tau_2 = \left(g_2^r, g^{r_1.h(F_2)}\right)$ of the files F_1 and F_2, and uses the bilinear pairing technique and hash function to verify whether the two tags are equal. Since $h(F_1)$ and $h(F_2)$ are equal, the data tags are equal when the malicious RSC provides the same data. Therefore, it can prevent the malicious RSC from providing the same data and resist data deduplication attacks.

6   Performance Analysis

In this section, we first analyze the performance of CCDAS from the theoretical level, and then conduct simulation experiments.

6.1   Theoretical Analysis

We compare our CCDAS with the scheme of MHT, which has the same functions [25]. We divide the main process of CCDAS into three stages: initialization, register auditing, and data auditing. Table 3 compares the calculation costs of the MHT and the CCDAS. For initialization, the difference between the MHT and the CCDAS is about coefficient n. Although fewer multipliers for nk in the CCDAS, $E_G + M_G$ is significantly more than H_{Z_p}. For register auditing, nk in the CCDAS is less than the MHT, though $k(H_G + E_G)$ is more than the costs in the MHT. In data auditing, there are significantly fewer multipliers in yl, though introducing $l(E_G + M_G)$ and $y(4M_G + E_G)$.

Table 3. Comparison of calculation costs

Scheme	Initialization	Register auditing	Data auditing
MHT	$2nk(H_Zp) + E_G$ $+ nk(HG + MG + 2EG)$	$4PG + 2HG$ $+ nk(HG + 3EG +$ $2MG)$	$4PG + 2HG$ $+ yl(HG + 3EG + 2MG)$
CCDAS	$n(E_G + M_G) + 2E_G + h_Zp$ $+ nk(HG + MG + 2EG)$	$k(HG + EG) + HG +$ $2PG$ $+ nk(2HG + 2EG)$	$l(EG + MG) + 2PG +$ $4EG$ $+ yl(HG + EG + MG)$

Table 4 compares communication costs about the MHT and the CCDAS. In initialization, $n|G|$ is significantly less than $nk|G|$, so communication costs are obvious superiority. In register auditing, the main advantage of the CCDAS is less multiplier in coefficient nk. But the CCDAS has extra $n(2|Z_p| + |G|) + nk|Z_p| + |G|$. So the actual size will depend on the instantiation of the coefficients. In data auditing, it is obvious that $k(|G| + |Z_P|) + 2ty|Z_p|$ is less than $ty(2|Z_p| + |G|)$.

Table 4. Comparison of communication costs

Scheme	Initialization	Register auditing	Data auditing
MHT	$2|Z_p| + 2|G| + nk|G|$	$nk(2|Z_p| + |G|) + |Z_p| +$ $2|G|$	$ky(2|Z_p| + |G|) + |Z_p| +$ $2|G|$
CCDAS	$3|G| + |Z_p| + n|G|$	$n(2|Z_p| + |G|) + nk|Z_p| +$ $|G|$	$k(|G| + |Z_p|) + 2ky|Z_p| +$ $|Z_p| + |G|$

6.2 Experimental Analysis

This article selects the Medical Data dataset, which contains 14 attributes [26]. We set up a simulation environment and constructed experiments to compare the practical time cost of CCDAS, MHT, and Dredas [27]. The experiments were run on a computer with a 3.50 GHz Intel i7-4710HQ CPU and 16 GB RAM. The experiment uses the pair-based cryptographic library JPBC (java encapsulation of the PBC library) [28] to implement the encryption algorithm and sets the security parameter to 256bit. For the initialization and register auditing stages, We set $n = 10$, and k goes from 100 to 1000. For the data auditing stage, we set $l = 5$, and y goes from 100 to 1000. The results of each experiment are calculated 20 times and averaged.

Figure 3 shows the computational overhead of MHT, CCDAS, and Dredas for the initialization phase. Since CCDAS and Dredas require registration time, we can see from the figure that MHT has advantages over CCDAS and Dredas. And as the number of data blocks increases, the advantage becomes larger.

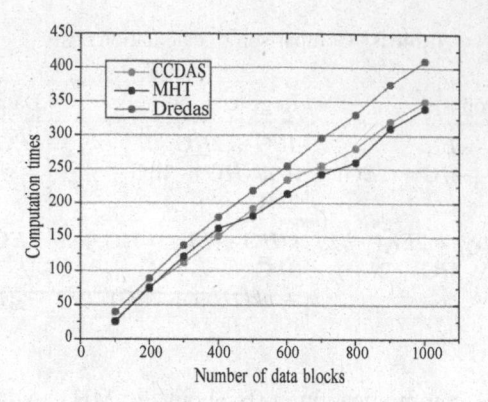

Fig. 3. Initialization time comparison

Figure 4 shows the calculation overhead of MHT, CCDAS, and Dredas for the register audit phase. We can see from the figure CCDAS has apparent advantages over MHT and Dredas. With the increase in the number of data blocks, the slope of the curve of MHT and Dredas gradually increases while the angle of CCDAS remains flat.

Figure 5 shows the computational overhead of the MHT, CCDAS, and Dredas about data auditing phases. The figure shows that CCDAS has an obvious advantage over MHT and Dredas. And with the increase in the number of data blocks, the slope of CCDAS is no longer stable, while MHT and Dredas keep a steady growth. In addition, CCDAS has a significantly lower slope than MHT and Dredas. In this stage, CCDAS combines each attribute in batches to complete the data audit, while MHT and Dredas protocols are single audit, so CCDAS has a significant advantage in computing overhead.

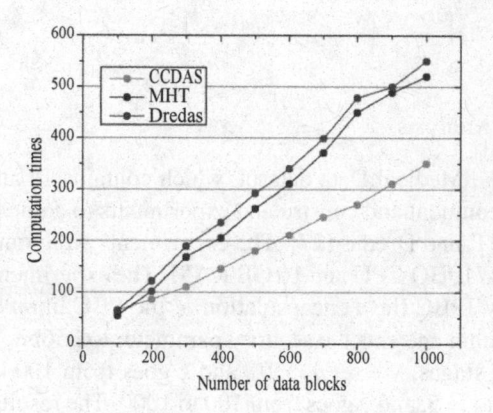

Fig. 4. Register auditing time comparison

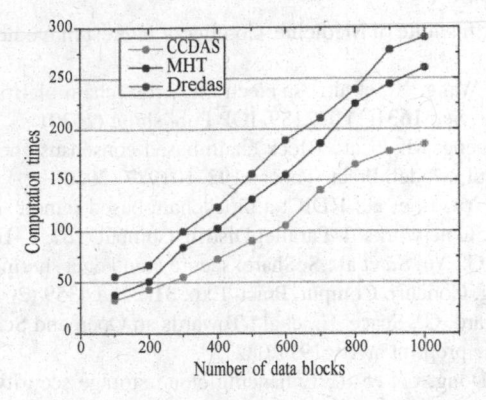

Fig. 5. Data auditing time comparison

7 Conclusion

With the increasingly extensive application of block chain data management technology and framework, cross-chain data sharing has gradually become a more common data circulation business. In this paper, we propose a cross-chain shared data audit scheme to ensure the consistency and integrity of shared data. Firstly, we propose a cross-chain data-sharing architecture based on the relay chain. Secondly, we analyze the data consistency and data. Based on the Challenge-Response method and the idea of batch auditing, we designed the audit protocol. Thirdly, the security analysis demonstrates that the desired security requirements are satisfied. Performance evaluation and comparison show that the scheme is practical. For future work, we will focus on defining and improving the usability of the proposed solution.

Acknowledgments. This work was supported by the National Natural Science Foundation of China (Nos. 62072092, 62072093, U1708262, and 62102075); the China Postdoctoral Science Foundation(No. 2019M653568); the Key Research and Development Project of Hebei Province (No. 20310702D); the Natural Science Foundation of Hebei Province (No. F2020501013); the Fundamental Research Funds for the Central Universities (No. N2023020).

References

1. Shen, M., Deng, Y., Zhu, L., et al.: Privacy-preserving image retrieval for medical IoT systems: a blockchain-based approach. IEEE Network **33**(5), 27–33 (2019)
2. Qiao, R., Luo, X.Y., Zhu, S.F., et al.: Dynamic autonomous cross consortium chain mechanism in e-healthcare. IEEE J. Biomed. Health Inform. **24**(8), 2157–2168 (2020)
3. DeBaun, M.R., et al.: American society of hematology 2020 guidelines for sickle cell disease: prevention, diagnosis, and treatment of cerebrovascular disease in children and adults. Blood Adv. **4**(8), 1554–1588 (2020)
4. Pournaghi, S.M., Bayat, M., Farjami, Y.: MedSBA: a novel and secure scheme to share medical data based on block chain technology and attribute-based encryption. J. Ambient Intell. Humaniz. Comput. **11**(11), 4613–4641 (2020)

5. Lo, B., Field, M.J.: Institute of Medicine. Conflict of interest in medical research, education, and practice (2009)
6. Wang, H., He, D., Wang, X., et al.: An electricity cross-chain platform based on sidechain relay. J. Phys. Conf. Ser. **1631**(1) 012189. IOP Publishing (2020)
7. Zhu, Z., Qi, G., Zheng, M., et al.: Block chain based consensus checking in decentralized cloud storage. Simul. Model. Pract. Theory **102**, 101987 (2020)
8. Wang, H., He, D., Yu, J., et al.: RDIC: a blockchain-based remote data integrity checking scheme for IoT in 5G networks. J. Parallel Distrib. Comput. **152**, 1–10 (2021)
9. Huang, L., Zhang, G., Yu, S., et al.: SeShare: secure cloud data sharing based on block chain and public auditing. Concurr. Comput. Pract. Exp. **31**(22), e4359 (2019)
10. Hardjono, T., Howard, G., Scace, E., et al.: Towards an Open and Scalable Music Metadata Layer (2019). arXiv preprint arXiv:1911.08278
11. Fan, K., Liu, M., Dong, G., et al.: Enhancing cloud storage security against a new replay attack with an efficient public auditing scheme. J. Supercomput. **76**(7), 4857–4883 (2020)
12. Duan, H., Du, Y., Zheng, L., et al.: Towards practical auditing of dynamic data in decentralized storage. IEEE Trans. Dependable Secure Comput. (2022)
13. Xue, J., Xu, C., Zhao, J., et al.: Identity-based public auditing for cloud storage systems against malicious auditors via block chain. Sci. China Inf. Sci. **62**(3), 1–16 (2019)
14. Jiang, Y., Wang, C., Wang, Y., et al.: A cross-chain solution to integrating multiple block chains for IoT data management. Sensors **19**(9), 2042 (2019)
15. Li, D., Yu, J., Gao, X., et al.: Research on multidomain authentication of IoT based on cross-chain technology. Secur. Commun. Netw. **2020** (2020)
16. Zhao, F., Yu, J., Yan, B.: Towards cross-chain access control model for medical data sharing. Procedia Comput. Sci. **202**, 330–335 (2022)
17. Chang, L., Yu, M., Xu, Z., Yuan, L., Bo, L.: Research on epidemic data sharing model based on cross-chain mechanism. In: Liang, Q., Wang, W., Liu, X., Na, Z., Zhang, B. (eds.) Communications, Signal Processing, and Systems. CSPS 2021. LNEE, vol. 878, pp. 424–430. Springer, Singapore (2022). https://doi.org/10.1007/978-981-19-0390-8_52
18. Zhou, L., Fu, A., Yang, G., et al.: Efficient certificateless multi-copy integrity auditing scheme supporting data dynamics. IEEE Trans. Dependable Secure Comput. (2020)
19. Xu, Y., Zhang, C., Wang, G., et al.: A block chain-enabled deduplicatable data auditing mechanism for network storage services. IEEE Trans. Emerg. Top. Comput. **9**(3), 1421–1432 (2020)
20. Hahn, C., Kwon, H., Kim, D., et al.: Enabling fast public auditing and data dynamics in cloud services. IEEE Trans. Serv. Comput. (2020)
21. Zhang, C., Xu, Y., Hu, Y., et al.: A blockchain-based multi-cloud storage data auditing scheme to locate faults. IEEE Trans. Cloud Comput. (2021)
22. Gao, X., Yu, J., Chang, Y., et al.: Checking only when it is necessary: Enabling integrity auditing based on the keyword with sensitive information privacy for encrypted cloud data. IEEE Trans. Dependable Secure Comput. (2021)
23. Ali, I., Chen, Y., Ullah, N., et al.: Bilinear pairing-based hybrid signcryption for secure heterogeneous vehicular communications. IEEE Trans. Veh. Technol. **70**(6), 5974–5989 (2021)
24. Dupressoir, F., Zain, S.: Machine-checking unforgeability proofs for signature schemes with tight reductions to the computational diffie-hellman problem. In: 2021 IEEE 34th Computer Security Foundations Symposium (CSF), pp. 1–15. IEEE (2021)
25. Wang, C., Chow, S.S.M., Wang, Q., Ren, K., Lou, W.: Privacy-preserving public auditing for secure cloud storage. IEEE Trans. Comput. **62**(2), 362–375 (2013)
26. Kaggle. https://www.kaggle.com/datasets

27. Fan, K., Bao, Z., Liu, M., et al.: Dredas: decentralized, reliable and efficient remote outsourced data auditing scheme with block chain smart contract for industrial IoT. Futur. Gener. Comput. Syst. **110**, 665–674 (2020)
28. JPBC Library. http://gas.dia.unisa.it/projects/jpbc/

Outsourced Privacy-Preserving SVM Classifier Model over Encrypted Data in IoT

Chen Wang[1], Yan Dong[1], Jiarun Li[1], Chen Chen[2], and Jian Xu[1,3(✉)]

[1] Software College, Northeastern University, Shenyang 110169, China
xuj@mail.neu.edu.cn
[2] Northeastern University, Shenyang 110169, China
[3] State Key Laboratory of Information Security, Institute of Information Engineering, Chinese Academy of Sciences, Beijing 100093, China

Abstract. The Internet of Things (IoT) enables the development of cloud computing by combining machine learning (ML) and big data technologies. Frameworks supporting ML typically process and classification manufacturing data services via cloud-based technologies. In order to achieve secure and efficient data collection and application, we design, implement and evaluate a new system employing a SVM classifier model over encrypted data (SVMCM-ED) based on multi-key Fully Homomorphic Encryption (multi-key FHE) in IoT. We first propose a new scheme that uses the cloud server and edge node to jointly implement SVM classification over the ciphertext to ensure the security of data and classification model. Our system significantly transfers cloud processing to the edge, and safely uses the model obtained from the data analysis to implement SVM classification among multiple users. We further design secure protocols based on multi-key FHE, which supports multiple users and satisfies the semi-honest security model where cloud computing is outsourced. Our protocol requires no interaction from the data analysis and users during online secure classification. Performance evaluation demonstrates that our new system can securely train a logistic regression model of multiple users. Performance evaluation demonstrates that our new system can securely implement the SVM classification model of multiple users in IoT, as well as share communication and computation overhead of the cloud.

Keywords: Multi-key FHE · cloud-edge · privacy-preserving · Internet of Things (IoT) · SVM

1 Introduction

Classification is a very important data mining method [1,2]. The concept of classification is to learn classification functions or build classification models based on existing data. This function or model maps the data records in the database

© ICST Institute for Computer Sciences, Social Informatics and Telecommunications Engineering 2023
Published by Springer Nature Switzerland AG 2023. All Rights Reserved
Q. Jiang et al. (Eds.): SPNCE 2022, LNICST 496, pp. 82–94, 2023.
https://doi.org/10.1007/978-3-031-30623-5_6

to one of the given categories, which can be applied to data prediction. The basic model of support vector machine (SVM) is to find the best separation hyperplane in the feature space to maximize the separation of positive and negative samples on the training set. SVM is a supervised learning algorithm for binary classification. After introducing kernel method, support vector machine can also be used to solve nonlinear problems.

Machine learning has brought great benefits to various application fields of the Internet of Things (IoT) [3], and put forward higher requirements for computing and storage resources. On the one hand, the processing capacity of personal terminals in practical applications is extremely limited, and they need to process massive data with the help of a trusted third-party cloud server. At the same time, centralized storage and processing of large amounts of data in a single cloud server will cause serious bandwidth and power consumption problems. Edge nodes are introduced to reduce the bandwidth and computing burden of the cloud server [4,5]. On the other hand, data storage in the cloud server and edge nodes brings about data leakage [6,7]. If any private data is disclosed, all personal information related to the record will be violated. How to protect data privacy and security in edge-assisted computing of the Internet of Things is an important issue. At present, SVM based privacy preserving research is mainly based on homomorphic encryption methods, but there are still the following defects:

First, once the classifier is handed over to the cloud server for processing, the copyright of the user classifier model will be damaged, and encryption is required for processing. Raymond et al. [8] proposed a privacy preserving classifier evaluation protocol for both parties. Compared with existing technologies, the protocol significantly improves efficiency. Zhou et al. [9] proposed a new scheme to achieve secure outsourced storage and k-NN query in the cloud, protect the privacy of users from the cloud, and users do not need to query online. However, the models of the above two schemes are stored in the server, and the adversary attacks the server and steals the models.

Second, users in the existing scheme use the same public key when uploading encrypted query data, and the security assumption is that the server cannot collude with any user. Once they collude with each other, cloud server can decrypt and obtain all users' query data and models. Recently, Meng et al. [10] proposed a scheme to support multiple users through privacy protection, allowing users to encrypt image features with the same key, thus realizing efficient image retrieval of images collected from multiple sources. However, since the data source has the same public key and private key, as long as one party obtains the encrypted data of the other party, it can decrypt the data.

Third, in the existing scheme, users and model owners must be online at the same time, interact with the cloud server, and participate in the classification stage in the whole process. Although users only need to bear a small part of computing and storage costs, they need to participate in the whole classification stage. However, in practical applications, users may not be able to maintain "online" all the time due to network conditions and other reasons, especially when there are multiple users, which brings inconvenience to data analysis.

In this paper, we further proposed a SVM classifier model over encrypted data (SVMCM-ED) based on multi-key FHE in IoT. We highlight our contributions below.

- Firstly, we propose a SVM classifier model over encrypted data in IoT to obtain multiple user classification results. The classification process is completed by the edge node and the cloud server. After sending the query data, the user can go offline. In this process, not only can data leakage be prevented, but also communication overhead of cloud server can be reduced.
- Secondly, we design two secure computing protocols based on multi-key FHE to prevent collusion between users, and provide security proof. This protocol allows encrypted calculation under different public keys and protects the data and models. Since each users has a different public and private key, no information will be leaked to the cloud server and edge node even if any users colludes with it.

2   Related Work

At present, researchers have done a lot of research work on privacy protection issues [11–14]. In the research of privacy protection data mining based on cryptography, there are the following problems: 1) The privacy and security of training data. 2) User query data and classification results are private data of users, including sensitive data, and their security and privacy should also be protected. Since user query data and classification results are the input and output of the classification stage, this is the privacy of the classification stage. protection issues. 3) The data is transmitted in plain text, and there is no guarantee that the data will not be stolen during the transmission process, resulting in privacy leakage. 4) For encrypted data, although fully homomorphic encryption can satisfy arbitrary operations, it is inefficient, and does not support comparison and maximal value operations.

In other works, edge computing is proposed to aid the training of industrial clouds. Edge node is composed of network devices that can be deployed anywhere over a network connection. Edge nodes have certain computing, storage and autonomous capabilities, which can reduce the data processing load on resource-constrained Internet of Things devices [15]. Since the research usually assumed that the edge node and industrial cloud are in a semi-honest model [7], the edge node will honestly implement the protocols and steal their private information by interaction with other participants, which will bring some security problems. Usually adopt data perturbation, fully homomorphic encryption, secure multi-party computation to protect privacy of edge computing outsourcing, among which fully homomorphic encryption are more common. Scholars at home and abroad pay more attention to how to perform machine learning over lightweight outsourced computing model under multiple users. Zhou et al.

[6] proposed a lightweight secure multi-key outsourced computing scheme under the cooperative but non-collusive double servers, and studied an efficient privacy preserving integer comparison protocol for wireless Internet of vehicles on this basis. Both user's location and interest privacy are effectively protected, which can resist the collusive between roadside units and semi-honest servers. However, users need to participate in the training process and bear part of the cost. The training process of the model we designed is jointly completed by the edge node and the industrial cloud. After smart device sends the training data, it can go offline without any communication overhead. The work [16] designed a privacy protection edge intelligent data aggregation solution to ensure data confidentiality, integrity, and real-timeness. The work [17] proposes a secure and smart communication solution for pervasive edge computing in infrastructure supporting IIoT. In the proposed scheme, the IIoT device detects the counterfeit identity of the adversary and shares it with the edge server to prevent the upstream transmission of its malicious data. The work [18] proposes a device-oriented anonymous privacy protection scheme with identity verification for data aggregation applications in the fog-enhanced IoT system. It also supports multiple permissions to locally manage smart devices and fog nodes.

At present, there is no Multi-key FHE system based on svm classification algorithm.

3   Our Proposed Design

The system architecture is shown in Fig. 1. There are four entities: User (U_i), Data Analysis (DA), Cloud Server (CS), and edge node (EN). User (e.g., client) has a large amount of user privacy data, which will be disclosed when it is handed over to EN and CS for computing, so it needs to be encrypted before uploading. In the medical environment, users (e.g., residents) submit personal information (e.g., weight, height, blood pressure, medical history and other personal information) to the CS to obtain their health condition. The model is stored in the DA. The model is proprietary intellectual property and cannot be disclosed to unauthorized entities. Therefore, it is necessary to send the encrypted model to the ED and CS. After the classification results are calculated, the user downloads it to the local for decryption to obtain the classification results (e.g., condition). The outstanding advantage of our system is that it allows U_i and DA to go offline completely after providing data, while the ED share the computing cost of the CS.

4   Our Proposed Design

4.1   Overview

There are n users $U_1, U_2, ..., U_n$, and each of them has a piece of private breast cancer disease data, respectively $m_1, m_2, ..., m_n$. DA has a trained SVM classifier model for breast cancer, and the classifier decision function is $f(x) =$

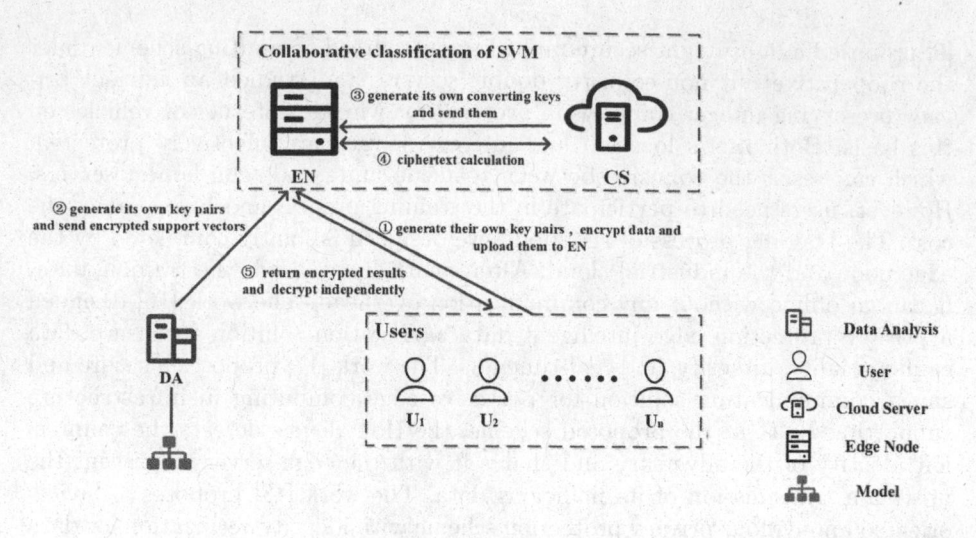

Fig. 1. The system architecture.

$sign(\sum\limits_{j=1}^{t} \alpha_j^* y_j K(g_j, x) + b^*)$. U wants to use CS to classify data through the SVM classifier model. U and DA must ensure that any unauthorized third party can obtain private data information in this process.

The privacy-preserving SVM classifier requirements in this scenario can be summarized as follows:

(1) The privacy data $m_1, m_2, ..., m_n$ of any U cannot be disclosed to other users, CS, and DA;
(2) The support vector $g_1, g_2, ..., g_t$ contained in the SVM classifier model owned by the DA cannot be disclosed to $U_1, U_2, ..., U_n$ and CS;
(3) The final classification results cannot be disclosed to CS and DA;
(4) Users bear as little computing and communication load as possible and do not need to participate in the whole classification process, that is, they do not need to be online all the time.

To meet the above requirements, this paper proposes a SVM classifier model over encrypted data (SVMCM-ED) based on multi-key homomorphic encryption to achieve the binary classification of encrypted data. The SVMCM-ED scheme uses CZW multi-key FHE algorithm to protect data privacy. Each user independently generates a public key to encrypt data and then uploads it. The DA independently generates a public key to encrypt data related to the classification model and then uploads it. Introduce an edge node ED that does not conspire with CS. The SVM classification process is jointly completed by CS and ED through interaction, without the participation of other parties. After the classification is completed, each user downloads CS's ciphertext results and decrypts them locally with the corresponding private key.

4.2 Communication Protocol

This paper mainly considers privacy-preserving SVM algorithm of classification process, namely privacy-preserving SVM classifier. Based on different kernel functions, different SVM classifiers can be constructed. In order to achieve data privacy protection, we in this paper use CZW multi-key FHE algorithm, and construct secure protocols to implement classification decision functions in different types of privacy-preserving SVM classifiers, which are secure inner product classification decision protocol and secure polynomial classification decision protocol.

Secure Inner Product Classification Decision Protocol. Given the unlabeled data object $m_i = (m_1, m_2, ..., m_d)$, the support vector $g_1, g_2, ..., g_t$ included in the training model, the corresponding class label $y_1, y_2, ..., y_t$ and lagrange multiplier $\alpha_1{}^*, \alpha_2{}^*, ..., \alpha_t{}^*$ of the support vector, and the hyperplane displacement b^*. The inner product between the data object $m_i = (m_1, m_2, ..., m_d)$ and the support vector $g_1, g_2, ..., g_t$ can be expressed as:

$$K(g_j, m_i) = \sum_{z=1}^{d} g_{jz} m_{iz} \tag{1}$$

Let $h_i = \sum_{j=1}^{t} \alpha_z^* y_j K(g_j, m_i) + b^*$ represent the decision value of the classification decision function. If $h(g, m_i) = 1$, then $y_i = +1$; If $h(g, m_i) = 0$, then $y_i = -1$. The security inner product classification decision protocol aims to calculate the ciphertext decision value without disclosing the plaintext.

Let $C_i = (c_1, c_2, ..., c_d)$ represent the ciphertext encrypted by m_i under public key $pk_{l,i}$, and the corresponding decryption private key is $sk_{l,i}$; Let $SV_1, SV_2, ..., SV_t$ represent the ciphertext encrypted by the support vector under public key $pk_{l,j}$, and the corresponding decryption private key is $sk_{l,j}$. A and B are used to represent the participants of the protocol, where A owns the ciphertext $C_i, SV_1, SV_2, ..., SV_t$ and model data $y_1, y_2, ..., y_t, \alpha_1{}^*, \alpha_2{}^*, ..., \alpha_t{}^*$ and b^* and B owns the corresponding private key $sk_{l,i}$ and $sk_{l,j}$ to decrypt.

The secure inner product classification decision protocol is shown below.

Secure Polynomial Classification Decision Protocol. Given the unlabeled data object $m_i = (m_1, m_2, ..., m_d)$, the support vector $g_1, g_2, ..., g_t$ included in the training model, the corresponding class label $y_1, y_2, ..., y_t$ and lagrange multiplier $\alpha_1{}^*, \alpha_2{}^*, ..., \alpha_t{}^*$ of the support vector, and the hyperplane displacement b^*. The polynomial kernel function between the data object $m_i = (m_1, m_2, ..., m_d)$ and the support vector $g_1, g_2, ..., g_t$ can be expressed as:

$$K(g_j, m_i) = (\sum_{z=1}^{d} g_{jz} m_{iz} + 1)^u \tag{2}$$

Protocol 2 is a description of the dot product protocol.

Protocol 1. Secure inner product classification decision protocol

Input A: $C_i, SV_1, SV_2, ..., SV_t, y_1, y_2, ..., y_t, \alpha_1{}^*, \alpha_2{}^*, ..., \alpha_t{}^*$ and b^*;

Input B: private key $sk_{l,i}$ and $sk_{l,j}$;

Output A: classification result $C(h_i)$

1: A:

2: **if** $pk_{l,i} \neq pk_{l,j}$ **then**

3:    expand $C_i, SV_1, SV_2, ..., SV_t$ to $\overline{C_i}, \overline{SV_1}, \overline{SV_2}, ..., \overline{SV_t}$, and the corresponding key is $sk_{l,\overline{U}} = (sk_{l,i}|sk_{l,j})$, where $\overline{U} = \{i, j\}$

4:    compute $s_i = \sum\limits_{j=1}^{t} \alpha_j^* y_j s_{j,i}$, and the corresponding key is $sk'_{l,\overline{U}} = (sk_{l,\overline{U}} \otimes sk_{l,\overline{U}})$

5: **else**

6:    compute $s_i = \sum\limits_{j=1}^{t} \alpha_j^* y_j s_{j,i}$, where the corresponding key is $sk'_{l,\overline{U}} = (sk_{l,i} \otimes sk_{l,j})$

7: **end if**

8: refreshing s_i is $s_i{}'$, and the corresponding key of $s_i{}'$ is $sk_{l-1,\overline{U}}$

9: select random number r, and encrypt r, b^* under public key $pk_{l-1,\overline{U}}$ to get $\overline{C}(r), \overline{C}(b^*)$

10: compute $\widetilde{h_i} = s_i' + \overline{C}(b^*) + \overline{C}(r)$ and send $\widetilde{h_i}$ to B

11: B:

12: decrypt $\widetilde{h_i}$ to $\widetilde{h_i}{}'$, and encrypt $C(\widetilde{h_i}{}')$ to A

13: A:

14: encrypt r under public key $pk_{l,i}$ to $C(r)$ and calculate $C(h_i) = C(\widetilde{h_i}{}') - C(r)$

4.3 Classification Process

SVMCM-ED includes three stages, namely, secure data encryption and upload stage, security data classification stage and secure decryption stage. The specific description is as follows:

Secure Data Encryption and Upload Stage. In this stage, each user $U_i(i \in [n])$ must independently generate its own key pair $\{pk_{l,i}, sk_{l,i}\}_{l=\{L,...,1,0\}}$, encrypt the private data m_i with the public key $pk_{L,i}$, and generate the converting key $\{\tau_{sk_{L,j} \to sk_{L,S}}\}$.

$$\{\tau_{sk_{L,i} \to sk_{L,S}}\} \leftarrow MKFHE.SwitchKeyGen(pp, sk_{L,j}, pk_{L,S})a \qquad (3)$$

The data analysis (DA) independently generates its own key pair $\{pk_{l,DA}, sk_{l,DA}\}$, and encrypts $g_1, g_2, ..., g_t$ under the public key $pk_{l,DA}$ to obtain the ciphertext $SV_1, SV_2, ..., SV_t$, and generates the converting key $\{\tau_{sk_{L,DA} \to sk_{L,S}}\}$.

$$\{\tau_{sk_{L,DA} \to sk_{L,S}}\} \leftarrow MKFHE.SwitchKeyGen(pp, sk_{L,DA}, pk_{L,S}) \qquad (4)$$

CS generates its own key pair $\{pk_{l,s}, sk_{l,s}\}_{l=\{L,...,1,0\}}$ independently and the converting key $\{\tau_{sk_{l,S} \to sk_{l-1,S}}\}$ for refresh the ciphertext.

In this stage, each data owner $U_i(i \in [n])$ independently uploads its ciphertext data C_i, public key $pk_{L,i}$ and the converting key $\{\tau_{sk_{L,j} \to sk_{L,S}}\}$ to the edge node

---

Protocol 2. Secure polynomial classification decision protocol

---

Input A: $C_i, SV_1, SV_2, ..., SV_t, y_1, y_2, ..., y_t, \alpha_1{}^*, \alpha_2{}^*, ..., \alpha_t{}^*$ and b^*;

Input B: private key $sk_{l,i}$ and $sk_{l,j}$;

Output A: classification result $C(h_i)$

1: A:

2: **if** $pk_{l,i} \neq pk_{l,j}$ **then**

3:    expand $C_i, SV_1, SV_2, ..., SV_t$ to $\overline{C}_i, \overline{SV}_1, \overline{SV}_2, ..., \overline{SV}_t$, and the corresponding key is $sk_{l,\overline{U}} = (sk_{l,i}|sk_{l,j})$, where $\overline{U} = \{i, j\}$

4:    compute $s_i = \sum\limits_{j=1}^{t} \alpha_j^* y_j s_{j,i}$, and the corresponding key is $sk'_{l,\overline{U}} = (sk_{l,\overline{U}} \otimes sk_{l,\overline{U}})$

5: **else**

6:    compute $s_i = \sum\limits_{j=1}^{t} \alpha_j^* y_j s_{j,i}$, where the corresponding key is $sk'_{l,\overline{U}} = (sk_{l,i} \otimes sk_{l,j})$

7: **end if**

8: refreshing s_i is s_i', and the corresponding key of s_i' is $sk_{l-1,\overline{U}}$

9: select random number r, and encrypt r, b^* under public key $pk_{l-1,\overline{U}}$ to get $\overline{C}(r), \overline{C}(b^*)$

10: compute $\widetilde{h}_i = \sum\limits_{j=1}^{t} \alpha_z^* y_j p_{j,i} + \overline{C}(b^*) + \overline{C}(r)$, where the corresponding key is $sk_{l-u,\overline{U}} = (sk_{l-u,i}|sk_{l-u,j})$ and send $\widetilde{h}_i$ to B

11: B:

12: decrypt $\widetilde{h}_i$ to $\widetilde{h}_i{}'$, and encrypt $C(\widetilde{h}_i{}')$ to A

13: A:

14: encrypt r under public key $pk_{l',i}$ to $C(r)$ and calculate $C(h_i) = C(\widetilde{h}_i{}') - C(r)$

ED through the secure channel. The DA independently uploads the kernel function $K(x, z)$, ciphertext $SV_1, SV_2, ..., SV_t$, plaintext $y_1, y_2, ..., y_t, \alpha_1{}^*, \alpha_2{}^*, ..., \alpha_t{}^*$, public key $pk_{l,DA}$ and converting key $\{\tau_{sk_{L.DA} \to sk_{L,S}}\}$ used in the SVM classifier to the ED through a secure channel. The CS uploads public key $pk_{l,S}$ and converting keys $\{\tau_{sk_{l.S} \to sk_{l-1,S}}\}$ to ED. At this time, ED runs the key exchange sub-algorithm to convert $C_1, C_2, ..., C_n$, $SV_1, SV_2, ..., SV_t$ into $C_{S1}, C_{S2}, ..., C_{Sn}$, $SV_{S1}, SV_{S2}, ..., SV_{St}$. After conversion, the private keys corresponding to the ciphertext are $sk_{L,S}$.

Secure Classification Decision Stage. In this stage, CS and ED complete the classification decision of data object $m_i = (m_1, m_2, ..., m_d)$ through security protocols, and different kernel functions select different security protocols. ED gets the ciphertext decision value $h_{S1}, h_{S2}, ..., h_{Sn}$, and converts the ciphertext to $C(h_1), C(h_2), ..., C(h_n)$.

$$C(h_i) \leftarrow MKFHE.SwitchKey(\tau_{sk_{l'},s \to sk_{l'},i}, h_{Si}) \tag{5}$$

Secure Decryption Stage. In this stage, U_i downloads ciphertext $C(h_i)$ from ED and decrypts decision value h_i independently with private key $sk_{l',i}$.

$$h_i \leftarrow MKFHE.Dec(pp, ct = (h, i, l'), sk_{l',i}) \tag{6}$$

That is, the classification label of m_i is $y_i = sign(h_i)$. If $h_i = 1$, then $y_i = 1$; If $h_i = 0$, then $y_i = -1$.

5   Security Analysis

This section analyzes the security of the communication protocol and SVMCM-ED under the semi-honest model. Both CS and EN are semi-honest participants, they honestly follow the execution of the protocol and allow inferences from the data obtained during the execution of the protocol. Its input data is private data and can only be known by the individual.

It is divided into the following three parts to discuss the security of the classifier under the semi honest model:

(1) Secure data encryption and upload stage: At this stage, $U_1, U_2, ..., U_n$ generates ciphertext C_i and converting key $\{\tau_{sk_{L.j} \rightarrow sk_{L,s}}\}$ independently and stores them on ED. DA generates ciphertext $SV_1, SV_2, ..., SV_t$ and converting key $\{\tau_{sk_{L.DA} \rightarrow sk_{L,s}}\}$ independently and stores them on ED. The independent generation key $\{\tau_{sk_{l.s} \rightarrow sk_{l-1,s}}\}$ of CS is stored on ED. The ED then converts $C_1, C_2, ..., C_n,\ SV_1, SV_2, ..., SV_t$ into $C_{S1}, C_{S2}, ..., C_{Sn}$, $SV_{S1}, SV_{S2}, ..., SV_{St}$.

(2) Secure classification decision stage: At this stage, ED and CS calculate the decision value of privacy data through different secure classification decision protocols according to different kernel functions $K_{(x,z)}$.

In the semi honest model, protocol participants A and B perform protocol operations honestly, but A is curious about data objects m_i, support vectors $g_1, g_2, ..., g_t$, and decision value h_i, and is curious about decision value h_i.

The secure inner product classification decision protocol only involves the addition and multiplication homomorphic operations between ciphertext. Similarly, the power function calculation in the secure polynomial classification decision protocol is converted into multiple ciphertext multiplication calculations, so the protocol only involves the addition and multiplication homomorphic operations between ciphertext. For A, without the private key $sk_{l,i}$ and $sk_{l,j}$, according to the semantic security of the CZW scheme, A cannot infer any information of the corresponding plaintext from the ciphertext C_i, $SV_1, SV_2, ..., SV_t$, $C(h_i)$. Since A introduces random number r, B cannot recover the decision value h_i from $\tilde{h}_i$.

In conclusion, the secure inner product classification decision protocol and the secure polynomial classification decision protocol mentioned in this section are safe under the semi-honest model. Therefore, ED cannot obtain any data information in the classification decision. Although CS has a private key that can be decrypted, because ED is disturbed by calculation or random number before sending the ciphertext, CS cannot obtain any private data information during the classification decision process.

(3) Secure decryption stage: At this stage, $U_1, U_2, ..., U_n$ decrypts $h_1, h_2, ..., h_n$ independently and judges the classification label $y_1, y_2, ..., y_n$ of $m_1, m_2, ..., m_n$. According to the semantic security of CZW multi-key FHE algorithm, any third-party without the corresponding decryption private key $sk_{l,1}, sk_{l,2}, ..., sk_{l,n}$ can obtain the information of $h_1, h_2, ..., h_n$ and $y_1, y_2, ..., y_n$.

To sum up, the proposed SVMCM-ED scheme is safe under the semi honest model.

6 Experiments

Our protocols are implemented in C++ on Ubuntu 18.04.2 64-bit version, Inter(R) Core(TM) i7-9700M CPU (3.00 GHz) 32 GB RAM. The server with the same configuration were used to simulate the edge node (EN) and the cloud server (CS) to collaborative implement the SVM model together in order to reduce the burden on the cloud server.

Four FCPS [18] standard datasets are used, namely: Hepta, Lsun, Tetra, and Wingnut public datasets, which are specially used for classification analysis. To facilitate the experiment, the range of security parameters of the encryption algorithm selected in this paper is $5 < \kappa < 60$. Wingnut dataset is used.

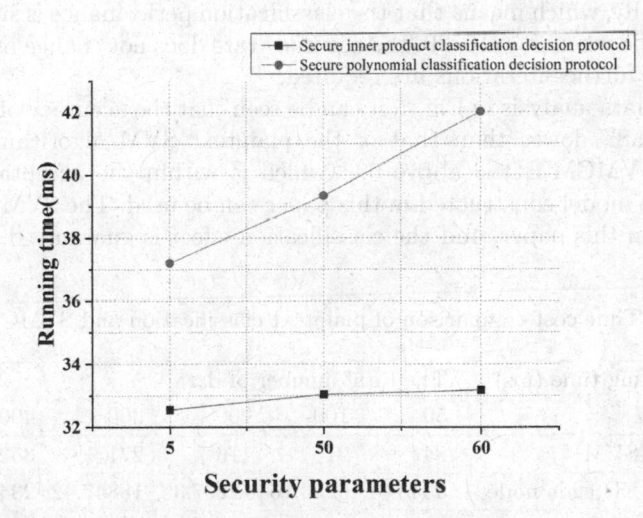

Fig. 2. Running time of two communication protocols.

The efficiency of each protocol is shown below. Figure 2 respectively shows the running time of the secure inner product classification decision protocol and secure polynomial classification decision protocol when the security parameter $\kappa = 5, 50, 60$.

The following experiments were conducted under the condition of $\kappa = 50$. As shown in Table 1, the feature descriptions of the four datasets are given. The effect of iteration number T on the classification effect of plaintext SVM and SVMCM-ED is discussed through experiments and analysis.

Table 1. Accuracy comparison of SVM and SVMCM-ED

Data	Model	Accuracy					
		$T = 5$	$T = 10$	$T = 15$	$T = 20$	$T = 25$	$T = 30$
Hepta	plaintext SVM	0.714	0.733	0.742	0.742	0.735	0.743
	SVMCM-ED	0.682	0.694	0.704	0.711	0.706	0.706
Lsun	plaintext SVM	0.708	0.724	0.731	0.734	0.741	0.736
	SVMCM-ED	0.687	0.693	0.706	0.702	0.698	0.704
Tetra	plaintext SVM	0.711	0.719	0.728	0.736	0.739	0.739
	SVMCM-ED	0.679	0.684	0.695	0.697	0.701	0.697
Wingnut	plaintext SVM	0.704	0.716	0.729	0.724	0.727	0.726
	SVMCM-ED	0.667	0.681	0.688	0.690	0.692	0.687

The accuracy is used to measure the classification effect. Table 1 and Fig. 3 show the comparison of the accuracy of plaintext SVM and SVMCM-ED with different values of T selected. When $T = 5$–15, the accuracy rate increases rapidly, which means that the classification performance is significantly improved; while when $T = 15$–30, the accuracy rate does not change much. After 15 rounds, no further iterations are required.

From the data analysis in Fig. 3, it can be seen that the accuracy of SVMCM-ED is 2.9%–5.8% lower than that of the plaintext SVM algorithm, and the accuracy of SVMCM-ED is above 0.6, which is within the acceptable range. Therefore, the model constructed in this paper can be used. The SVM algorithm is completed in this paper, and the classification effect is guaranteed.

Table 2. Time cost comparison of plaintext classification and SVMCM-ED

The running time (ms)	The total number of data				
	50	100	200	300	400
plaintext SVM	84	91	176	271	352
SVMCM-ED egde node	3343.81	6253.16	12207.36	18847.42	23497.92
SVMCM-ED cloud server	2788.11	5218.49	10284.21	15745.26	20935.43

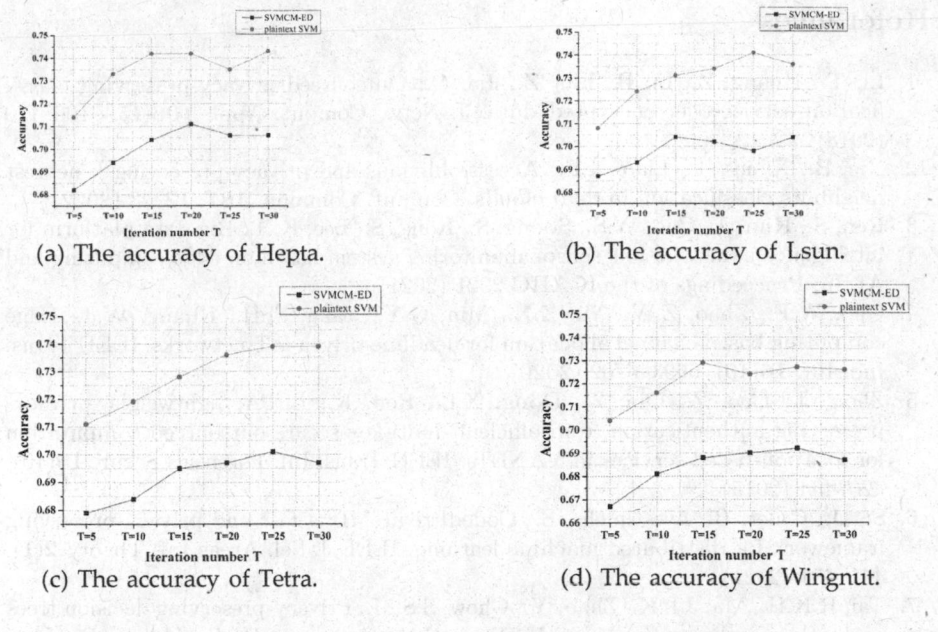

Fig. 3. Accuracy comparison of SVM and SVMCM-ED.

Using the Lsun data set, n represents the total number of data, taking n = 50, 100, 200, 300, 400, and conduct experiments respectively. Table 2 shows the classification of the plaintext SVM algorithm and the running time of the SVMCM-ED egde node and cloud server when n changes. The data in the table shows that its running time increases linearly with n, and the running time of ciphertext classification is between 1 s and 24 s, which is within the acceptable range. The egde node bears the main overhead, reducing the burden on the cloud server.

7 Conclusion

In this paper, a SVM classifier model over encrypted data (SVMCM-ED) is implemented instead of using the SVM classifier model directly. It allows data analysis to provide their encrypted model so that edge nodes can cooperate with cloud server and outsource SVM classifier services. We give the entity structure of the model and design the communication protocols, including the secure inner product classification decision protocol and secure polynomial classification decision protocol. More importantly, the module sequence combination is constructed based on the above protocol. Then, we give the security analysis. The experiments show that SVMCM-ED can realize the SVM classification over encrypted data, and the edge nodes can share the burden of cloud servers.

References

1. Li, T., Huang, Z., Li, P., Liu, Z., Jia, C.: Outsourced privacy-preserving classification service over encrypted data. J. Netw. Comput. Appl. **106**(15), 100–110 (2018)
2. Xie, B., Xiang, T., Liao, X.F.: Access-oblivious and privacy-preserving k nearest neighbors classification in dual clouds. Comput. Commun. **187**, 12–23 (2022)
3. Ren, S., Kim, J., Cho, W.S., Soeng, S., Kong, S., Lee, K.H.: Big data platform for intelligence industrial IoT sensor monitoring system based on edge computing and AI. In: Proceedings of the ICAIIC 2021 (2021)
4. Gao, W.F., Zhao, Z.W., Yu, Z.X., Min, G.Y., Yang, M.H., Huang, W.J.: Edge computing based channel allocation for deadline-driven IoT networks. IEEE Trans. Ind. Inf. **16**(10), 6693–6702 (2020)
5. Zhou, J., Cao, Z., Qin, Z., Dong, X.L., Ren, K.: LPPA: lightweight privacy-preserving authentication from efficient multi-key secure outsourced computation for location-based services in VANETs. IEEE Trans. Inf. Forensics Secur. **15**(10), 420–434 (2019)
6. So, J., Guler, B., Avestimehr, S.: CodedPrivateML: a fast and privacy-preserving framework for distributed machine learning. IEEE J. Sel. Areas Inf. Theory **2**(1), 441–451 (2021)
7. Tai, R.K.H., Ma, J.P.K., Zhao, Y., Chow, S.S.M.: Privacy-preserving decision trees evaluation via linear functions. In: Foley, S.N., Gollmann, D., Snekkenes, E. (eds.) ESORICS 2017. LNCS, vol. 10493, pp. 494–512. Springer, Cham (2017). https://doi.org/10.1007/978-3-319-66399-9_27
8. Lu, Z., Zhu, Y., Castiglione, A.: Efficient k-NN query over encrypted data in cloud with limited key-disclosure and offline data owner. Comput. Secur. **69**, 84–96 (2017)
9. Shen, M., Cheng, G., Zhu, L., Du, X., Hu, J.: Content-based multi-source encrypted image retrieval in clouds with privacy preservation. Future Generation Computer Systems
10. Bost, R., Pop, R., Tu, S.: Machine learning classification over encrypted data. In: Network & Distributed System Security Symposium (2014)
11. Zheng, Y., Duan, H., Wang, C., Wang, R.: Securely and efficiently outsourcing decision tree inference. IEEE Trans. Dependable Secure Comput. 1 (2020)
12. Xu, R., Joshi, K., Li, C.: NN-EMD: efficiently training neural networks using encrypted multi-sourced datasets. IEEE Trans. Dependable Secure Comput. 1 (2021)
13. Crawford, J.L.H., Gentry, C., Halevi, S., Platt, D.: Doing Real Work with FHE: The Case of Logistic Regression (2018)
14. Chamikara, M., Bertok, P., Khalil, I., Liu, D., Camtepe, S.: Privacy preserving distributed machine learning with federated learning. Comput. Commun. **171**(4), 112–125 (2021)
15. Xiong, J., et al.: A personalized privacy protection framework for mobile crowd-sensing in IIoT. IEEE Trans. Ind. Inform. **16**(/6), 4231–4241 (2020)
16. Khan, F., Jan, M.A., Rehman, A., Mastorakis, S., Alazab, M., Watters, P.: A secured and intelligent communication scheme for IIoT-enabled pervasive edge computing. IEEE Trans. Ind. Inf. **17**(7), 5128–5137 (2021)
17. Guan, Z.T., et al.: APPA: an anonymous and privacy preserving data aggregation scheme for fog-enhanced IoT. J. Netw. Comput. Appl. (2019)
18. FCPS[EB/OL]. http://uni-marburg.de/fb12/datenbionik/data?languagesvnc=1/

A Scheme of Anti Gradient Leakage of Federated Learning Based on Blockchain

Xin Zhang[1], Yuanzhen Liu[1], Yanbo Yang[1]([✉]), Jiawei Zhang[2], Teng Li[2], and Baoshan Li[1]

[1] School of Information Engineering, Inner Mongolia University of Science & Technology, Bao Tou 014010, China
lz@stu.imust.edu.cn, yangyanbo@imust.edu.cn
[2] School of Cyber Engineering, Xidian University, Xi'an 710071, China

Abstract. Federated learning provides a new solution for data security and privacy protection in the process of machine learning. In distributed learning, interactive gradient rather than direct exchange of data avoids the direct acquisition of data by malicious participants. The latest research shows that the gradient will also leak the data privacy during user training, current solutions to gradient leakage problems are mainly divided into two categories: 1. Encrypt the parameters of the model updating process by using the cryptography scheme; 2. Increase the interference noise for the gradient through thinning, gradient compression, adding noise and other schemes. However, the cryptographic scheme cannot be targeted at the aggregator, and the noise scheme has too much impact on the performance of the model. This paper uses the trust mechanism of blockchain to design an anti gradient leakage scheme for this problem: when the participants upload the gradient, the noise is added through the blockchain smart contract, and the noise value is randomly divided into multiple copies and stored in the blockchain. The central server obtains the noise sum of all participants through the smart contract, and aggregates the gradient to remove the noise. In the training process, all participants can only obtain the aggregation gradient and noise gradient, and cannot recover user data. At the same time, due to the automatic execution and tamper proof characteristics of blockchain smart contracts, malicious interference in the data exchange process is avoided.

Keywords: Federated Learning · Blockchain · Ring signature · Deep Leakage from Gradients · Gradient Update

1 Introduction

With the further development of network communication, the Internet also needs a higher level of security and stronger privacy protection. Various countries and regions have issued a series of regulations related to privacy protection, which put forward strict requirements for data security and privacy protection [1]. Machine learning needs to use a large amount of data for training, but the protection of data and privacy makes it difficult

© ICST Institute for Computer Sciences, Social Informatics and Telecommunications Engineering 2023
Published by Springer Nature Switzerland AG 2023. All Rights Reserved
Q. Jiang et al. (Eds.): SPNCE 2022, LNICST 496, pp. 95–108, 2023.
https://doi.org/10.1007/978-3-031-30623-5_7

for data to circulate and form data islands, which cannot release the greater value of data. Traditional machine learning based on central servers faces serious privacy and security challenges and cannot achieve ubiquitous secure AI for future networks. Furthermore, traditional centralized machine learning schemes may not be suitable for ubiquitous AI due to the huge overhead introduced by centralized data aggregation and processing [2]. As an emerging distributed machine learning scheme, federated learning provides new solutions to the privacy and security issues faced by machine learning. In federated learning, participating devices collaboratively train a shared model through their local data. Unlike traditional machine learning schemes, only model updates are uploaded to the centralized parameter server instead of the original data, providing tighter privacy for machine learning. Under federated learning, the original data is always stored locally, avoiding direct leakage of privacy [2]. However, according to the latest research, the process of model updating still faces the risk of privacy leakage. For example, malicious participants can infer user data by obtaining gradient updates during user training, which poses a great threat to data security and user privacy in federated learning [3].

With the rapid development of blockchain technology in recent years, its own "Trust" feature has created a reliable cooperation mechanism. It can provide a trusted environment in an untrustworthy network and can provide secure and trusted services in numerous scenarios, solving the problems faced by traditional centralized servers. The combined use of blockchain and distributed learning effectively improves the confidentiality of data and the security of computing and can meet a variety of different application scenarios.

We designed a blockchain-based solution for federal learning gradient leakage, using smart contracts to add noise to the gradient when users submit gradient data, while storing the noise value in the blockchain by secret sharing, and the central server removes the noise after aggregating the model, which ensures the machine learning training accuracy and solves the gradient leakage problem at the same time. The main contributions of this paper are as follows:

(1)In this paper, a federated learning improvement protocol is designed to add noise to the model to prevent gradient leakage when participants submit data and to remove noise after the central server aggregates the model to avoid affecting training accuracy.
(2)Using blockchain and smart contracts to store several copies of noise values obtained by gradient hash recalculation and a smart contract to calculate all the shared noise and return to the central server, storing the noise values shared by each participant in the blockchain, avoiding the malicious participant from directly obtaining the noise data to recover the gradient and then infer the real data of the user. The application of ring signature in the process guarantees the identity security of data uploaders.

2 Related Work

Jin et al. [4] proposed an advanced data leakage attack and theoretically demonstrated that the attack can effectively recover bulk data from shared aggregation gradients. Zhao et al. [5] proposed a simple but reliable method to extract accurate data from the gradients. Wu et al. [6] proposed a new method called gradient privacy leakage (PLFG) to infer sensitive information through gradients only. Shafee et al. [7] point out the attacks on privacy by deep learning models and some solutions to them. Wang et al. [8] proposed a generalized gradient privacy attack called SAPAG, which attacks user privacy based on gradient differences as a distance metric; Wei et al. [9] proposed a principled framework for evaluating and comparing different forms of client-side privacy leakage attacks, showing how an adversary can reconstruct private local training data by simply analyzing shared parameter updates from local training (e.g., local gradient or weight update vectors). Ren et al. [10] describe the attack as a regression problem and optimize two branches of the generative model by minimizing the distance between gradients; Wainakh et al. [3, 11] propose using LLG to extract training data labels from user-shared gradients; Jia et al. [12] speed up image reconstruction by imposing a priori image information and improving initialization. Hu et al. [1] propose a new inference attack, called Source Inference Attack (SIA), which optimally estimates the source of training members; Huang et al. [13] evaluated the advantages of three defense mechanisms against gradient inversion attacks, showed the trade-offs of these defense methods in terms of privacy disclosure and data utility, and found that combining them in an appropriate way reduces the effectiveness of the attack; Yuan et al. [14] made the first attempt to explore record-level privacy leakage for NLP tasks in FL by exploiting the complexity of language modeling to study the exposure of records of interest in federation aggregation. Two related attacks are proposed by monitoring exposure patterns to identify the corresponding clients when extracting specific records.

Lin et al. [15] used sparsification to reduce exchange costs and achieve reasonable accuracy with various model structures. Zheng et al. added a dropout layer before feeding data to the classifier and obtained better results with an appropriate dropout rate; Wei et al. [16], for example, clarified that the traditional server-coordinated differential privacy approach is insufficient to protect the privacy of training data reasons, analyzed the privacy utility tradeoff for Fed-CDP to provide differential privacy guarantees, and proposed a dynamic attenuation noise injection strategy to further improve Fed-CDP's accuracy and resilience. Fu et al. understood the utility of differential privacy in FL by adjusting the number of iterations performed and formally derived the convergence under differential privacy noise in FL based on the FedAvg algorithm speed; Wang et al. [17] suggested reshaping and tailoring gradient methods for differentially private distributed optimization and proposed two differentially privacy-oriented gradient methods to ensure privacy and optimality; Wu et al. [18] applied local differential privacy techniques to local gradients to protect user privacy and combined randomly sampled items into pseudo-interaction items in order to protect the items with which users interact in order to achieve anonymity. Zhao et al. [19] proposed a new CDL framework, PrivateDL, which allows efficient transfer of relational knowledge from sensitive data to public data in a privacy-preserving manner and enables participants to learn local models together based on public data with noise-proof labels. PrivateDL creates a privacy gap between local models and private datasets, thus ensuring privacy from attacks launched against local models through gradient sharing. Hya et al. [20] proposed a privacy-preserving network transformation method using random permutations in software protection extensions (SGX), which protects model parameters from being inferred by curious servers and dishonest clients; Dxa et al. [21] proposed an entropy-based gradient compression

(EGC) mechanism to reduce communication overhead, where EGC selects the transmission based on the entropy of the gradient terms gradient, which can achieve a high compression ratio without sacrificing accuracy; So et al. [22] introduced a new metric to quantify the privacy assurance checkout of joint learning over multiple training sessions and to develop a structured user selection policy to ensure the long-term privacy of each user.

Current responses to the gradient leakage problem mainly have two solution ideas: 1. Use cryptographic schemes such as homomorphic encryption to encrypt the updated model parameters and then upload them to the central server, which will encrypt the updated model parameters using cryptographic schemes, and only the central server can decrypt and aggregate them into a new model, In such schemes, it is difficult for other participants to obtain the user gradient, but the central server can decrypt the user gradient parameters, thereby revealing the user privacy; 2. Add noise to the model, and when users upload the gradient parameters, add appropriate noise to the data so that the participants cannot directly access each round of training gradients, thus making it difficult to recover the data.

3   Preliminary Knowledge

3.1   Blockchain

In blockchain technology, decentralization is its most essential feature. Each node in the network backs up the complete ledger information and provides a credible transaction environment in an untrustworthy network, laying a solid foundation of "trust" and creating a reliable cooperation mechanism that has a wide range of application prospects.

The consensus mechanism contained in the blockchain enables each unrelated node to verify and confirm the data in the network, thus generating trust and reaching consensus; the cryptographic algorithm escorts the anonymity, immutability and unforgeability of the blockchain, which is the bottom line of whether a chain is trustworthy and has basic security; a smart contract is a contract defined in digital form that can automatically enforce its terms. It puts the contract in the form of code on the blockchain and executes it automatically under the agreed conditions. The immutable and traceable nature of the blockchain provides a secure and trusted environment for smart contracts to operate.

The protocols through smart contracts means that the participants can only execute according to the protocols specified in the contract, and the contract can be executed automatically when the contract trigger conditions are met, which brings into play its advantages in cost efficiency and greatly avoids the interference of malicious behaviors during the normal execution of the contract.

3.2   Federated Learning

Federated learning as an emerging distributed machine learning scheme provides a new solution to address the privacy and security issues faced by machine learning. In federated learning, the core idea is to build a global model based on virtual fused data by exchanging model parameters or intermediate results without exchanging local individual or sample data through distributed model training among multiple data sources with local data, so as to achieve a balance between data privacy protection and data sharing computation, i.e., the new paradigm of "The New Application Paradigm" of "data available but not visible, data not moving model moving".

3.3 Ring Signature

A Ring signature is a simplified group signature that eliminates the need for signature group creation and group administrators. It provides a clever way to achieve unconditional anonymity of the signer's identity while avoiding the problem of excessive group administrator privileges. In ring signatures, the signer cannot be confirmed as the identity of the signer, and this unconditional anonymity is very useful in special environments where information needs to be protected for a long time.

In a ring signature, the attacker can also not determine which member of the ring generated the signature. The signature generated by one member of the ring can be verified by all others, while other members of the ring cannot forge the signature of the real signer. An external attacker can not forge a signature for the data even if it is based on obtaining a valid ring signature.

The unique nature of ring signatures can be widely used in anonymous electronic elections, e-government, e-money systems, key distribution, and multi-party secure computing, thus becoming a hot topic of current research.

3.4 Gradient Leaks

It has long been assumed that gradients can be shared securely, i.e., gradient exchange does not disclose training data. Instead, studies have shown that malicious participants can obtain private training data from publicly shared gradients [23].

In the training process of machine learning, the machine learning model is optimized by continuously updating the gradient to obtain the optimal model. The gradient was calculated as described in Eq. (1):

$$\nabla W_{t,i} = \frac{\partial l(F(x_{t,i}, W_t), y_{t,i})}{\partial W_t} \tag{1}$$

where W_t is the model weight parameter for round t, $x_{t,i}$, $y_{t,i}$ are the data inputs and labels for round t of participant i, $F(\bullet)$ is the predicted value of the input data under the current model parameters, and $l(\bullet)$ is the loss function constructed using the predicted values with the true labels.

Under the condition that the learning rate is η, the weights are updated in each round as described in Eq. (2):

$$W_{t+1} = W_t - \eta \overline{\nabla W_t} \tag{2}$$

Federation learning, in which the gradients computed separately for each participant need to be aggregated as described in Eq. (3).

$$\nabla W_{t+1} = \frac{1}{N} \sum_i^N \nabla W_{t,i} \tag{3}$$

To recover the data from the gradient, we first initialize a random virtual input x' and label input y'. Then, we input these "virtual data" into the model and obtain the "virtual gradient" $\nabla W'$, as described in Eq. (4):

$$\nabla W' = \frac{\partial l\big(F(x', W), y'\big)}{\partial W} \tag{4}$$

Optimizing the spurious gradients close to the original also brings the dummy data close to the real training data. Given the gradient at a particular step, we obtain the training data by minimizing the following objectives, as described in Eq. (5).

$$x', y' = \arg\min_{x', y'} \left\| \nabla W' - \nabla W \right\|^2 \tag{5}$$

The paradigm distance $||\nabla W' - \nabla W||^2$ in the objective function is differentiable, and the virtual input x' and label y' can be optimized using a standard gradient-based approach. After several iterations of optimization, the real data can be recovered (Fig. 1).

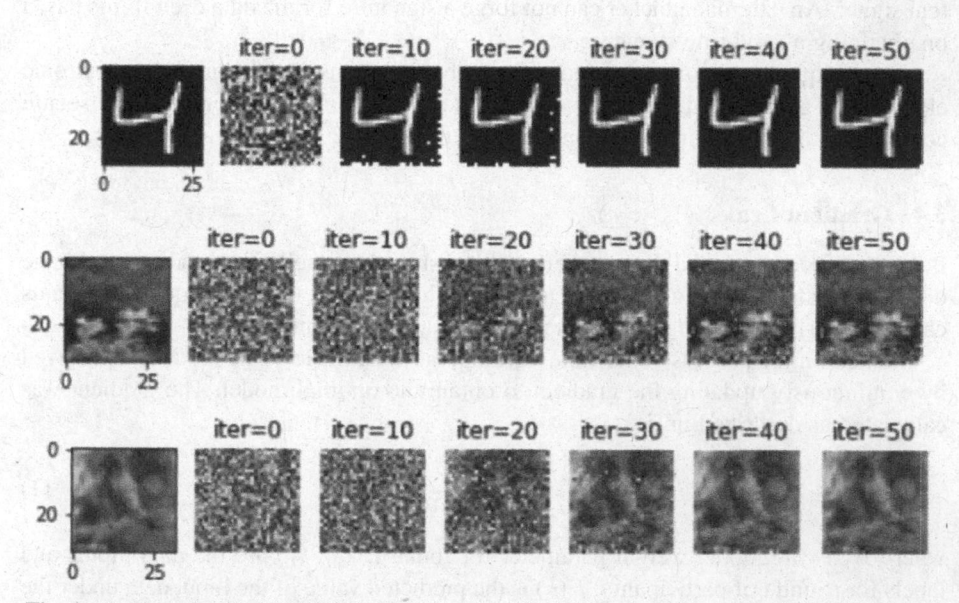

Fig. 1. Recover data from MNIST, cifar-100 and cifar-10 datasets by gradient leakage method

4   Gradient Protection Principles

As shown in Fig. 2, although adding noise to the gradient parameters of the training model can enhance the privacy protection in the machine learning process, the noise has a serious impact on the machine learning training effect; adding too little noise cannot achieve effective privacy protection, and adding too much noise causes serious degradation to the machine learning training accuracy [23].

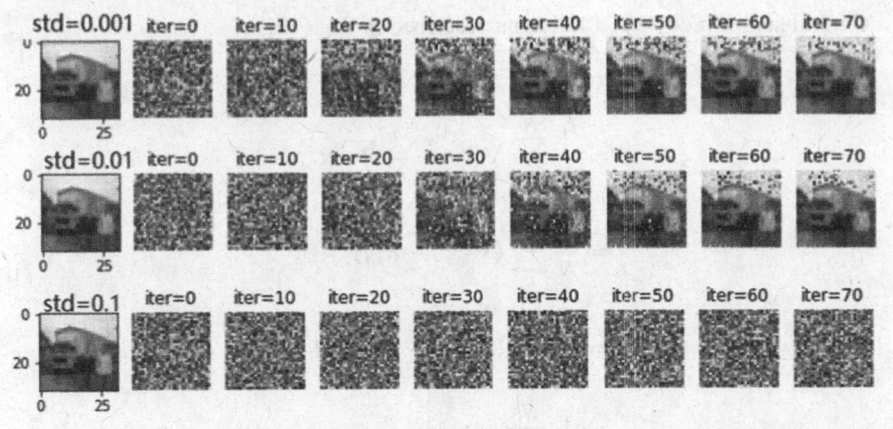

Fig. 2. Gradient leakage data recovery with noise distributions with variance of 0.001, 0.01 and 0. 1 respectively

In the scheme we design, each participant adds noise R_t to the gradient $\nabla W_{t,i}$ updated in each round and sends it to the central server, which receives the gradient $\nabla W'_{t,i}$ asdescribed in Eq. (6):

$$\nabla W'_{t,i} = \nabla W_{t,i} + R_{t,i} \tag{6}$$

The central server aggregates the incoming gradients as described in Eq. (7):

$$\overline{\nabla W_t}' = \frac{1}{N} \sum_i^N \nabla W'_{t,i} \tag{7}$$

The participant sends the generated noise to multiple participants using secure multi-party computation $F_s(\bullet)$ as described in Eq. (8):

$$r_1, r_2, ..., r_s = F_s(R_{t,i}) \tag{8}$$

Multiple security calculations in Eq. 8 establish a security protocol. The security protocol enables each participant to obtain the corresponding information without including other information output, preventing the malicious node and other participants to know which participant the information belongs to and the privacy of the participants.

The participants jointly calculate the sum of all random numbers as described in Eq. (9).

$$R_t = \frac{1}{N} \sum_i^N R_{t,i} = F_s^{-1}(r_1, r_2 ..., r_s) \tag{9}$$

Central server recovery gradient as described in Eq. (10).

$$\nabla W_t = \overline{\nabla W_t'} - R_t$$

$$= \frac{1}{N} \sum_i^N \nabla W_{t,i}' - \frac{1}{N} \sum_i^N R_{t,i}$$

$$= \frac{1}{N} \sum_i^N (\nabla W_{t,i}' - R_{t,i})$$

$$= \frac{1}{N} \sum_i^N (\nabla W_{t,i} + R_{t,i} - R_{t,i})$$

$$= \frac{1}{N} \sum_i^N \nabla W_{t,i}$$

$$(10)$$

It can be seen that the data recovered by the central server is the same as the aggregated gradient without any added noise, which ensures that the training accuracy will not be affected by the added noise. By passing the added noise through the secure multi-party computation, neither any participant nor the central server can directly recover the noise value or infer the true gradient, thus ensuring the user's privacy.

5   An Overview of the System

5.1   System Model

As shown in Fig. 3, the whole system is composed of three parts: the blockchain network, participants, and central server. The details are described as follows.

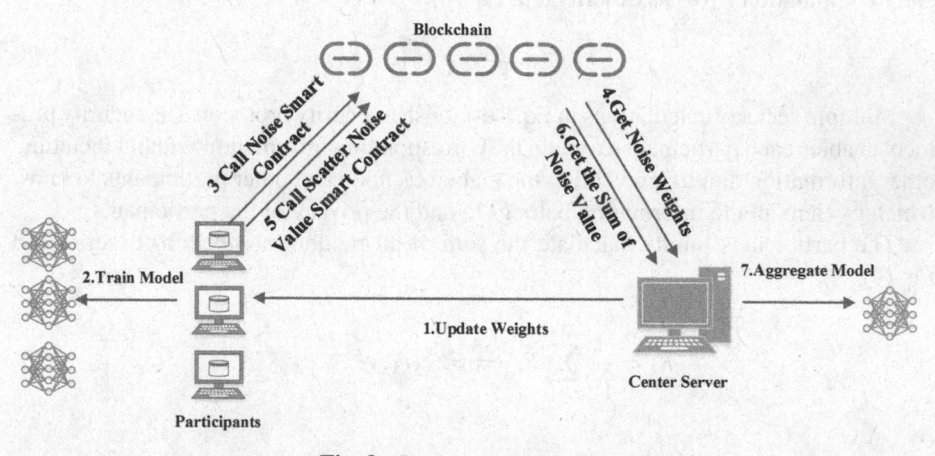

Fig. 3. System model diagram

(1)The Blockchain network, which provides a secure and trusted execution environment for the system, guarantees the reliable operation of smart contracts, stores data, and safeguards data security.

(2)The participant, the provider of the training data, trains the model parameters using the data he has.

(3)The central server, which is responsible for the aggregation of model gradients and updating of model weights.

5.2 Threat Model

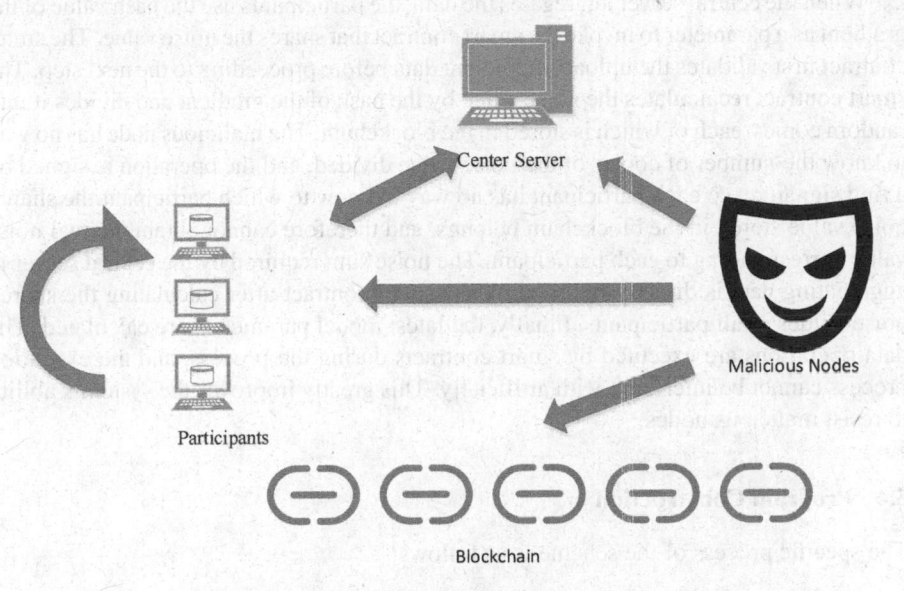

Fig. 4. Threat model diagram

Although blockchain provides a secure and trusted computing environment, it still faces the risk of attacks on user data and privacy. Figure 4 shows the threats faced by the system: Participants may send wrong data; the central server will infer user privacy based on the gradient data raised by participants; malicious nodes will disrupt the training process during the machine learning training, making the training of machine learning difficult and exposing the identity of data parties and data privacy; blockchain management users can, based on the data stored in the blockchain, recover the data of the participating parties, expose the user's identity based on the transaction records of the blockchain, etc.

5.3 Solution Principle

In the federal learning training process, the central server directly obtains the gradient parameters of the model trained by the participant to aggregate into new model parameters and can also directly recover the user data according to the gradient. In the whole process, not only can the central server directly obtain the gradient parameters, but also the transmission process is easy to leak the gradient data, which threatens the privacy and security of users.

In summary, we designed a blockchain-based solution for federal learning gradient leakage: when the participant finishes training and uploads the gradient data, the smart contract automatically adds the noise value associated with the gradient hash and saves the gradient after adding noise in the blockchain, i.e., it is impossible to recover the user's data directly through gradient leakage. The participants sign the model after adding noise by ring signature, and any participant can not confirm who uploaded the data after uploading.

When the central server aggregates the data, the participants use the hash value of the gradient as a parameter to invoke the smart contract that shares the noise value. The smart contract first validates the uploaded gradient data before proceeding to the next step. The smart contract recalculates the noise value by the hash of the gradient and divides it into random copies, each of which is stored in the blockchain. The malicious node has no way to know the number of copies of the noise value divided, and the operation is signed by a ring signature, so each participant has no way to know to which participant the shared noise value stored in the blockchain belongs, and therefore cannot obtain the real noise value corresponding to each participant. The noise sum required by the central server in aggregating data is directly returned by the smart contract after calculating the shared noise values of all participants. Finally, the latest model parameters are calculated. The data operations are executed by smart contracts during the process, and the execution process cannot be interfered with artificially. This greatly improves the system's ability to resist malicious nodes.

5.4   Program Construction

The specific process of the scheme is as follows:

(1) **Training of models**

The participants use the model parameters shared by the central server to train the machine learning and use their own data to calculate the gradient ∇W_i.

(2) **Gradient uploads**

Participant i invokes the add-noise smart contract with the gradient ∇W_i as a parameter, and the smart contract calculates the hash $H_i = Hash(\nabla W_i)$ of ∇W_i, generates the noise value $R_i = Random(H_i)$ with H_i as a random number seed, calculates the gradient $\nabla W_i' = \nabla W_i + R_i$ of the add-noise, and stores $\nabla W_i'$ in the blockchain.

(3) **Validate the data and share the noise values**

Participant i invokes the shared noise value smart contract with the hash value H_i of the gradient ∇W_i as an argument, and the smart contract first verifies whether the uploaded noise gradient contains the noise gradient $\nabla W_i'$ corresponding to H_i: The smart contract first calculates the noise value $R_i' = Random(H_i)$ with H_i. Using the noise value R_i' and the noise gradient $\nabla W_i'$, it calculates the gradient $\nabla W_i'' = \nabla W_i' - R_i'$ and checks whether the hash value $H_i' = Hash(\nabla W_i'')$ of $\nabla W_i''$ is consistent with H_i. If it is consistent, it means that the gradient ∇W_i uploaded by participant i has not been changed, otherwise, it means that the noise gradient stored in the blockchain does not match with the gradient uploaded by the participant.

After verifying the data, the smart contract divides $R_r{'}$ into n_i random copies, generates n_i random numbers $R_{i,1}, R_{i,2}, ..., R_{i,n_i}$, where $R_{i,1} + R_{i,2}+, ..., +R_{i,n_i} = R_i{'}$, and stores the random number $R_{i,1}, R_{i,2}, ..., R_{i,n_i}$ in the designated account address on the blockchain.

(4) **Obtain the noise value**

The central server aggregates the gradients by first obtaining the noise sum, which is obtained by the central server by invoking the smart contract that computes the noise sum. The smart contract sums up all the noise $R_{1,1}, R_{1,2}, ..., R_{1,n_1}, R_{2,1}, R_{2,2}, ..., R_{2,n_2}, ...$ in the account after division to obtain R, and returns R to the central server.

(5) **Polymerization gradient**

The central server obtains the noise gradient $\nabla W_1{'}, \nabla W_2{'}, ..., \nabla W_n{'}$ from the blockchain and calculates the average gradient using $\overline{\nabla W_t} = \frac{1}{n}(\sum_{i=1}^{n} \nabla W_i{'} - R)$.

The new round model parameters are $W_{t+1} = W_t - \eta \overline{\nabla W_t}$. After sharing the new model parameters with each participant, the next round of training is performed until a compliant machine learning model is obtained.

6 Analysis of Security

The federal learning gradient leakage solution proposed in this paper effectively prevents the user privacy problem caused by gradient leakage and improves the problem of model accuracy degradation caused by adding noise. At the same time, it protects the user's identity security through blockchain smart contract and ring signature technology, and greatly avoids malicious behaviors in the training process.

As shown in Table 1, compared with the recent method, the method protects the participant information, so that other participants cannot judge which participant the information belongs to; resist malicious nodes and central servers to recover information from the gradient; resist malicious nodes to tampering with information; ensure the accuracy of model parameters and ensure the training effect.

In the gradient uploading stage, the participant invokes the smart contract to add noise to the gradient, and what is stored in the blockchain is not the real gradient. At the same time, the data uploaded by the participants is signed by the ring signature technology, so others cannot tell which user the data in the blockchain belongs to and cannot find multiple rounds of training ladders for the same participant.

In the shared noise value phase, the participants invoke the smart contract with the gradient hash as a parameter, and first verify that the noise gradient stored in the blockchain matches the uploaded gradient based on the gradient hash, and subsequently, the noise value is randomly divided into multiple copies. Since a ring signature is used for the operation, a malicious attacker cannot confirm which participant the divided noise values belong to, and all the divided noise values are stored in the same account address, making it impossible to recover the true noise values. Therefore, it is impossible

Table 1. Compares with the most recent scheme

	The malicious nodes and other participants are unable to determine which participant the information belongs to	Resisting malicious nodes from recovering information from the gradient	Resthe central server to recover information from the gradient	The accuracy of the model parameters is not affected, and the training effect is guaranteed	Verify whether the malicious node destroys the information and determine whether the participant sends the error information
The method of this paper	√	√	√	√	√
ESMFL	-	√	-	√	-
FedGCN	-	√	-	-	-
Fed-CDP	-	√	-	√	-

to recover the true gradient based on the noise gradient and the divided noise value, and thus protect the user privacy and security.

In the acquire noise sum stage, the central server obtains the noise sum directly through the smart contract, avoiding the direct acquisition of noise values and thus recovering the true gradient.

In the aggregated gradient phase, the central server uses the noise gradient and the noise sum to calculate the average gradient and update the model parameters. Compared with other add-noise schemes, there is no loss of model parameter accuracy and the machine learning training effect is guaranteed.

In the improved scheme, the ring signature ensures the identity security of the participants; the data storage process is automatically completed by the smart contract in the blockchain and cannot be controlled by humans; the results are written in the blockchain; and the malicious nodes cannot destroy the training model due to the tamper-evident nature of the blockchain. In addition, due to the introduction of the blockchain network, the transmission of information between parties does not need to find a separate transmission channel, which greatly enhances the transmission security and reduces the network communication volume.

7   Conclusion

Aiming at the problem of gradient leaking privacy in federated learning, this paper proposes a federated learning training scheme based on blockchain. In this scheme, by adding enough noise to the gradient, malicious participants and the central server can not infer user privacy by using the gradient. The central server removes the noise after aggregating the gradient uploaded by the participants, so the final aggregated gradient will not affect the original gradient, The performance degradation of the final model is avoided. Because in the process of adding and removing noise, it is executed through blockchain, and the added noise is randomly divided, malicious participants can only obtain the aggregated model parameters, and cannot obtain the gradient parameters of each participant. Malicious participants cannot steal user privacy through gradient disclosure. Experiments show that this scheme provides a secure solution to the privacy security caused by gradient leakage in federated learning, and ensures the performance of the training model.

Acknowledgments. This research is supported by Natural Science Foundation of Inner Mongolia Autonomous Region (2020LH06006); Major science and technology projects of Inner Mongolia Autonomous Region (2019ZD025); Innovation fund of Inner Mongolia University of science and Technology (2019QDL-B51); Inner Mongolia discipline inspection and supervision big data open project (IMDBD2020021); Kundulun District Science and technology plan of Baotou City, Inner Mongolia (YF2021011).

References

1. Hu, H., Salcic, Z., Sun, L.: Source inference attacks in federated learning. In: 2021 IEEE International Conference on Data Mining (ICDM), pp. 1102–1107 (2021)
2. Jahani-Nezhad, T., Maddah-Ali, M.A., Li, S.: SwiftAgg: communication-efficient and dropout-resistant secure aggregation for federated learning with worst-case security guarantees. arXiv preprint arXiv (2022)
3. Wainakh, A., Ventola, F., Müig, T.: User label leakage from gradients in federated learning. arXiv preprint arXiv (2021)
4. Jin, X., Chen, P.Y., Hsu, C.Y.: CAFE: catastrophic data leakage in vertical federated learning. In: Advances in Neural Information Processing Systems, pp. 994–1006 (2021)
5. Zhao, B., Mopuri, K.R., Bilen, H.: iDLG: improved deep leakage from gradients. arXiv preprint arXiv (2020)
6. Wu, F.: PLFG: a privacy attack method based on gradients for federated learning. In: Yu, S., Mueller, P., Qian, J. (eds.) SPDE 2020. CCIS, vol. 1268, pp. 191–204. Springer, Singapore (2020). https://doi.org/10.1007/978-981-15-9129-7_14
7. Shafee, A., Awaad, T.A.: Privacy attacks against deep learning models and their countermeasures. J. Syst. Archit. **114**, 101940 (2020)
8. Wang, Y., Deng, J., Guo, D.: SAPAG: a self-adaptive privacy attack from gradients. arXiv preprint arXiv (2020)
9. Wei, W., Liu, L., Lope,r M.: A framework for evaluating gradient leakage attacks in federated learning. arXiv preprint arXiv (2020)
10. Ren, H., Deng, J., Xie, X.: GRNN: generative regression neural network – a data leakage attack for federated learning. ACM Trans. Intell. Syst. Technol. (TIST) **13**(4), 1–24 (2022)
11. Wainakh, A., Müig, T., Grube, T.: Label leakage from gradients in distributed machine learning. In: 2021 IEEE 18th Annual Consumer Communications & Networking Conference (CCNC). IEEE (2021)
12. Jia, Q., Hansen, L.K.: What can we learn from gradients? (2020)
13. Huang, Y., Gupta, S., Song, Z.: Evaluating gradient inversion attacks and defenses in federated learning. arXiv e-prints. Advances in Neural Information Processing Systems, vol. 34, pp. 7232–7241 (2021)
14. Yuan, X., Ma, X., Zhang, L.: Beyond class-level privacy leakage: breaking record-level privacy in federated learning. IEEE Internet Things J. **99** (2021)

15. Lin, S., Wang, C., Li, H.: ESMFL: efficient and secure models for federated learning. arXiv preprint arXiv (2020)
16. Wei, W., Liu, L., Wu, Y.: Gradient-leakage resilient federated learning. In: 2021 IEEE 41st International Conference on Distributed Computing Systems (ICDCS). IEEE (2021)
17. Wang, Y., Nedic, A.: Tailoring gradient methods for differentially-private distributed optimization. arXiv preprint arXiv (2022)
18. Wu, C., Wu, F., Cao, Y.: FedGNN: federated graph neural network for privacy-preserving recommendation. arXiv preprint arXiv (2021)
19. Zhao, Q., Zhao, C., Cui, S.: PrivateDL: privacy-preserving collaborative deep learning against leakage from gradient sharing. Int. J. Intell. Syst. **35**(8), 1262–1279 (2020)
20. Hya, D., Li, H., Xxa, D.: PPCL: privacy-preserving collaborative learning for mitigating indirect information leakage. Inf. Sci. **548**, 423–437 (2021)
21. Dxa, B., Yuan, M., Di, K.: EGC: entropy-based gradient compression for distributed deep learning - ScienceDirect. Inf. Sci. **548**, 118–134 (2021)
22. So, J., Ali, R.E., Guler, B.: Securing secure aggregation: mitigating multi-round privacy leakage in federated learning. arXiv preprint arXiv (2021)
23. Zhu, L., Liu, Z., Han, S.: Deep leakage from gradients. In: Advances in Neural Information Processing Systems 32 (2019)

Analysis of a New Improved AES S-Box Structure

Rong Cheng[✉], Yu Zhou, Xudong Miao, and Jianyong Hu

Science and Technology on Communication Security Laboratory,
Chengdu 610041, China
xidian_chengrong@163.com

Abstract. S-boxes are very important nonlinear components in symmetric ciphers and have a great role in the security of cryptographic algorithms. In algorithm design, 4-bit and 8-bit S-boxes are most commonly used. The S-box of the AES is the best 8-bit S-box in terms of nonlinearity and differential uniformity at present. However, other properties are not the best.

In this paper, we improve and propose a new algebraic structure that can be used to generate S-boxes with excellent performance. The main enhanced properties of the new S-boxes are: strict avalanche criterion (SAC), distance to SAC, the bit independence criterion (BIC), algebraic complexity, inverse algebraic complexity, and periodicity. After comparing with existing S-boxes, the properties of S-boxes proposed in this paper are the best.

Keywords: S-box · AES · Affine transformation · Strict avalanche criterion · Periodicity · Algebraic complexity

1 Introduction

The S-box is a nonlinear function that is widely used in symmetric ciphers. In block ciphers with substitution-permutation network (SPN) structure, S-boxes can provide nonlinearity to the encryption algorithm and greatly improve the difficulty of cryptanalysis. For different cryptanalysis methods, S-boxes have many performance indicators, such as nonlinearity for resistance to linear analysis, difference uniformity for resistance to differential analysis, algebraic degree for resistance to algebraic attacks, and so on. A strong S-box should have good properties.

In addition to the three properties nonlinearity, difference uniformity and algebraic degree, the main properties that is needed to be considered in the design of S-boxes are strict avalanche criterion (SAC), distance to SAC [25], the bit independence criterion [9], and algebraic complexity, as well as the algebraic complexity of inverse S-boxes [5], etc. The AES algorithm [8] is the most widely used cryptographic algorithm with SPN structure, and its S-box reaches the

© ICST Institute for Computer Sciences, Social Informatics and Telecommunications Engineering 2023
Published by Springer Nature Switzerland AG 2023. All Rights Reserved
Q. Jiang et al. (Eds.): SPNCE 2022, LNICST 496, pp. 109–125, 2023.
https://doi.org/10.1007/978-3-031-30623-5_8

current optimum in terms of resistance to differential and linear attacks, but there are still many properties being not good, such as algebraic complexity is only 9 and possible periods are 2, 27, 59, 81 and 87.

In order to improve the AES S-box, many people have made attempts. Liu et al. enhanced the algebraic complexity of AES S-box to 255 [13]. However, the algebraic complexity of the inverse of improved S-box is 9, and other properties such as distance to SAC and periodicity are still very poor. Cui et al. made improvements to the affine transform of the S-box of AES [7] and proved that the upper bound on the algebraic complexity of the S-box of the AES-like structure is 9, which is much smaller than the 255 optimum. Cui et al. further improved [6] on [7] by considering more properties to obtain a better 8-bit S-box. Nitaj et al. proposed a new structure [17] and searched for a better S-box and analyzed it. However, Nitaj et al. did not perform a deeper analysis of the structure, and this novel structure has greater potential for discovery. Based on the [17], Said Eddahmani et al. improved the distance to SAC of the S-box [10]. However, the mean of SAC and the maximal BIC of S-box became worse.

In this paper, we propose a new S-box structure and analyze its properties. Further, we show that they are all affine equivalent to AES S-box. For the most commonly used 4-bit and 8-bit S-boxes in cryptographic algorithms, we find many S-boxes with better properties than other existing S-boxes in our new structure, then compare it with S-boxes in [7] and [17], finally we think it has the best comprehensive performance. It can be used as a better S-box in encryption algorithms.

This paper is organized as follows: In Sect. 2, we introduce several types of S-box generation structures and propose an improved structure in this paper. In Sect. 3, we analyze affine equivalence of S-boxes. In Sect. 4, we propose a 4-bit S-box and an 8-bit S-box. Then we analyze their properties and compare them with existing S-boxes. In Sect. 5, we summary the data in the Table 16 and Table 17, and then conclude in Sect. 6.

2   Preliminaries

Let $A \in \mathbb{F}_2^{n \times n}$ be a matrix and $a \in \mathbb{F}_2^n$ be a vector. Let $a = (t_{n-1}, t_{n-2}, \cdots, t_0)$, then a can be uniquely represented as a number $a \in \mathbb{F}_{2^n}$,

$$a = 2^{n-1}t_{n-1} + 2^{n-2}t_{n-2} + \cdots + t_0.$$

For the convenience of understanding, this paper uses a and a directly without describing their transformation process. In addition, we use a^{-1} and a^{-1} to denote both the inverse of $a \in \mathbb{F}_{2^n}$ and omit the transformation process. In this paper, all 8-bit S-boxes use the finite field $\mathbb{F}_{2^8} = \mathbb{F}_2[t]/(t^8 + t^4 + t^3 + t + 1)$.

2.1   Algebraic Expression of the S-Box

A Boolean function $f : \mathbb{F}_2^n \to \mathbb{F}_2$ is a function with n input variables and only one output variable in $\mathbb{F}_2$. Let $\mathcal{B}_n$ be the set of n-variable Boolean functions.

Similar to Boolean functions, the S-box $F : \mathbb{F}_2^n \rightarrow \mathbb{F}_2^m$ is an n-input, m-output function, and which variables can be seen as Boolean functions:

$$F = (f_{m-1}, f_{m-2}, \ldots, f_0),$$

where $f_i \in \mathcal{B}_n$ $(0 \leq i \leq m-1)$ is the *coordinate function* of F. In this paper, we consider only the case where $n = m$.

Affine equivalent is a really important definition in the study of the properties of S-box. Two S-boxes $F : \mathbb{F}_2^n \rightarrow \mathbb{F}_2^n$ and $G : \mathbb{F}_2^n \rightarrow \mathbb{F}_2^n$ are affine equivalent, if there exists affine invertible matrices $\boldsymbol{B_1} \in \mathbb{F}_2^{n \times n}$ and $\boldsymbol{B_2} \in \mathbb{F}_2^{n \times n}$, s.t.

$$G = \boldsymbol{B_2}(F(\boldsymbol{B_1}x + a)) + b$$

for $x \in \mathbb{F}_2^n$, where $a, b \in \mathbb{F}_2^n$. In the following, we use the symbol $G \sim F$ to indicate that G is affine equivalent to F.

In the following, we give three algebraic structures of S-boxes. The algebraic expression of AES-like S-box consists of two transformations: $f : x \longmapsto x^{-1}$ and $g : x \longmapsto \boldsymbol{A}x + b$, where $\boldsymbol{A}$ is an invertible matrix in $\mathbb{F}_2^{8 \times 8}$ and $b \in \mathbb{F}_2^8$. That is $S_{AES}(x) = g \circ f(x)$, then

$$S_{AES}(x) = \boldsymbol{A}x^{-1} + b.$$

The matrix $\boldsymbol{A}$ in the AES algorithm is a cyclic matrix and $b = 0x63$ ($0x$ means it is a hexadecimal number, and similarly, $(01100011)_2$ means a binary number).

$$S_{AES}(x) = \boldsymbol{A}x^{-1} + b = \begin{bmatrix} 1 & 1 & 1 & 1 & 1 & 0 & 0 & 0 \\ 0 & 1 & 1 & 1 & 1 & 1 & 0 & 0 \\ 0 & 0 & 1 & 1 & 1 & 1 & 1 & 0 \\ 0 & 0 & 0 & 1 & 1 & 1 & 1 & 1 \\ 1 & 0 & 0 & 0 & 1 & 1 & 1 & 1 \\ 1 & 1 & 0 & 0 & 0 & 1 & 1 & 1 \\ 1 & 1 & 1 & 0 & 0 & 0 & 1 & 1 \\ 1 & 1 & 1 & 1 & 0 & 0 & 0 & 1 \end{bmatrix} \begin{bmatrix} x_7 \\ x_6 \\ x_5 \\ x_4 \\ x_3 \\ x_2 \\ x_1 \\ x_0 \end{bmatrix} + \begin{bmatrix} 0 \\ 1 \\ 1 \\ 0 \\ 0 \\ 0 \\ 1 \\ 1 \end{bmatrix}.$$

To overcome the shortcomings of AES S-box, [6] and [7] proposed improved structure for AES S-box. It consists of three transformations, that is $S_{APA}(x) = g \circ f \circ g(x)$. Then

$$S_{APA}(x) = \boldsymbol{A}(\boldsymbol{A}x + b)^{-1} + b,$$

where $\boldsymbol{A}$ is an invertible matrix in $\mathbb{F}_2^{8 \times 8}$ and $b \in \mathbb{F}_2^8$. The structure named *Affine-Power-Affine* S-box in [7]. The properties of S-box in [7] can be found in Table 17.

Although $S_{APA}(x)$ is greatly improved compared to AES S-box, many of its properties are not optimal. [17] presented the structure of a new improved AES S-box $S_{new20}(x)$. That is

$$S_{new20}(x) = \begin{cases} \dfrac{\boldsymbol{A}x + \alpha}{\boldsymbol{A}x + \beta} & \text{if } x \neq \boldsymbol{A}^{-1}\beta \\ 0x01 & \text{if } x = \boldsymbol{A}^{-1}\beta \end{cases},$$

where A is an invertible matrix in $\mathbb{F}_2^{8\times 8}$ and $\alpha, \beta \in \mathbb{F}_2^8$. The properties of S-box in [17] can be found in Table 17.

Based on the [17], Said Eddahmani et al. improved the distance to SAC of the S-box [10]. The structure is

$$S_{new21}(x) = \begin{cases} \dfrac{aA \cdot x + b}{cA \cdot x + d} & \text{if } x \neq A^{-1}\dfrac{d}{c} \\ \dfrac{a}{c} & \text{if } x = A^{-1}\dfrac{d}{c} \end{cases},$$

where A is an invertible matrix in $\mathbb{F}_2^{8\times 8}$ and $a, c \in \mathbb{F}_2^8/\{0\}$, $b, d \in \mathbb{F}_2^8$. $S_{new21}(x)$ is a permutation in $\mathbb{F}_{2^n}$ if $ad + bc \neq 0$. The properties of $S_{new21}(x)$ can be found in Table 17.

2.2   An Improved S-Box Structure

The properties of $S_{APA}(x)$ and $S_{new20}(x)$ are greatly enhanced relative to AES-like S-box. In [17], the authors found an 8-bit S-box with better properties (see Table 17). However, the structure $S_{new20}(x)$ has not been further explored. We propose a new structure as an extension of $S_{new20}(x)$ and study the properties of such structures.

Let $F : \mathbb{F}_2^n \to \mathbb{F}_2^n$ be an n-bit S-box. For $x \in \mathbb{F}_{2^n}$, the algebraic expression of $F(x)$ is

$$F(x) = (\alpha + \beta)(Ax + \beta)^{-1} + \gamma, \tag{1}$$

where $\alpha \neq \beta$, and $\alpha, \beta, \gamma \in \mathbb{F}_{2^n}$, the matrix A is an invertible matrix in $\mathbb{F}_2^{n\times n}$, the inverse of 0 is 0, that is $F(A^{-1}\beta) = \gamma$.

In the following, the n-bits S-box in Eq. (1) is denoted by $F_{new}^n(x)$. If $\gamma = 0x01$ then $F_{new}^8(x) = S_{new20}(x)$, because

$$S_{new20}(x) = \begin{cases} \dfrac{Ax + \alpha}{Ax + \beta} = \dfrac{Ax + \beta + \alpha + \beta}{Ax + \beta} = (\alpha + \beta)(Ax + \beta)^{-1} + 1 & \text{if } x \neq A^{-1}\beta \\ 0x01 & \text{if } x = A^{-1}\beta \end{cases},$$

so it is obvious that $S_{new20}(x)$ is a special case of F_{new}^n.

3   Affine Invariant Properties of F_{new}^n

The S-boxes generated by Eq. (1) have the same properties in some respects. In this section, we study its affine invariants.

The number of invertible matrix [26] in $\mathbb{F}_2^{n\times n}$ is $|GL(n, \mathbb{F}_2)| = \prod_{k=0}^{n-1}(2^n - 2^k)$, then the total number of n-bit S-boxes in F_{new}^n can be obtained.

Proposition 1 (The number of F_{new}^n). Let α, β and $\gamma \in \mathbb{F}_{2^n}$, then the upper bound on the number of S-boxes that can be generated by Eq. (1) is

$$2^{2n}(2^n - 1)\prod_{k=0}^{n-1}(2^n - 2^k).$$

Table 1. Different parameters generate the same S-box.

α	1	2	3	4	5
β	10	7	13	14	4
A	(10, 3, 7, 11)	(11, 1, 3, 7)	(1, 2, 3, 12)	(7, 12, 1, 3)	(13, 15, 6, 8)
α	6	7	8	9	10
β	9	3	15	5	8
A	(12, 13, 2, 4)	(6, 14, 5, 15)	(3, 4, 12, 1)	(9, 7, 11, 10)	(8, 5, 15, 6)
α	11	12	13	14	15
β	2	1	11	6	12
A	(2, 6, 8, 13)	(4, 8, 13, 2)	(14, 11, 10, 9)	(15, 9, 14, 5)	(5, 10, 9, 14)

Remark 1. In fact, for $n = 2, 3, 4$ and any fixed γ, an S-box generated by Eq. (1) will be repeated $2^n - 1$ times for all invertible matrix $A \in \mathbb{F}_2^{n \times n}$, for all $\alpha \in \mathbb{F}_{2^n}$ and $\beta \in \mathbb{F}_{2^n}$ in our experiments. We find that the number of different S-boxes in F_{new}^n is $2^{2n}|GL(n, \mathbb{F}_2)|$ for $n = 2, 3, 4$. So we have a guess: the number of different S-boxes generated by Eq. (1) is $2^{2n}|GL(n, \mathbb{F}_2)|$ for $n \geq 2$.

Example 1. Let $n = 4$, $\gamma = 7$, the S-box [10,15,9,8,14,5,12,4,1,13,7,2,6,11,0,3] can be generated by 15 different parameters (A, α, β) in Table 1. It is important to note that the value of A in Table 1 indicates the four row vectors of matrix A. For example, $A = (1, 2, 3, 12)$ means the first row of A is [0, 0, 0, 1], the second row is [0, 0, 1, 0], the third row is [0, 1, 0, 0] and the last row is [1, 1, 0, 0]. This S-box uses the finite field $\mathbb{F}_{2^4} = \mathbb{F}_2[t]/(t^4 + t + 1)$.

In order to prove the equivalence of F_{new}^n and x^{-1} in $\mathbb{F}_{2^n}$, we introduce Lemma 1.

Lemma 1. *Let $a, b \in \mathbb{F}_{2^n}$, then there exists one matrix A, s.t. $ab = Ab$, where A is an invertible matrix in $\mathbb{F}_2^{n \times n}$.*

The above result means that the multiplication in the finite field $\mathbb{F}_{2^n}$ can be expressed in the form of an affine transformation.

Proposition 2 (Affine Equivalent). *All n-bit S-boxes in F_{new}^n are affine equivalents.*

Proof. Let $x \in \mathbb{F}_{2^n}$, then

$$x^{-1} \sim A'(Ax + a)^{-1} + b, \tag{2}$$

where A, A' are invertible matrices in $\mathbb{F}_2^{n \times n}$, $a, b \in \mathbb{F}_{2^n}$.

It is easy to find that Eq. (2) and Eq. (1) are affine equivalents for the same irreducible polynomial in $\mathbb{F}_{2^n}$, if and only if

$$\begin{cases} a = \beta \\ b = \gamma \\ A'(Ax + a)^{-1} = (\alpha + \beta)(Ax + \beta)^{-1}. \end{cases} \tag{3}$$

Table 2. Representatives of 16 classes of optimal 4-bit S-boxes [16].

Class	Distributions of S-boxes
G_0	0, 1, 2, 13, 4, 7, 15, 6, 8, 11, 12, 9, 3, 14, 10, 5
G_1	0, 1, 2, 13, 4, 7, 15, 6, 8, 11, 14, 3, 5, 9, 10, 12
G_2	0, 1, 2, 13, 4, 7, 15, 6, 8, 11, 14, 3, 10, 12, 5, 9
G_3	0, 1, 2, 13, 4, 7, 15, 6, 8, 12, 5, 3, 10, 14, 11, 9
G_4	0, 1, 2, 13, 4, 7, 15, 6, 8, 12, 9, 11, 10, 14, 5, 3
G_5	0, 1, 2, 13, 4, 7, 15, 6, 8, 12, 11, 9, 10, 14, 3, 5
G_6	0, 1, 2, 13, 4, 7, 15, 6, 8, 12, 11, 9, 10, 14, 5, 3
G_7	0, 1, 2, 13, 4, 7, 15, 6, 8, 12, 14, 11, 10, 9, 3, 5
G_8	0, 1, 2, 13, 4, 7, 15, 6, 8, 14, 9, 5, 10, 11, 3, 12
G_9	0, 1, 2, 13, 4, 7, 15, 6, 8, 14, 11, 3, 5, 9, 10, 12
G_{10}	0, 1, 2, 13, 4, 7, 15, 6, 8, 14, 11, 5, 10, 9, 3, 12
G_{11}	0, 1, 2, 13, 4, 7, 15, 6, 8, 14, 11, 10, 5, 9, 12, 3
G_{12}	0, 1, 2, 13, 4, 7, 15, 6, 8, 14, 11, 10, 9, 3, 12, 5
G_{13}	0, 1, 2, 13, 4, 7, 15, 6, 8, 14, 12, 9, 5, 11, 10, 3
G_{14}	0, 1, 2, 13, 4, 7, 15, 6, 8, 14, 12, 11, 3, 9, 5, 10
G_{15}	0, 1, 2, 13, 4, 7, 15, 6, 8, 14, 12, 11, 9, 3, 10, 5

According to Lemma 1, the Eq. (3) always holds. That is

$$F_{new}^n(x) \sim x^{-1},$$

then all n-bit S-boxes in F_{new}^n are affine equivalents.   □

Remark 2. For $n = 4$, all S-boxes in F_{new}^4 are affine equivalent to G_3 (see in Table 2). The upper bound on the number of S-boxes that affine equivalent to G_3 is 104, 044, 953, 600 (= $20160 \times 20160 \times 16 \times 16$), and the upper bound on the number of S-boxes of F_{new}^4 is 82, 575, 360 (= 20160×2^{12}). So F_{new}^4 is a subset of G_3 equivalence class.

Remark 3. For $n = 8$, all S-boxes in F_{new}^8 are affine equivalent to AES S-box. In fact, it is easy to find from the proof of Proposition 2 that

$$F_{new}^8(x) \sim S_{new20}(x) \sim S_{new21}(x) \sim S_{APA}(x) \sim S_{AES}(x) \sim x^{-1},$$

where $x \in \mathbb{F}_{2^8}$.

The nonlinearity [19] represents the degree of correlation between the S-box and the linear function.

Proposition 3 (Nonlinearity). *The nonlinearity of F_{new}^n is*

$$\mathcal{NL}(F_{new}^n) = 2^{n-1} - 2^{\frac{n}{2}},$$

where n is even.

Table 3. Proposed 4-bit S-box.

x	0	1	2	3	4	5	6	7	8	9	10	11	12	13	14	15
$F_{this}^4(x)$	13	15	10	6	7	14	9	8	0	5	11	4	3	1	2	12

Differential uniformity [18] describes whether S-boxes can resist differential attacks.

Proposition 4 (Differential Uniformity). *The differential uniformity of* F_{new}^n *satisfies*

$$\mathcal{U}(F_{new}^n) \leq 4$$

Proof. The differential uniformity is an affine invariant, and we have proved that $F_{new}^n \sim S_{APA}$, then the proof is given in [13]. □

Remark 4. In fact, it can be seen from the experiment that

$$\mathcal{U}(F_{new}^n) = \begin{cases} 2 \text{ if } n \text{ is odd,} \\ 4 \text{ if } n \text{ is even.} \end{cases}$$

In general, the higher the algebraic degree [5] of the S-box, the stronger the resistance to algebraic attacks.

Proposition 5 (Algebraic degree). *The algebraic degree of* F_{new}^n *is*

$$Deg(F_{new}^n) = n - 1.$$

4   Proposed S-Box Performance Analysis

We will analyze the characteristics of the proposed S-box in this section from the aspects of Strict Avalanche Criterion (SAC), distance to SAC, periodicity, algebraic complexity and Bit Independence Criterion (BIC).

In the practical encryption algorithm, 4-bit and 8-bit S-boxes are the most commonly used S-boxes. In this section, we focus on the properties of a 4-bit S-box and an 8-bit S-box.

For $n = 4$, we have tested all parameters $(\boldsymbol{A}, \alpha, \beta, \gamma)$. The number of matrices $\boldsymbol{A}$ is 20160 and there are 5,160,960 different S-boxes in total. Finally, we find 131 S-boxes with good properties. Table 3 is a 4-bit S-box proposed by this paper denoted by F_{this}^4, whose parameters are $\boldsymbol{A} = (9, 7, 10, 5)$ and $(\alpha, \beta, \gamma) = (7, 13, 3)$. In addition, F_{this}^4 uses the finite field $\mathbb{F}_{2^4} = \mathbb{F}_2[t]/(t^4 + t + 1)$.

For $n = 8$, considering that the number of matrices $\boldsymbol{A}$ is too large to calculate, we just tested all the cyclic invertible matrices (the number is 128), and find 158 S-boxes with good properties. Table 4 is an 8-bit S-box our proposed denoted by F_{this}^8, which parameters are $\boldsymbol{A} = (32, 64, 128, 1, 2, 4, 8, 16)$ and $(\alpha, \beta, \gamma) = (34, 251, 1)$.

F_{this}^4 and F_{this}^8 will be analyzed in the following section.

Table 4. Proposed 8-bit S-box.

F_{this}^8	0	1	2	3	4	5	6	7	8	9	A	B	C	D	E	F
0	9c	e5	06	05	be	24	23	1c	e1	4b	bc	64	21	3b	43	45
1	42	fb	90	78	5c	02	0c	a1	28	75	d0	41	7f	89	f6	85
2	b1	61	00	cd	57	dd	94	df	5f	07	32	bb	d6	5a	ac	1b
3	70	e6	77	fa	76	a9	44	14	c5	0a	eb	fd	5d	12	50	f4
4	10	d3	8f	c2	18	4c	93	c0	8a	a2	c4	ad	04	a6	16	30
5	c6	2a	8c	59	97	88	9f	6c	ae	b7	3a	b4	4f	35	c7	40
6	48	80	46	84	b2	47	d7	dc	4e	4a	ca	ef	7e	2b	a5	8b
7	6a	d5	af	a8	4d	e8	3f	66	1e	27	56	b9	34	f0	f2	a3
8	09	39	0f	1d	d2	71	20	11	72	9b	9a	33	e4	98	f7	3e
9	cb	65	60	2c	95	2e	da	e7	58	54	6d	0b	74	63	a4	2f
A	f3	5b	38	c3	ee	c9	87	8e	25	08	19	36	91	db	62	26
B	81	15	b8	d9	e9	ab	53	b3	1f	69	ea	9d	a7	83	f5	96
C	82	9e	03	73	c1	b5	7a	fe	51	8d	b0	7c	37	a0	de	b6
D	6e	6f	67	31	0d	13	bd	49	86	55	f1	ff	f9	0e	7b	52
E	ec	aa	ed	68	d4	29	e3	1a	ba	c8	2d	99	79	cf	3c	7d
F	e2	22	ce	cc	17	d1	92	3d	bf	f8	d8	6b	e0	5e	01	fc

4.1   Strict Avalanche Criterion

Strict avalanche criterion (SAC) [25] is a indicator that must be considered in S-box design. In fact, SAC is a diffusion criterion. It requires the S-box satisfy that the probability that any single bit reversed in the input will result in a change in each output bits is 0.5. Therefore, SAC can be described as: Let $F = (f_0, f_1, \ldots, f_{n-1})$ be an S-box, for any $a \in \mathbb{F}_2^n$, and $wt(a) = 1$, satisfies $\sum_{x \in \mathbb{F}_2^n} f_i(x) \oplus f_i(x \oplus a) = 2^{n-1}$, $i \in \{0, 1, \cdots, n-1\}$. We have tested the SAC of the two S-boxes $F_{this}^4(x)$ and $F_{this}^8(x)$, and the results are shown in Table 5 and Table 6, respectively.

Table 5. SAC of F_{this}^4.

Reverse	Bit 3	Bit 2	Bit 1	Bit 0
0001	8	8	8	8
0010	12	8	8	8
0100	8	8	4	8
1000	8	8	8	8

Table 6. SAC of F_{this}^8.

Reverse	Bit 7	Bit 6	Bit 5	Bit 4	Bit 3	Bit 2	Bit 1	Bit 0
00000001	132	124	140	128	120	120	128	124
00000010	124	124	124	124	120	120	120	128
00000100	128	132	124	144	132	120	120	120
00001000	124	132	140	128	128	136	136	128
00010000	128	132	132	120	132	128	136	136
00100000	136	124	132	140	124	132	128	136
01000000	136	116	124	128	128	124	132	128
10000000	128	140	116	124	120	128	124	132

Remark 5. For F_{this}^4, we find that 4 occurs 1 time, 8 occurs 14 times and 12 occurs 1 time. For F_{this}^8, 116 occurs 2 times, 120 occurs 10 times, 124 occurs 14 times, 128 occurs 15 times, 132 occurs 11 times, 136 occurs 7 times, 140 occurs 4 times and 144 occurs 1 time.

In generally, the mean value of the SAC matrix is often used to represent the SAC property. However, this expression does not completely account for the SAC of the S-box. For example, 4 and 12 respectively appear once in Table 5, and their effects cancel each other out, resulting in the mean value of SAC is 8.

Describing the diffusion properties of the S-box, distance to SAC is better than the mean value of SAC. The distance to SAC [25] is the sum of bias that the elements in the SAC matrix with respect to 2^{n-1}. That is, let $F = (f_0, f_1, \ldots, f_{n-1})$ be an S-box, for any vectors $x \in \mathbb{F}_2^n$, $a = (a_{n-1}, a_{n-2}, \cdots, a_0) \in \mathbb{F}_2^n$, and $wt(a) = 1$, then

$$DSAC(F) = \sum_{j=0}^{n-1} \sum_{i=0}^{n-1} \left| \sum_{x,a \in \mathbb{F}_{2^n}} f_i(x) \oplus f_i(x \oplus a_j) - 2^{n-1} \right|.$$

One S-box F satisfies SAC if and only if $DSAC(F) = 0$, that is all elements in the SAC matrix is 2^{n-1}.

S-boxes with good diffusion criterion should have a small DSAC. The DSAC values of F_{this}^4 and F_{this}^8 are shown in Table 7 and Table 8, respectively.

Table 7. DSAC and mean of SAC of 4-bit S-boxes.

	Distance to SAC	Mean of SAC
Optimal value	0	8
F_{this}^4 (Table 3)	8	8
PRESENT [3]	32	10
Piccolo [20]	44	8.25
TWINE [23]	28	9.25
QARMA [1]	24	6.5
KLEIN [11]	24	9.5
GIFT [2]	40	10

Table 8. DSAC and mean of SAC of 8-bit S-boxes.

		Distance to SAC	Mean of SAC
Optimal value		0	128
F_{this}^8 (Table 4)		324	128.06
AES [8]		432	129.25
SM4 [22]		492	127.94
FOX [14]		688	130.38
AIRA [15]	S_1	432	129.25
	S_2	488	126.88
CLEFIA [21]	S_1	848	138
	S_2	488	126.88
S_{APA} [7]		452	128.19
S_{new20} [17]		328	128.25
S_{new21} [10]		324	130.44

4.2 Periodicity

The periodicity of the S-box [24] is a property about the distribution. Let F : $\mathbb{F}_{2^n} \to \mathbb{F}_{2^n}$ be an S-box. For $x \in \mathbb{F}_{2^n}$, the period of x is the smallest r such that $F^r(x) = x$.

A well-distributed S-box should have only one period path, that is the period of the S-box is 2^n. The input x is called a fixed point of S-box if there exist special period $r = 1$ for x. An S-box has a poor periodicity, if fixed points exist for it.

The periodicity of AES S-box is not optimal value, which possible periods are 2, 27, 59, 81 and 87. There is no fixed point in AES S-box, but the minimum period reaches 2. F_{this}^4 and F_{this}^8 have the largest period 2^n (see in Table 9 and Table 10, respectively).

Table 9. The periodicity of 4-bit S-boxes.

S-box	Periodicity
Optimal value	16
F_{this}^4 (Table 3)	16
PRESENT [3]	2, 3, 4, 7
Piccolo [20]	3, 13
TWINE [23]	1, 3, 6
QARMA [1]	1, 2
KLEIN [11]	2
GIFT [2]	7, 9

Table 10. The periodicity of 8-bit S-boxes.

		Periodicity
Optimal value		256
F_{this}^8 (Table 4)		256
AES [8]		2, 27, 59, 81, 87
SM4 [22]		1, 2, 3, 6, 9, 24, 35, 56, 120
FOX [14]		1, 2, 8, 21, 94, 120
AIRA [15]	S_1	2, 27, 59, 81, 87
	S_2	2, 3, 9, 21, 36, 64, 121
CLEFIA [21]	S_1	4, 5, 17, 109, 116
	S_2	256
S_{APA} [7]		2, 12, 26, 176
S_{new20} [17]		256
S_{new21} [10]		256

Proposition 6. *Let* $F : \mathbb{F}_{2^n} \to \mathbb{F}_{2^n}$ *be an S-box. For* $x \in \mathbb{F}_{2^n}$, $a \in \mathbb{F}_{2^n}$, *the new S-box* $G : \mathbb{F}_{2^n} \to \mathbb{F}_{2^n}$ *has new distribution of periods.*

$$G(x) = I_n F(x) + a,$$

where I_n *is an* $n \times n$ *identity matrix.*

Example 2. The periods of S-box $F_1(x) = [12, 5, 6, 11, 9, 0, 10, 13, 3, 14, 15, 8, 4, 7, 1, 2]$ are 2, 3, 4, 7. If $a = 3$, then the periods of new S-box $I_4 F_1(x) + 3$ are 15 and 1. However, the S-box $F_2(x) = [11, 2, 15, 13, 0, 14, 4, 5, 6, 10, 7, 8, 9, 12, 3, 1]$ has periods 3, 5, 8. If $a = 6$, then the period of $I_4 F_2(x) + 6$ can reach 16.

From Proposition 6, we know that the parameter γ is used to change the periodicity of S-boxes in Eq. (1).

4.3   Algebraic Complexity

An S-box can be uniquely represented as a univariate polynomial. Let $F : \mathbb{F}_2^n \to \mathbb{F}_2^n$ be any n-bit S-box. The univariate polynomial representation of F is

$$F(X) = \sum_{i=0}^{n-1} u_i X^i,$$

where $u_i \in \mathbb{F}_{2^n}$. The number of terms of $F(X)$ is defined as the algebraic complexity [5].

The algebraic complexity of the S-box indicates the resistance to interpolation attacks. If the algebraic complexity of the S-box is too small, it may lead to efficient interpolation attacks [12].

The univariate polynomial $F(X) = \sum_{i=0}^{n-1} u_i X^i$ and the algebraic degree of S-box are related as follows [4]: $\mathrm{Deg}(S) = \max\{wt(i), u_i \neq 0\}$. This means that the maximum algebraic complexity is $2^n - 1$ for an n-bit S-box. The algebraic complexity data about F_{this}^4 and F_{this}^8 are shown in Table 11 and Table 12, respectively.

Table 11. The algebraic complexity of 4-bit S-boxes.

S-box	Algebraic complexity	Inverse Algebraic complexity
Optimal value	15	15
F_{this}^4 (Table 3)	15	15
PRESENT [3]	14	13
Piccolo [20]	15	15
TWINE [23]	15	15
QARMA [1]	14	14
KLEIN [11]	14	14
GIFT [2]	15	12

Table 12. The algebraic complexity of 8-bit S-boxes.

		Algebraic complexity	Inverse Algebraic complexity
Optimal value		255	255
F_{this}^8 (Table 4)		255	255
AES [8]		9	255
SM4 [22]		255	255
FOX [14]		247	246
AIRA [15]	S_1	9	255
	S_2	9	254
CLEFIA [21]	S_1	247	245
	S_2	253	255
S_{APA} [7]		254	255
S_{new20} [17]		255	254
S_{new21} [10]		255	254

One of the ways to obtain $F(X)$ is using lagrange interpolation in $\mathbb{F}_{2^n}$. The algebraic complexity of AES S-box is 9, which univariate polynomial is

$$S_{AES}(X) = 05X^{254} + 09X^{253} + f9X^{251} + 25X^{247} + f4X^{239}$$
$$+ 01X^{223} + b5X^{191} + 8fX^{127} + 63.$$

However, the algebraic complexity of the inverse of AES S-box is 255, so it is optimal in only one aspect. In fact, the upper bound on the algebraic complexity of AES-like S-boxes is 9 [7]. The algebraic complexity of F_{this}^4 and F_{this}^8 all reache the upper bound. The coefficients of univariate polynomial of F_{this}^8 are shown in Table 13.

Table 13. The coefficients of univariate polynomial of F_{this}^8.

	0	1	2	3	4	5	6	7	8	9	A	B	C	D	E	F
0	e9	7e	5d	7b	52	7b	96	8e	11	2e	51	5b	43	0f	ae	0f
1	51	18	a8	d0	ff	1f	be	bd	b2	fb	5c	68	23	ac	56	2d
2	03	d8	57	be	a6	ff	eb	35	fc	17	63	87	95	44	45	70
3	34	b5	dc	75	f8	87	9d	d8	89	ee	14	68	b5	46	0b	9a
4	05	b4	06	aa	cb	66	9b	ef	af	e6	72	4c	fb	6c	33	1c
5	16	21	aa	e6	fd	cb	60	36	6e	05	05	61	ab	9a	0f	f2
6	7d	b4	01	54	6a	e0	14	85	f9	c0	76	32	16	cd	a7	53
7	0a	95	c5	79	dd	6b	d4	4e	6a	a4	93	1d	ca	9d	df	ab
8	f1	f5	64	58	29	91	c9	66	96	5a	f7	e7	e6	aa	95	88
9	f5	f7	c8	01	18	11	0e	a6	21	f5	66	82	14	bd	7f	e5
A	bb	85	f2	1c	4a	fe	a3	f9	2f	a4	63	78	82	fb	3e	62
B	e6	31	3e	3e	3f	ed	5b	43	e3	fd	d4	a1	8b	7e	97	a6
C	f3	c4	58	1f	a5	56	47	c4	a5	84	3c	9d	33	62	a8	a9
D	3f	33	70	14	38	11	4d	03	6b	51	5d	d4	67	92	a4	c7
E	7e	a1	15	f5	a4	86	b4	56	f8	7a	3a	2b	61	13	46	9c
F	e8	1c	e0	44	82	a5	fc	15	8f	19	39	cf	fa	42	33	00

and the univariate polynomial of F_{this}^4 is

$$F_{this}^4(X) = 14X^{14} + 4X^{13} + 12X^{12} + 7X^{11} + 11X^{10} + 7X^9 + 10X^8 + 11X^7$$
$$+ 13X^6 + 13X^5 + 11X^4 + 5X^3 + 15X^2 + 15X + 13.$$

4.4 Bit Independence Criterion

The bit independence criterion (BIC) means that the change in output bits is statistically independent when the input any bit changed. For a good S-box, the correlation between output bits should be as small as possible. According to the definition of S-box BIC given in [9], we conducted a BIC test on the proposed S-boxes. The experimental results of F_{this}^4 and F_{this}^8 are shown in Table 14 and 15, respectively.

Table 14. The BIC of S-box F_{this}^4.

	$k = 3$	$k = 2$	$k = 1$	$k = 0$
$j = 3$	1.0	0.5	0.5	**0.577**
$j = 2$	0.5	1.0	0.5	**0.577**
$j = 1$	0.5	0.5	1.0	**0.577**
$j = 0$	**0.577**	**0.577**	**0.577**	1.0

Table 15. The BIC of S-box F_{this}^8.

	$k = 7$	$k = 6$	$k = 5$	$k = 4$	$k = 3$	$k = 2$	$k = 1$	$k = 0$
$j = 7$	1.0	0.063	**0.126**	0.095	0.094	0.096	0.125	0.094
$j = 6$	0.063	1.0	0.124	0.125	0.095	0.096	0.125	**0.126**
$j = 5$	**0.126**	0.124	1.0	0.097	0.094	0.1	0.1	0.125
$j = 4$	0.095	0.125	0.097	1.0	0.094	0.065	0.095	0.064
$j = 3$	0.094	0.095	0.094	0.094	1.0	0.094	0.125	0.096
$j = 2$	0.096	0.096	0.1	0.065	0.094	1.0	0.094	0.125
$j = 1$	0.125	0.125	0.1	0.095	0.125	0.094	1.0	0.094
$j = 0$	0.094	**0.126**	0.125	0.064	0.096	0.125	0.094	1.0

In Table 14 and 15, j and k denote the output bits of the S-box, the elements in the table are the maximum value of the correlation coefficient between j and k, when the input bits $a \in \mathbb{F}_{2^n}, wt(a) = 1$ are changed.

The BIC of the S-box is generally described by the maximum value of the BIC matrix for $j \neq k$, and the optimal value is 0. For the S-boxes F_{this}^4, the maximum BIC value is 0.577. For F_{this}^8, the maximum BIC value is 0.126.

5 Comparison with Some Known S-boxes

In Table 16 and Table 17, we list F_{this}^4 and $F_{this}8$ for all properties in this paper, then compared with the S-boxes in some public algorithms or proposed by other scholars. After comparison, it is clear that F_{this}^4 and $F_{this}8$ are the best results at present.

Finally, we check the affine equivalence class of the S-boxes. For 4-bit S-boxes in Table 16, it can be seen that only the S-box of GIFT is not optimal. For 8-bit S-boxes in Table 17, it can be seen that the S-boxes with good linear and differential properties are all affine equivalent to AES S-box.

Table 16. Comparison of F_{this}^4 with other S-boxes.

	PRESENT [3]	Piccolo [20]	TWINE [23]	QARMA [1]	KLEIN [11]	GIFT [2]	F_{this}^4	Optimal
Nonlinearity	4	4	4	4	4	6	**4**	4
Differential Uniformity	4	4	4	4	4	4	**4**	4
Algebraic Degree	3	3	3	3	3	3	**3**	3
Mean of SAC	10	8.25	9.25	6.5	9.5	10	**8**	8
Distance to SAC	32	44	28	24	24	40	**8**	0
Possible periods	2, 3, 4, 7	3, 13	1, 3, 6	1, 2	2	7, 9	**16**	16
Algebraic Complexity	14	15	15	14	14	15	**15**	15
InverseAlgebraic Complexity	13	15	15	14	14	12	**15**	15
Maximal BIC	1	0.577	0.577	0.577	0.577	1	**0.577**	0
Affine equivalent (see in Table 2)	G_0	G_8	G_3	G_9	G_4	NOT Equivalent	G_3	

Table 17. Comparison of F_{this}^8 with other S-boxes.

	AES [8]	SM4 [22]	FOX [14]	AIRA [15]		CLEFIA [21]		S_{APA} [7]	S_{new20} [17]	S_{new20} [10]	F_{this}^8	Optimal
				S_1	S_2	S_1	S_2					
Nonlinearity	112	112	96	112	112	100	112	112	112	112	**112**	120
Differential Uniformity	4	4	16	4	4	10	4	4	4	4	**4**	4
Algebraic Degree	7	7	6	7	7	6	7	7	7	7	**7**	7
Mean of SAC	129.25	127.94	130.38	129.25	128.75	138	126.88	128.19	128.25	130.44	**128.06**	128
Distance to SAC	432	492	688	432	400	848	488	452	328	324	**324**	0
Possible periods	2, 27, 59 81, 87	1, 2, 3, 6 9, 24, 35 56, 120	1, 2, 8, 21 94, 120	2, 27, 59 81, 87	2, 3, 9, 21 36, 64, 121	4, 5, 17 109, 116	256	2, 12 26, 176	256	256	**256**	256
Algebraic Complexity	9	255	247	9	9	247	253	254	255	255	**255**	255
Inverse Algebraic Complexity	255	255	246	255	254	245	255	254	254	254	**255**	255
Maximal BIC	0.134	0.135	0.377	0.134	0.134	0.333	0.132	0.129	0.126	0.129	**0.126**	0
Affine equivalence with AES S-box	YES	YES	NO	YES	YES	NO	YES	YES	YES	YES	**YES**	

6   Conclusion

In this paper, we propose a new S-box structure to improve the existing 4-bit and 8-bit S-boxes. The new structure gives more possibilities for improving the Strict avalanche criterion (SAC), distance to SAC, the bit independence criterion (BIC), algebraic complexity, inverse algebraic complexity, and periodicity while maintaining good differential and linear properties. By comparing them with the S-boxes in public algorithms and other improved S-boxes, it can be observed that F_{this}^4 and F_{this}^8 in this paper have better properties.

Acknowledgements. The first author and the second author were supported in part by the Sichuan Science and Technology Program (No. 2021ZYD0011, 2020JDJQ0076).

References

1. Avanzi, R.M.: The QARMA block cipher family. IACR Trans. Symmetric Cryptol. **2017**(1), 4–44 (2017). https://doi.org/10.13154/tosc.v2017.i1.4-44
2. Banik, S., Pandey, S.K., Peyrin, T., Sasaki, Yu., Sim, S.M., Todo, Y.: GIFT: a small present. In: Fischer, W., Homma, N. (eds.) CHES 2017. LNCS, vol. 10529, pp. 321–345. Springer, Cham (2017). https://doi.org/10.1007/978-3-319-66787-4_16
3. Bogdanov, A., et al.: PRESENT: an ultra-lightweight block cipher. In: Paillier, P., Verbauwhede, I. (eds.) CHES 2007. LNCS, vol. 4727, pp. 450–466. Springer, Heidelberg (2007). https://doi.org/10.1007/978-3-540-74735-2_31
4. Canteaut, A.: Lecture Notes on Cryptographic Boolean Functions. Inria, Paris, France (2016)

5. Carlet, C.: Vectorial Boolean Functions for Cryptography. Boolean Models Methods in Mathematics (2006)
6. Cui, J., Huang, L., Zhong, H., Chang, C., Yang, W.: An improved AES S-box and its performance analysis. Int. J. Innov. Comput. Inf. Control **7**(5), 2291–2302 (2011)
7. Cui, L., Cao, Y.: A new S-box structure named affine-power-affine. Int. J. Innov. Comput. Inf. Control **3**(3), 751–759 (2007)
8. Daemen, J., Rijmen, V.: AES proposal: Rijndael. Gaithersburg, MD, USA (1999)
9. Detombe, J., Tavares, S.: Constructing large cryptographically strong S-boxes. In: Seberry, J., Zheng, Y. (eds.) AUSCRYPT 1992. LNCS, vol. 718, pp. 165–181. Springer, Heidelberg (1993). https://doi.org/10.1007/3-540-57220-1_60
10. Eddahmani, S., Mesnager, S.: A suitable proposal of s-boxes (inverse-like) for the AES, their analysis and performances. In: Stănică, P., Mesnager, S., Debnath, S.K. (eds.) ICSP 2021. CCIS, vol. 1497, pp. 49–63. Springer, Cham (2021). https://doi.org/10.1007/978-3-030-90553-8_4
11. Gong, Z., Nikova, S., Law, Y.W.: KLEIN: a new family of lightweight block ciphers. In: Juels, A., Paar, C. (eds.) RFIDSec 2011. LNCS, vol. 7055, pp. 1–18. Springer, Heidelberg (2012). https://doi.org/10.1007/978-3-642-25286-0_1
12. Jakobsen, T.P., Knudsen, L.R.: Attacks on block ciphers of low algebraic degree. J. Cryptol. **14**(3), 197–210 (2001). https://doi.org/10.1007/s00145-001-0003-x
13. Jinomeiq, L., Baoduui, W., Xinmei, W.: One AES S-box to increase complexity and its cryptanalysis. J. Syst. Eng. Electron. **18**(2), 427–433 (2007). https://doi.org/10.1016/S1004-4132(07)60108-X
14. Junod, P., Vaudenay, S.: FOX: a new family of block ciphers. In: Handschuh, H., Hasan, M.A. (eds.) SAC 2004. LNCS, vol. 3357, pp. 114–129. Springer, Heidelberg (2004). https://doi.org/10.1007/978-3-540-30564-4_8
15. Kwon, D., et al.: New block cipher: ARIA. In: Lim, J.-I., Lee, D.-H. (eds.) ICISC 2003. LNCS, vol. 2971, pp. 432–445. Springer, Heidelberg (2004). https://doi.org/10.1007/978-3-540-24691-6_32
16. Leander, G., Poschmann, A.: On the classification of 4 bit S-boxes. In: Carlet, C., Sunar, B. (eds.) WAIFI 2007. LNCS, vol. 4547, pp. 159–176. Springer, Heidelberg (2007). https://doi.org/10.1007/978-3-540-73074-3_13
17. Nitaj, A., Susilo, W., Tonien, J.: A new improved AES S-box with enhanced properties. In: Liu, J.K., Cui, H. (eds.) ACISP 2020. LNCS, vol. 12248, pp. 125–141. Springer, Cham (2020). https://doi.org/10.1007/978-3-030-55304-3_7
18. Nyberg, K.: Differentially uniform mappings for cryptography. In: Helleseth, T. (ed.) EUROCRYPT 1993. LNCS, vol. 765, pp. 55–64. Springer, Heidelberg (1994). https://doi.org/10.1007/3-540-48285-7_6
19. Nyberg, K.: S-boxes and round functions with controllable linearity and differential uniformity. In: Preneel, B. (ed.) FSE 1994. LNCS, vol. 1008, pp. 111–130. Springer, Heidelberg (1995). https://doi.org/10.1007/3-540-60590-8_9
20. Shibutani, K., Isobe, T., Hiwatari, H., Mitsuda, A., Akishita, T., Shirai, T.: *Piccolo*: an ultra-lightweight blockcipher. In: Preneel, B., Takagi, T. (eds.) CHES 2011. LNCS, vol. 6917, pp. 342–357. Springer, Heidelberg (2011). https://doi.org/10.1007/978-3-642-23951-9_23
21. Shirai, T., Shibutani, K., Akishita, T., Moriai, S., Iwata, T.: The 128-bit blockcipher CLEFIA (extended abstract). In: Biryukov, A. (ed.) FSE 2007. LNCS, vol. 4593, pp. 181–195. Springer, Heidelberg (2007). https://doi.org/10.1007/978-3-540-74619-5_12

22. SM4: ISO/IEC 18033–3:2010/AMD 1:2021 information technology—security techniques—encryption algorithms—part 3: block ciphers—amendment 1: SM4 homepage. https://www.iso.org/standard/81564.html

23. Suzaki, T., Minematsu, K., Morioka, S., Kobayashi, E.: *TWINE*: a lightweight block cipher for multiple platforms. In: Knudsen, L.R., Wu, H. (eds.) SAC 2012. LNCS, vol. 7707, pp. 339–354. Springer, Heidelberg (2013). https://doi.org/10.1007/978-3-642-35999-6_22

24. Wang, Y.B.: Analysis of structure of AES and its S-box. J. PLA Univ. Sci. Technol. (Nat. Sci.) (2002)

25. Webster, A.F., Tavares, S.E.: On the design of S-boxes. In: Williams, H.C. (ed.) CRYPTO 1985. LNCS, vol. 218, pp. 523–534. Springer, Heidelberg (1986). https://doi.org/10.1007/3-540-39799-X_41

26. Wilson, R.A.: The Finite Simple Groups. Springer, London (2009). https://doi.org/10.1007/978-1-84800-988-2

Network Security

Social Internet of Tings Trust Management Based on Implicit Social Relationship

Hongbin Zhang[1,2], Fan Fan[1], Dongmei Zhao[2(✉)], Bin Liu[3,4], Yanxia Wang[5], and Jian Liu[1]

[1] School of Information Science and Engineering, Hebei University of Science and Technology, Shijiazhuang 050000, China
[2] Hebei Key Laboratory of Network and Information Security, Hebei Normal University, Shijiazhuang 050024, Hebei, China
zhaodongmei666@126.com
[3] School of Economics and Management, Hebei University of Science and Technology, Shijiazhuang 050000, China
[4] Research Center of Big Data and Social Computing, Hebei University of Science, Shijiazhuang, China
[5] Hebei Geological Workers' University, Shijiazhuang 050081, China

Abstract. The "Social Internet of Things (SIoT)" is a combination of the Internet of Things (IoT) and social networks to form a new paradigm. The SIoT promotes the development of smart cities, smart transportation, and many other fields. In SIoT, the openness and mobility of objects are enhanced. However, this tends to lead to network data sparsity problems. By distinguishing explicit and implicit social relationships, we introduce an implicit social relationship-based trust management model (IRTM) for reliable service delivery in SIoT. IRTM establishes implicit social relationships among nodes by mining their latent characteristics and trust transitivity. It models SIoT by creating sub-networks for each social relationship as a way to fuse the impact of different types of social relationships on trust management. To address the problem of malicious attacks by malicious nodes in the network to protect their interests, it considers two metrics, node relationship strength, and recommendation reliability, to filter malicious recommendations. Experiments conducted in the presence of data sparsity and malicious objects show that IRTM can improve the accuracy and convergence of trust evaluation compared to other methods that ignore implicit social relationships when computing trust. In addition, our scheme can improve resistance to trust-related attacks.

Keywords: Social Internet of Things · Trust Management · Malicious Attack · Implicit Social Relationship · Multiple Social Relationships

1 Introduction

Information and intelligence are important features of modern development, and the realization of "interconnection of all things and intelligent interoperability" is an important goal of modern development. To further promote the "Internet of Everything", a

Q. Jiang et al. (Eds.): SPNCE 2022, LNICST 496, pp. 129–139, 2023.
https://doi.org/10.1007/978-3-031-30623-5_9

new paradigm, the Social Internet of Things, has been proposed. The Social Internet of Things (SIoT) will further promote the development of health care (telemedicine, e-health, etc.), smart cities (connected cars, smart weather, etc.), smart homes (home lighting control systems, home security systems, etc.) and other fields by establishing social networks among smart devices [1–3]. However, in this environment where frequent interactions occur, some bad nodes can maliciously attack other nodes. The service request process of good nodes will be disturbed. Therefore, trust plays a crucial role in ensuring reliable service delivery [4–6]. The concept, metrics, and assessment methods of trust are not uniform in different fields [7]. For example, in real life, trust represents the intimacy between people, and trust also indicates recognition of people's abilities in some specific scenarios, etc. In SIoT, trust represents the reliability of the services provided by objects. Therefore, trust management in SIoT is essential for a more reliable and satisfactory service to the principals.

It is important to note that in traditional IoT, the location of smart objects is relatively fixed. However, in SIoT, the mobility of smart objects becomes stronger. And mobility tends to lead to dense nodes in some areas and sparse nodes in others. Objects can build social relationships autonomously is the characteristic of SIoT. The social relationship is an important evaluation metric in SIoT trust management. When the data where the nodes are located is sparse, it means that there is a lack of information about the social relations of the nodes, which leads to the inability to accurately evaluate trust. Therefore, we propose an implicit social relationship-based trust management model (IRTM). The model extends the social relationship network by mining the implicit social relationships among nodes, making its scheme applicable in sparse networks as well. Two metrics, node relationship strength, and recommendation reliability are considered to filter malicious recommendations so that its model is still robust in a hostile environment. An example diagram for seeking the most reliable service using trust management is given in Fig. 1. And the detailed part of the IRTM trust management model we will discuss in detail in Sect. 4.

The remainder of this paper is organized as follows. Section 2 reviews the related work. Section 3 describes the preparatory work. In Sect. 4, we detail the design of an implicit social relationship-based trust management model (IRTM) for SIoT. In Sect. 5, we verify the effectiveness of the model through experimental simulations. Finally, we summarize the work in this paper and outline future work in Sect. 6.

2 Related Work

This section reviewed and analyzed the related work on trust management of the Social Internet of Things in recent years.

M. Nitti et al. [8] model subjective trust management based on social network characteristics; an objective trust model was built based on P2P related approach and using some characteristics of social networks. In Ref [9], multiplicative attribute maps were used to quantify predefined social relationships and calculate the trust strength between nodes in the context of SIoT. The Ref [10] considers four attributes of closeness, service feedback, sociality, and transaction importance for the trust management of nodes. Fang-Yu Gai [11] introduced the theory of social networks in in-vehicle networks so that they can better serve the trust model. The accuracy of trust assessment models can be improved by quantifying social relationships. In Ref [12], context-aware trust quantification methods based on feature-attribute matching methods were proposed. And ability, willingness, and social relationship elements were used to measure trust. In Ref [13], a differentiated perceptual trust management model is proposed. This model introduces social relations in the computation of trust to better understand some discriminatory behaviors. However, the above references are more homogeneous in considering social relationships and only use the social similarity between nodes to represent the strength of ties. It is not possible to integrate the impact of multiple social relationships on trust management.

The Ref [14] considers trust attributes such as honesty, collaboration, community interest, and node energy of trust and calculates trust based on direct observation, indirect recommendation, the centrality of nodes, and reliability factors. In Ref [15], an adaptive trust management protocol under SIoT is proposed. In Ref [16], the authors propose a temporal similarity-based trust model for social IoT that incorporates the impact of three attributes, namely the community interest attribute, friend attribute, and collaborative work attribute, on trust assessment. However, the above references only exploit explicit social relationships and completely ignore implicit social relationships. It is not able to effectively solve the network sparsity problem.

Therefore, this paper effectively alleviates the network data sparsity problem and the cold start problem by establishing implicit social relationships. Inspired by the subnet composite approach in Ref [17] and Ref [18], the multi-subnet composite complex network idea is used to model the SIoT. In the following, the system model will be elaborated.

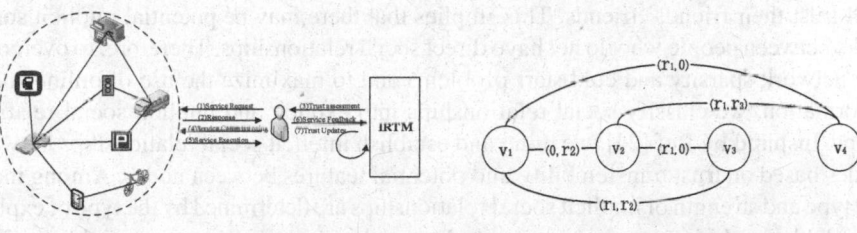

Fig. 1. SIoT trust management process   **Fig. 2.** Composite network example diagram

3 Preliminaries

3.1 Types of Social Relationships

The SIoT enhances the navigability of the network. Each type of social relations has a different impact on navigability and represents a different level of trust [18, 19]. According to the object-specific socialization model of SIoT defined in Ref [20], objects create different types of social relationships. The initial trust value of social relationships is set according to the definition of social relationships and the analysis of the type of navigability and importance of social relationships in SIoT by Ref [21] and [22].

In this paper, the trust value range is set within (0, 1), when the higher trust value indicates that the more reliable the smart object is, the higher the interaction success rate. When objects such as cell phones and laptops belong to the same owner, they will have a higher probability of having similar behaviors. Therefore, we set the highest initial trust value of 0.9 to the Ownership Object Relationship (OOR). There is a higher similarity between objects produced by the same manufacturer in the same period. Therefore, we set a higher initial trust value of 0.8 for the Parental Object Relationship (POR). There is a high probability of interaction and collaboration between objects such as sensors and actuators used in the same environment such as a smart home or smart city to accomplish tasks. Therefore, we give a slightly higher initial trust value of 0.7 to Co-Location Object Relationship (C-LOR). Co-Work Object Relationship (C-WOR) are established between objects that are far away from each other according to the task type, such as telemedicine. Since the longer distance makes the objects more likely to suffer from malicious attacks, we give a low initial trust value of 0.6 to the Co-Work Object Relationship. The initial trust value between objects without social relations is 0.5.

3.2 Implicit Social Relationship

In most of the previous studies on trust management in SIoT, only explicit social relationships between nodes have been utilized, and the role of implicit social relationships in trust management has been completely ignored. Explicit social relationships are explicitly establishable social relationships between nodes. The types of explicit social relationships in SIoT are described in Sect. 3.1. Implicit social relationships are implicit social links established through the transferability of trust between two nodes that do not have social relationships. For example, in real life, people tend to trust their friends and will trust their friends' friends. This implies that there may be potential implicit social links between people who do not have direct social relationships. Therefore, to overcome the network sparsity and cold start problems and to maximize the use of online social information, we classify social relationships into explicit and implicit social relationships. Inspired by Ref [24], we mine and establish implicit social relationships between nodes based on trust transferability and potential features between nodes. Among them, the type and strength of implicit social relationships are determined by the type of explicit social relationships that exist between nodes and the number of common neighbors. Thus many nodes may be related to each other through implicit social relationships.

Based on the explicit social relationship types described in Sect. 3.1, we can establish implicit parent-object relationships, implicit collaborative location relationships, etc. Objects have both explicit and implicit social relationships with each other, and there may be multiple social relationships. And different types of explicit and implicit social relationships have different impacts on trust evaluation. Considering one type of social relationship alone will affect the accuracy of the evaluation results. Therefore, we use the idea of the composite network to build a composite SIoT network with explicit and implicit social relationships by loading multiple explicit and implicit single-relationship sub-networks. The composite network is introduced as described in Sect. 3.3.

3.3 Multi-relationship Composite Network

Smart objects are abstracted as nodes, and the relationships between smart objects are abstracted as connected edges in SIoT. The SIoT composite network model can be represented by a quadruplet $G = (V, E, R, F)$, and an example diagram is shown in Fig. 2.

- $V = \{v_1, v_2, v_3, \ldots, v_m\}$ represents the set of nodes, which is the number of nodes in the set.
- $E = \{\langle v_h, v_l \rangle | v_h, v_l \in V\}$ denotes the set of connected edges between nodes.
- $R = \{r_1, r_2, r_3, \ldots, r_n\}$ denotes the set of social relations between nodes, and is the number of types of relations in the set.
- F denotes the function to calculate the degree of multiple social relations.

4 The Proposed Trust Management Model

The Implicit Social Relationships (IRTM) based social IoT trust management model consists of six components: SIoT composite network construction, trust propagation, trust aggregation, filtering mechanism, outcome processing, and trust evaluation. Honesty, cooperativeness, and community interest are considered to be the most prominent indicators for characterizing SIoT systems [15]. The trust management model is elaborated below using the community interest attribute as an example and describing the attribute in terms of POR and C-LOR between nodes, as shown in Fig. 3 below.

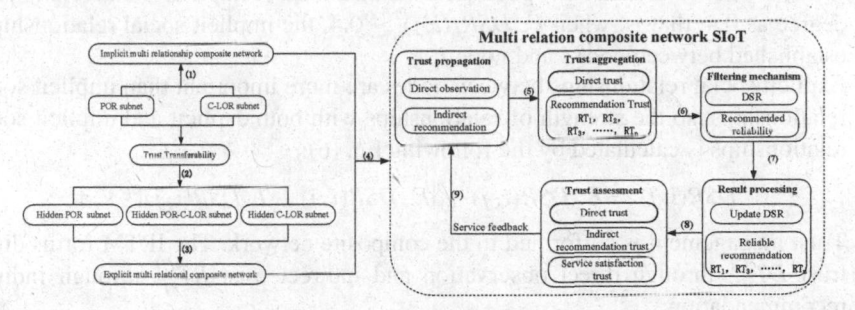

Fig. 3. IRTM model

1. Based on the social relationship matrix ES and the corresponding initial trust values, we obtain the dominant relationship trust matrix E_DSR_1 and E_DSR_2. The relationship trust values of both social relationships are calculated by Eq. (1), and the dominant multi-relationship composite network is constructed.

$$F\_DSR_E(i, j) = \max(E\_DSR_1(i, j), E\_DSR_2(i, j)) + |E\_DSR_1(i, j) - E\_DSR_2(i, j)|^{\eta} \times \sigma \quad (1)$$

where the parameter σ controls the trust value within the range, $\sigma = 0.01$ in this paper; The size of the parameter η depends on the type of the node social relationship and takes values in the range $(0, 1)$;

2. The relational strength of implicit social relationships decays from the strength of explicit social relationships and evolves according to the type of social relationships and the number of indirect friends. Thus, the implicit social relationship matrix is calculated as shown in (2):

$$IS = ES \otimes ES \cdot RM \tag{2}$$

where $\otimes$ denotes the outer product operation and $\cdot$ denotes the inner product operation; the regularization matrix RM is used to exclude the node from establishing an implicit trust relationship with itself; in the implicit social relationship matrix, the value 0 indicates that there is no implicit social relationship between two nodes, and other values indicate the number of times the node appears as an indirect friend;

The calculation of the strength of implicit social relations between nodes is given in Eq. (4):

$$I\_DSR(i,j) = (1-r) \times E\_DSR(i,j) - (r \times E\_DSR(i,j))^{IS(i,j)^{\eta}} \tag{3}$$

where $IS(i,j)$ denotes the number of times the node j appears as an indirect friend of the node i; the parameter r is the trust decay factor, and the value range is $(0, 1)$;

3. We give the calculation of the relationship trust level with both implicit social relationships as shown in Eq. (5):

$$F\_DSR_I(i,j) = \max(I\_DSR_1(i,j), I\_DSR_2(i,j)) + |I\_DSR_1(i,j) - I\_DSR_2(i,j)|^{\eta} \times \sigma \tag{4}$$

To prevent the establishment of implicit social relationships from leading to too dense network links, this paper sets the threshold of implicit social relationship degree as 0.4, that is, when $F\_DSR_I(i,j) > 0.4$, the implicit social relationship is established between node i and node j;

4. Explicit social relationships between nodes are more important than implicit social relationships, so the strength of relationships with both explicit and implicit social relationships is calculated by the following Eq. (6):

$$DSR(i,j) = E\_DSR(i,j) + |E\_DSR(i,j) - I\_DSR(i,j)|^{\eta} \times \sigma \tag{5}$$

5. Trust management is performed in the composite network. The IRTM forms direct trust DT_{ij}^{CI} through direct observation and indirect trust RT_{kj}^{CI} through indirect recommendation.

6. To prevent malicious nodes from making dishonest recommendations, this paper sets up a filtering mechanism in the IRTM model. The recommendation trust is filtered according to the degree of social relationship between node i and node k and the reliability of node k' recommendation values. The relationship degree threshold is set to 0.5, which means that node i only accepts recommendations from recommenders whose relationship trust degree is higher than 0.5. We calculated the reliability of the recommended values by considering the difference between the mean and median of the recommended values. Assuming that the node i has n recommenders, the calculation formula is as follows:

$$RT_{rel}(k) = 1 - \frac{\left| 2n \times RT_{kj}^{CI} - \sum_{k=1}^{n} RT_{kj}^{CI} - 2n \times RT_{med} \right|}{\sum_{k=1}^{n} RT_{kj}^{CI} + n \times RT_{med}} \tag{6}$$

7. Based on the results of the filtering mechanism, m reliable recommendation values are obtained. Thus, a reliable indirect trust can be formed.
8. At the end of the interaction at moment t, node i will rate the satisfaction of the service provided by node j to provide feedback for the next interaction, which is calculated as follows:

$$S_{ij}(t) = \begin{cases} T_{ij}^{CI}(t - \Delta t) \times 1, & \text{if satisfied} \\ T_{ij}^{CI}(t - \Delta t) \times (-1), & \text{if dissatisfied} \end{cases} \quad (7)$$

9. The three trust measures of direct trust, indirect referral trust, and service satisfaction are considered for a comprehensive assessment of trust values, calculated as follows:

$$TT_{ij}^{CI} = \begin{cases} (1 - \mu) \times DT_{ij}^{CI}(t) + \frac{\mu}{2} \times RT_{ij}^{CI}(t) + \frac{\mu}{2} \times S_{ij}(t - \Delta t), & \text{if } j == k \\ \mu \times RT_{ij}^{CI}(t) + (1 - \mu) \times S_{ij}(t - \Delta t), & \text{if } j! = k \end{cases} \quad (8)$$

where μ ($0 \leq \mu \leq 1$) used to balance the contribution of direct trust, indirect trust, and service satisfaction to trust.

We will conduct experiments and analyze the accuracy, convergence, and resilience of the IRTM model in detail in Sect. 5.

5 Experimental Results and Analysis

In this section, we compare the IRTM model in detail with the approaches in Ref [14, 15], and [16]. Experiments show that the IRTM model improves accuracy, convergence, and resistance to attacks. In this paper, simulations are performed in MATLAB using the dataset from Ref [22]. This dataset is based on a real IoT dataset provided by the city of Santan-der. We randomly selected 30 users from this dataset and constructed SIoT networks for 100 objects owned by their users. The total experimental simulation time was 100 h.

5.1 Trust Evaluation of Nodes in the Good Condition

To verify that the IRTM model improves the accuracy of trust assessment, multiple groups of dynamic nodes are randomly selected in a good environment for trust assessment comparison experiments. The network environment in which half of the nodes are located exhibits obvious sparse characteristics. Sparse networks are a common and not negligible application scenario for SIoT. Therefore, we compare the convergence properties of trust evaluation algorithms in general non-sparse scenarios and sparse network scenarios. The evaluated nodes perform well for the first 50 h, after which they are transformed from good to malicious nodes. Ideally, the good node trust evaluation value tends to be 1 and the malicious node tends to be 0. The IRTM model is compared with the methods Ref [14, 15], and [16]. The results are shown in Fig. 4. The dashed line shows the empirical confidence interval at a 90% confidence level.

In Fig. 4(a), the trust value evaluated by the IRTM model proposed in this paper for good nodes in the normal network environment is closer to the true value1 than the trust

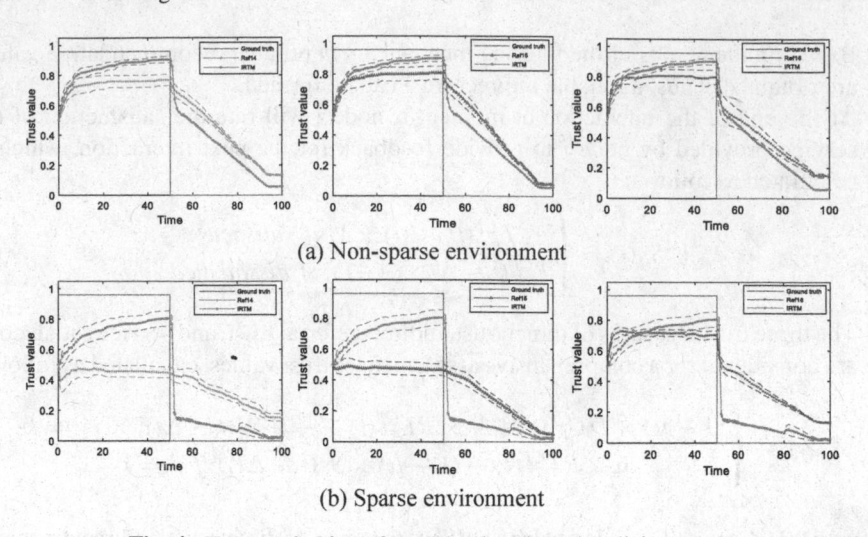

(a) Non-sparse environment

(b) Sparse environment

Fig. 4. Trust evaluation of a randomly selected malicious node

values evaluated by the methods in Ref [14, 15], and [16]; the trust value evaluated for malicious nodes is closer to the true value 0 and converges faster. This indicates that the IRTM model improves the accuracy of node trust assessment. This is because on the one hand the IRTM model incorporates service feedback trust in the trust evaluation, and on the other hand the trust between nodes is dynamically updated. When the nodes provide good services, the trust in the degree of relationship between nodes increases; when the nodes provide malicious services, the trust between nodes dynamically decreases.

As can be seen in Fig. 4(b), the IRTM model differs significantly from the evaluated values of the methods in Ref [14] and Ref [15]. This is due to the sparse data of the network environment in which the nodes are located, which affects the evaluation of the trust value of the nodes by comparing the methods of Ref [14] and Ref [15]. Compared with the evaluation results of the three comparative kinds of literature, it can be seen that the IRTM model is still close to the true value of the node trust value evaluation in the sparse network environment. This is because this paper solves the problem that the node trust cannot be evaluated correctly due to network sparsity by establishing implicit social relationships between nodes to populate the network. In addition, IRTM can converge to the new true value faster when the node becomes a malicious node. Comparing Fig. 4(a) and Fig. 4(b), we can see that IRTM improves the convergence speed and accuracy of trust evaluation regardless of whether the nodes are in the non-sparse or sparse scenario.

5.2 Trust Management in the Dynamic Hostile Change Conditions

To further validate the resilience of the IRTM model to trust attacks in SIoT environments with different levels of hostility. We consider two different malicious environments with a high malicious node percentage of 50% and a low malicious node percentage of 20%. In the experiments, the optimal parameter weights are set for the methods of Ref [14, 15], and [16]. In addition, to verify the importance of the degree of relationship between nodes in the trust management model, it is also compared with the case where malicious recommendations are filtered only by the reliability of the recommendation value without considering the degree of relationship in the model of this paper. For the sake of comparison and analysis, the above Case is referred to as "Case 1". The trust evaluation results of different models on randomly selected good nodes when malicious nodes launch attacks under two malicious node percentages, high and low, are shown in Fig. 5.

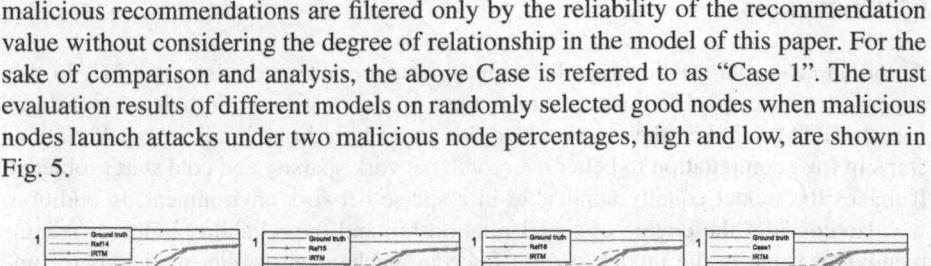

(a) 20% percentage of malicious nodes

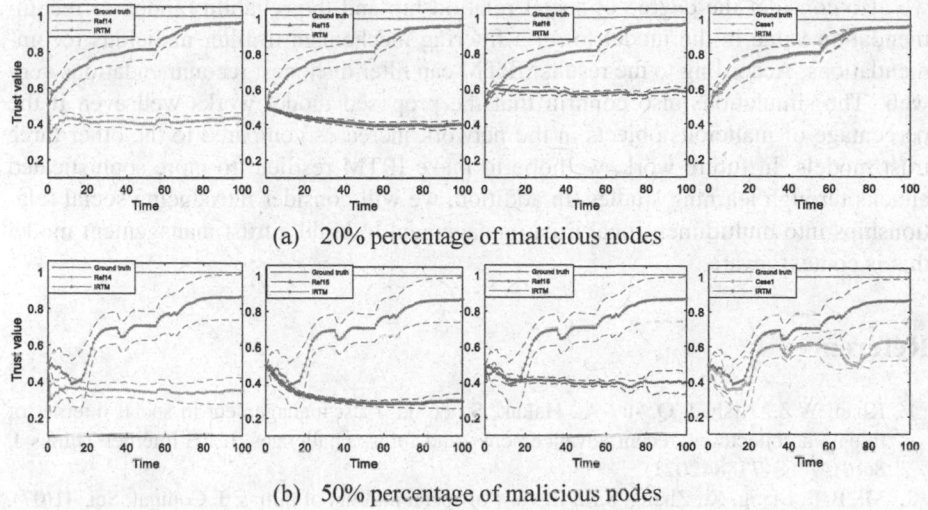

(b) 50% percentage of malicious nodes

Fig. 5. Trust evaluation of randomly selected nodes under malicious attacks

From Fig. 5(a), it can be seen that the result curves of trust evaluation of good nodes at low malicious node percentage for method case 1 in this paper are consistent. It is closer to the true value than the results of Ref [14, 15], and [16]. This indicates that this paper's model filters malicious recommendations and has a better stability. In contrast, the evaluation results of Ref [14] and Ref [15] differ more from the true value. On the one hand, it is because these two methods cannot filter malicious recommendations under defamation attack, which leads to lower trust value; on the other hand, it is because the network environment in which the nodes are located is more sparse, which makes the evaluation accuracy lower.

From Fig. 5(b), we can see that the evaluation result curves of this paper's model and "Case 1" are above the other three methods and closer to the true value 1. This indicates that the IRTM model has a strong ability to resist malicious attacks. The evaluation result curve of Case 1 fluctuates more and is below the curve of this paper's model. This is because under the high malicious node percentage, due to the increase in the number of malicious nodes, filtering malicious recommendations only by recommendation reliability will filter normal recommendations incorrectly as malicious recommendations, making the evaluation accuracy lower. In contrast, the evaluation result curve of the model in this paper is still smoother and closer to the true value than the evaluation result of Case 1. This indicates that introducing the degree of social relationship into trust management effectively improves the accuracy of evaluation results.

6 Conclusion

Autonomous social relationships between objects are a characteristic of SIoT. In this paper, we propose a SIoT trust management model based on implicit relationships, namely IRTM. Unlike other approaches, this paper introduces implicit social relationships in trust computation to better overcome network sparsity and cold start problems. It makes the model equally applicable in a sparse network environment. In addition, we also consider the degree of social relationship and the reliability index of recommendation value in the model to set a filtering mechanism to filter malicious recommendations. According to the results, IRTM can filter dishonest recommendations very well. The simulations also confirm that the proposed model works well even if the percentage of malicious objects in the network increases compared to the other three trust models. In future work, we hope to make IRTM resilient to more sophisticated attacks through learning studies. In addition, we will consider introducing social relationships into multidimensional trust management to build a trust management model that is context-aware.

References

1. Khan, W.Z., Arshad, Q. -u. -A., Hakak, S., et al.: Trust management in social internet of things: architectures, recent advancements, and future challenges. IEEE Internet Things J. **8**(10), 7768–7788 (2021)
2. Mi, B.T., Liang, X., Zhang, S.S.: Review of social internet of things. J. Comput. Sci. **41**(07), 1448–1475 (2018)
3. Xiong, J.B., Bi, R.W., Tian, Y.L., et al.: Mobile swarm intelligence perceives security and privacy: models, progress and trends. J. Comput. Sci. **9**, 1949–1966 (2021)
4. Khanfor, A., Hamrouni, A., Ghazzai, H., at al.: A trustworthy recruitment process for spatial mobile crowdsourcing in large-scale social IoT. In: 2020 IEEE Technology & Engineering Management Conference (TEMSCON), pp. 1–6. IEEE, Novi (2020)
5. Thirukkumaran, R., Muthu Kannan, P.: Survey: security and trust management in internet of things. In: 2018 IEEE Global Conference on Wireless Computing and Networking (GCWCN), pp. 131–134. IEEE, Lonavala (2018)
6. Wen, Y.Y., Xu, Z., Jiao, R.X.: A social IoT trust prediction model using deep learning. Telecommun. Technol. **61**(03), 269–275 (2021)
7. Artz, D., Gil, Y.: A survey of trust in computer science and the semantic web. J. Web Seman. **5**(2), 58–71 (2007)
8. Nitti, M., Girau, R., Atzori, L.: Trustworthiness management in the social internet of things. IEEE Trans. Knowl. Data Eng. **26**(5), 1253–1266 (2014)
9. Premarathne, U.S.: MAG-SIoT: a multiplicative attributes graph model based trust computation method for social internet of things. In: 2017 IEEE International Conference on Industrial and Information Systems (ICIIS), pp. 1–6. IEEE, Peradeniya (2017)
10. Ekbatanifard, G., Yousefi, O.: A novel trust management model in the social internet of things. J. Adv. Comput. Eng. Technol. **5**(2), 57–70 (2019)
11. Gai, F.Y.: Research on trust management based security mechanism in Internet of Things. National University of Defense Technology (2017)
12. Wei, L., Wu, J., Long, C.: On designing context-aware trust model and service delegation for social internet of things. IEEE Internet Things J. **8**(6), 4775–4787 (2021)

13. Jafarian, B., Yazdani, N., Haghighi, M.S.: Discrimination-aware trust management for social internet of things. Comput. Netw. **178**, 107254 (2020)
14. Meena Kowshalya, A., Valarmathi, M.L.: Dynamic trust management for secure communications in social internet of things (SIoT). Sādhanā **43**(9), 1–8 (2018). https://doi.org/10.1007/s12046-018-0885-z
15. Chen, I., Bao, F., Guo, J.: Trust-based service management for social internet of things systems. IEEE Trans. Dependable Secure Comput. **13**(6), 684–696 (2016)
16. Sagar, S., Mahmood, A., Kumar, J., et al.: A time-aware similarity-based trust computational model for social internet of things. In: GLOBECOM 2020 Global Communications Conference, pp. 1–6 (2020)
17. Zhou, S., Bin, S., Shao, F.J.: Material diffusion recommendation algorithm based on multi-subnet composite complex network model. Complex Syst. Complex. Sci. **15**(04), 77–84 (2018)
18. Sui, Y.: Study on multi-subnet complex network model and its related properties. Qingdao University (2012)
19. Nitti, M., Atzori, L., Cvijikj, I. P.: Network navigability in the social internet of things. In: 2014 IEEE World Forum on Internet Of Things (WF-IoT), pp. 405–410, IEEE. Seoul (2014)
20. Atzori, L., Iera, A., Morabito, G.: The social internet of things (siot)–when social networks meet the internet of things: concept, architecture and network characterization. Comput. Netw. **56**(16), 3594–3608 (2012)
21. Ouechtati, H., Nadia, B.A., Lamjed, B.S.: A fuzzy logic-based model for filtering dishonest recommendations in the social internet of things. J. Ambient Intell. Humanized Comput. 1-20 (2021).
22. Marche, C., Atzori, L., Nitti, M.: A dataset for performance analysis of the social internet of things. In: 2018 IEEE 29th Annual International Symposium on Personal, Indoor and Mobile Radio Communications (PIMRC), pp. 1–5. IEEE, Bologna (2018)
23. Marche, C., Atzori, L., Iera, A., et al.: Navigability in social networks of objects: the importance of friendship type and nodes' distance. In: 2017 IEEE Globecom Workshops (GC Wkshps), pp. 1–6. IEEE, Singapore (2017)
24. Qin, Q., Zhang, H.R.: Three-branch recommendation based on trust transfer mechanism. Pattern Recogn. Artif. Intell. **33**(07), 600–609 (2020)

Romeo: SGX-Based Software Anti-piracy Framework

Yanning Du[✉], Xin Song, and Yichuan Wang

Xi'an University of Technology, Xi'an, Shaanxi, China
duyanning@gmail.com

Abstract. Preventing software piracy has always been a concern of software developers. Since crackers can track and analyze the application code, any client-side anti-piracy mechanism can only increase the cost of crackers, but cannot really stop them, unless the anti-piracy mechanism is put on the server along with the core functionality of the software. However, this approach harms the user experience. In this paper, we propose a software anti-piracy framework that makes it possible for developer to integrate anti-piracy mechanisms into the client-side without compromising the user experience through the use of Intel's SGX technology.

Keywords: Anti-piracy · SGX · Enclave

1 Introduction

As an application developer, it is always a headache to protect your rights against software piracy. You cannot protect your rights just by a licensing agreement. You must also use technical means to defend your rights from infringement.

It is common practice to include anti-piracy logic in the application code, which detects piracy and refuses to work when piracy is detected. However, both the logic for detecting piracy and the logic for denying service to pirated copies run the risk of being bypassed by crackers [1, 2, 4–9].

The source of this risk is that, in order to provide services to users, our software, i.e., the code that provides services to users, is distributed to users, along with the code that detects piracy and refuses to provide services.

This means that crackers have access to these codes. You cannot hide any anti-piracy logic in the public code. Even the most sophisticated anti-piracy logic, once presented to the cracker, is breached.

Distributing software to a user means presenting anti-piracy logic to crackers. In order to prevent crackers from tracking the anti-piracy logic, many software developers are forced to adopt a "kill a thousand enemies, lose eight hundred" approach. In this approach, developers place only part of the services in the app distributed to users, and place the rest of the services, along with the anti-piracy logic, on a server that crackers

Q. Jiang et al. (Eds.): SPNCE 2022, LNICST 496, pp. 140–155, 2023.
https://doi.org/10.1007/978-3-031-30623-5_10

cannot touch. Since crackers cannot modify the code on the server, they cannot breach the anti-piracy logic.

However, this approach is a way to sacrifice the user experience in exchange for the benefit of software developers. Because this approach not only puts the anti-piracy logic on the server, it also requires that the code that provides services to users must also be placed on the server. The premise that the logic for denying service to pirate users can work is that the right to decide whether to provide service to users is in the hands of the software developer. When the software developer decides to refuse service, the user does not get the service.

The services that are placed on the server must be critical, because if they are not, the cracker may choose to throw them away. However, putting critical functionality on the server can seriously impact the user experience.

Intel's Software Guard eXtensions (SGX) technology gives app developers another possibility. With this technology, developers can achieve the same anti-piracy purpose without putting the anti-piracy logic on the developer's server. The anti-piracy logic is included in the app together with other functions of the software, distributed to the user and installed on the user's computer. Thanks to the protection of SGX technology, although the anti-piracy logic is installed on the user's machine, it is not visible to crackers. Thus, the purpose of protecting the anti-piracy logic is achieved.

In short, we have made the following contributions in this work: We have demonstrated the application of SGX technology in anti-piracy. We have designed an anti-piracy scheme. We have designed a prototype framework for integrating SGX technology into application software.

2   Background

2.1   Anti-piracy Mechanism

The anti-piracy logic of software consists of two parts: the first part is the piracy detection logic, and the second part is the denial-of-service logic. An attack on either part by a cracker will cause the software's anti-piracy mechanism to fail.

The piracy detection logic is the code that determines if a copy is pirated. If this code is deployed on the user's computer, a cracker can analyze it in a cracking environment (e.g., debugger, IDA) to figure out how the piracy detection logic works, and then bypass the piracy detection logic or cheat the piracy detection logic into believing the pirated software is genuine software.

Denial of service logic is the ability to deny service when the piracy detection logic determines that the copy is a pirated copy. Similarly, a cracker can analyze this part of the code and, after figuring out its logic, modify it. So that it no longer works in the way the application developer intended.

Some developers chose to scatter piracy detection logic and denial-of-service logic throughout the application to deal with crackers. However, this approach is essentially the opposite of the modularity advocated by software engineering. Once you implement the piracy detection logic and denial of service logic as a function in accordance with the idea of software engineering, and then call them from time to time in the software's business processes, these functions themselves will become the target of attack. If it is not implemented as a function, but directly scattered in the form of inlined code, it is also easy to find out by crackers using automated tools due to the same code pattern. It is very difficult for software developers to repeat the anti-piracy logic in different forms in every needed location, and it also interferes with the development of the software.

2.2 Software Guard Extensions

SGX technology [3–18] is an extension of the Intel processor. It provides a set of instructions through which an application can place a portion of its code in a memory area called an enclave. The enclave is still part of the process address space, but the content stored in the enclave, whether code or data, is not visible outside the enclave. This "outside" includes not only other parts of the process to which the enclave belongs, but also privileged software such as the operating system.

The data and code to be put in the enclave are encrypted and cannot be read by anyone until they are decrypted in the enclave. Only Intel processors that support SGX technology can decrypt them. The decrypted code and data are placed in the enclave where no one can access them. That is, nothing can access them except the code itself in the enclave.

Developers do not need to use the SGX instructions provided by the processor directly. They just need to call the SDK functions provided by Intel to utilize SGX [19–23]. The code and data to be put in the enclave is made into a dynamic library and distributed to the user in an encrypted form. The code and data in this dynamic library are decrypted by the processor and placed in the enclave. We can simply think of this dynamic library as existing in the enclave. The boundary between the enclave and the outside world is controlled by SGX. For the world outside the enclave, whether it is another part of the enclave's process or privileged software like an operating system, the code and data in the enclave seem like to exist in the memory of a remote computer, and cannot be touched directly. You can only call functions in the enclave indirectly by calling proxy functions, just like calling remote procedures. Here, as with RPCs, there is also a marshalling and unmarshalling of parameters. But by using the SDK from Intel, we can simply describe these functions in the Enclave Description Language (EDL), and the tools in the SDK will automatically generate the corresponding marshalling/unmarshalling code for us. The code in the enclave can also call external code, such as API functions provided by the operating system for network communication.

3   Overview

The design of anti-piracy mechanism is related to the following two aspects:

- The designer's vision of the user experience.
- The designer's vision of the developer experience.

The following is our view of these aspects. Finally, the basic working process of the framework and remote attestation is described.

3.1 User Experience

The following is an example to illustrate the user experience when using the application protected by Romeo framework.

The user has purchased the application and the license allows 3 instances to run simultaneously. The user has installed the application on four computers. When the user runs the application on the first, second and third computer in sequence, everything works fine. Keep the instances on these computers running, and then start the application on the fourth computer. At this point, the total number of instances running exceeds the maximum allowed by the license. However, the program starts normally on the fourth computer, without any complaint. But then the application on the first computer starts to strike. A dialog box pops up, telling the user that the number of instances running at the same time exceeds the limit allowed by the license the user purchased. When the user finds the dialog on the first computer, he restarts the application, and after the restart, the application works again, but then the application on the second computer goes into a strike.

That is, when the number of simultaneously online instances reaches the maximum allowed by the license, starting a new instance will cause the oldest instance to go into a strike state. The new instance does not tell the user that the number of simultaneously online instances has exceeded the limit. This solution penalizes a genuine user who has copied his software to others, thus creating the fact of piracy. For the genuine user, a new instance started by a pirate user will cause the genuine user's instance to strike. The user only knows that their rights have been compromised by the presence of pirate users. But he doesn't know which pirate user caused the problem.

3.2 Developer Experience

For the application developer, the software he sells to each user is the same. The only difference is the enclave DLL. In fact, the enclave DLL is basically the same from the point of view of source code, only the user ID (such as the user's email address provided when registering) string is different.

The process of regenerating the enclave DLL once for each user ID can be automated as part of the user registration process. When the user has completed registration and paid, the user downloads the resulting enclave DLL as an electronic license and copies it to the application directory.

This process is very easy for the developer to accomplish, whether he chooses to provide a registration system or to register the users manually himself. Because each time you only need to replace the user ID part in the source code of the enclave DLL, and then recompile to generate the enclave DLL.

The application developer needs to run a server. Each instance of the application communicates with this server so that the server can know how many instances of each sold copy are currently running. When the number of instances running simultaneously exceeds the maximum allowed by the license, the server notifies the oldest instance to go on strike.

3.3 Basic Working Process

When a critical service function of an application is executed in an enclave, the application sends a confession message to the server. The *confession message* consists of a *user ID*, a *random number*, and a *secret code*. The secret code is assigned to the instance by the server when the instance first confesses to the server. The confession message is sent in plaintext via a UDP packet.

When the server receives the message, it extracts the user ID and random numbers from the message and uses them to construct the *reassurance message*. The server encrypts the reassure message with its own private key $\{n, d\}$ and sends it back to the application instance.

$$E = R^d \bmod n \tag{1}$$

where E is the *encrypted reassurance message* and R is the *reassurance message*. R is the concatenation of the *user ID*, a *random number*, and an optional *secret code*.

$$R = id \| nonce \| secret^{opt} \tag{2}$$

Because the *reassurance message* is small, we encrypt it directly with the server's RSA private key. The customary hash process of signing is omitted.

After encryption and before it is transmitted over the network, the encrypted reassurance message is transformed from a binary block to a string to suit the requirements of JSON.

$$E' = mapping \cdot grouping \cdot serializing\ E \tag{3}$$

The function *serializing* is used to obtain the binary data block of E. The function *grouping* divides the binary data block into a grouping of 6 bits, and the function *mapping* maps each group to a printable character. The actual transmission is E'. Accordingly, an inverse transformation is performed when the reassurance message of this form is received.

$$E = unserializing \cdot merge \cdot unmapping E' \tag{4}$$

where *unmapping* converts E' from printable characters to 6-bit tuples, function *merge* combines these tuples, and *unserializing* restructures the merged binary data block.

Upon receiving the *reassurance message*, the instance decrypts it in the enclave with the server's public key $\{n, e\}$.

$$D = E^e \bmod n = \left(R^d\right)^e \bmod n \tag{5}$$

where D is the *decrypted reassurance message*, E is the *encrypted reassurance message*, and R is the *reassurance message*.

Accordingly, the verification process is simplified. We only need the RSA public key of the server to decrypt the received encrypted reassurance message.

The user ID and random number are extracted, and then compared with the user ID and random number of the previously sent *confession message*.

If the message contains the same information as in the previously sent confession message, the instance is validly reassured. Otherwise, the reassurance is considered invalid.

Effective reassurance causes a counter inside the enclave (which we call the *disappointment counter*) to be cleared to zero. Each execution of a critical service function of the application causes the disappointment counter to be incremented by one. When the value of the disappointment counter grows to a threshold due to the lack of timely reassurance messages, the critical service functions in the enclave will go on strike. This threshold is called the *heartbreak value*.

3.4   Remote Attestation

SGX provides integrity of code and confidentiality and integrity of data at run-time. However, it does NOT provide confidentiality of code offline as a binary file on disk. Adversaries can reverse engineer the binary enclave DLL. An adversary could disassemble it and then make a copy that bypasses checking for reassurance messages.

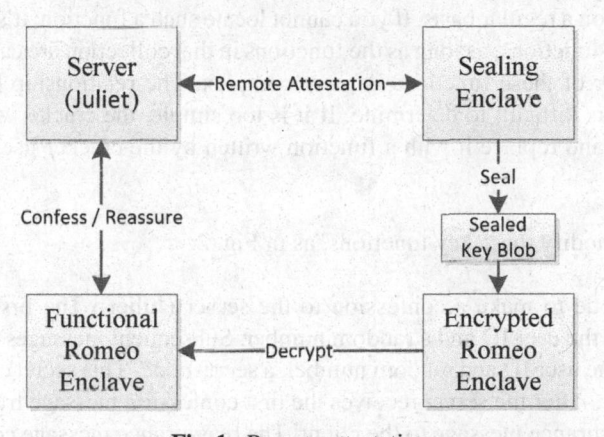

Fig. 1. Remote attestation

To solve this problem, we devised a sealing enclave in addition to the original enclave and called the original enclave Romeo Enclave (see Fig. 1). The Romeo Enclave DLL is provided to the user in an encrypted form that needs to be decrypted before it is run for the first time, with the key coming from the server. The sealing enclave communicates with the server and uses SGX's remote attestation mechanism to obtain the decryption key from the server, seals the key and saves it to a file. The client app reads this sealed key from the file and unseals it, then uses this key to decrypt itself (via SGX's Protected Code Loader) and restore itself to a functional Romeo enclave. The remote attestation is performed only once in the entire process. After that, Romeo Enclave communicates directly with servers, eliminating the need for remote attestation.

4 Implementation

The Romeo framework can be divided into two parts: the client part (which can be called Romeo), and the server part (which can be called Juliet).

4.1 Client

The client part is a library. The application code needs to be modified slightly to use this library. However, these modifications are quite easy. There is no impact on the logical structure of the application.

First, the developer needs to identify some core functions in the application and place them in the enclave for execution. These core functions should meet the following conditions:

- These functions are located on the critical path of the critical services provided by the application. We will achieve denial of service by controlling these critical functions.
- They are frequently invoked. Only then can we maintain the power to threaten pirate users with it on a regular basis. If you cannot locate such a function, it's fine to locate a collection of functions, as long as the functions in that collection are called frequently.
- The behavior of these functions is more complex. The relationship between inputs and outputs is difficult to determine. If it is too simple, the cracker will analyze the relationship and replace it with a function written by the cracker itself, which never strike.

Then, we modify these key functions, as in Fig. 2:

- Insert the code to make a confession to the server (Juliet). The first message sent contain only the user ID and a random number. Subsequent messages will contain, in addition to the user ID and random number, a secret code. This secret code is assigned by the server. After the server receives the first confession message from the client, it sends a reassurance message to the client. The reassurance message contains a secret code. The client will include this secret code in all future messages. The client will not send a new confession until the last one has been reassured by a confession message.
- Insert the strike logic. Each execution of the strike logic will add one to the *disappointment counter*, and when the value of the disappointment counter exceeds the heartbreak value, the client will enter the heartbroken state. Once it enters the heartbreak state, the enclave will refuse to execute core functions. After that, even if you receive a reassurance message from the server later, it does not help. In other words, once Remote's heart is broken, there is no way to recover.

In addition to these modifications of core functions in the enclave, the following additions need to be made to the code outside the enclave:

- Listen for reassurance messages from the server. Upon receiving the reassurance message, transport it into the enclave.

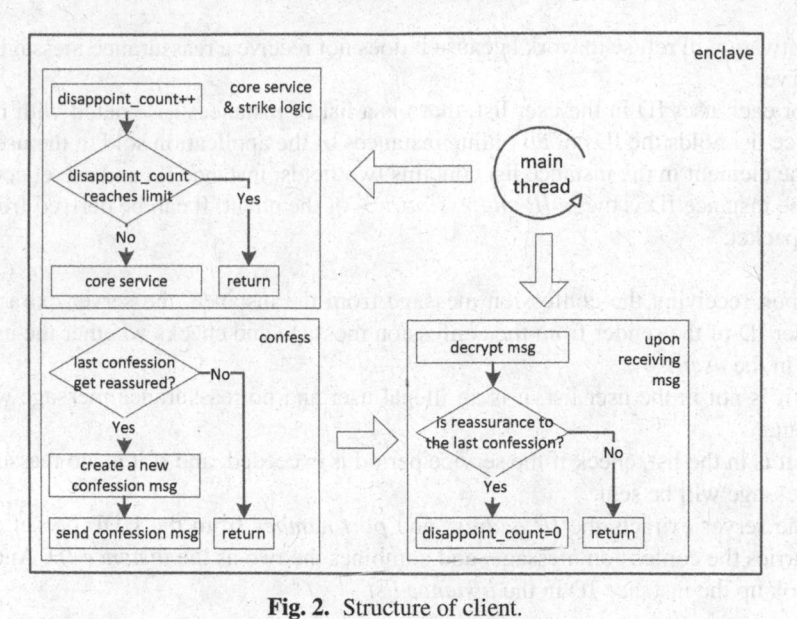

Fig. 2. Structure of client.

Then add code to the enclave to do the following:

- The enclave gets the incoming reassurance message from the outside world and decrypts the reassurance message with the server's public key.
- Extract the user ID and random number from the reassurance message, and then compare them with the user ID and random number from the previously sent confession message.
- If the information contained in the reassurance message is the same as the message sent in the last confession message, then the instance is validly reassured. Otherwise, the reassurance is considered invalid.
- Effective reassurance will cause the disappointment counter inside the enclave to be cleared.

4.2 Server

The server part is a separate program. We call it Juliet. Juliet's role is to receive confession messages from the client, and to send the appropriate reassurance messages. By controlling whether or not to send a reassurance message to Romeo, we can control whether or not to put Romeo into a heartbroken state. This allows us to control whether or not the application refuses to provide service (i.e., strike).

The confession message sent by the client contains the user ID. The user ID uniquely identifies each copy of the software.

As in Fig. 3, in the server, there is a list of users. The user IDs that appear in this list are the legitimate user IDs. Some IDs are in an expired state, which means that they purchased the software as a service, i.e. they can only use the software for a limited period of time. After the service period has expired, the software can be retained, but the software will refuse to work because it does not receive a reassurance message from the server.

For each user ID in the user list, there is a list of instances associated with it. The instance list holds the IDs of all online instances of the application sold to the user ID.

The element in the instance list contains two fields: instance ID and secret code.

The instance ID is the < *IP address:port* > of the client. It can be derived from the UDP packet.

1. Upon receiving the confession message from the instance, the server extracts the user ID of the sender from the confession message and checks whether the user ID is in the *user list*:
2. If it is not in the user list, it is an illegal user and no reassurance message will be sent.
3. If it is in the list, check if the service period is exceeded, and if it is, no reassurance message will be sent.
4. The server extracts the *IP address* and *port number* from the UDP packet which carries the confession message, and combines the two as the *instance ID*. And then look up the instance ID in the *instance list*.

If it does not exist, this may be due to one of the following conditions:

– It is a new instance.
– It may be a confession from old instances that have been neglected. These old instances have already been taken offline because of the start of new instances. But they don't know it yet, and send a confession message. The message will be neglected.
– This is an old instance that restarted after a strike. This situation is actually no different from a new instance starting up.
– At this time the server only needs to see whether the confession contains a secret code to do different processing:
– If the confession does not contain a *secret code*, then the confession is from a new instance (or an old instance after a restart, which is essentially a new instance). All it has to do at this point is to generate a new instance structure (which contains the newly generated secret code), add the instance structure to the instance list, and send a reassurance message, which contains the newly generated secret code, to the instance.
– If the message contains a secret code. This means that the confession message is sent by an old instance that had been neglected. Just ignore it.

4. If the instance ID exists in the instance list, it checks if the confession contains a secret code.
5. If not, this is a very strange phenomenon. While it's not the first time you confess, why would there be no secret code, the server will think this situation as a fake message sent by adversaries. Just ignore it.
6. If so, then compare the secret code in the confession with the secret code saved in the instance structure in the instance list.

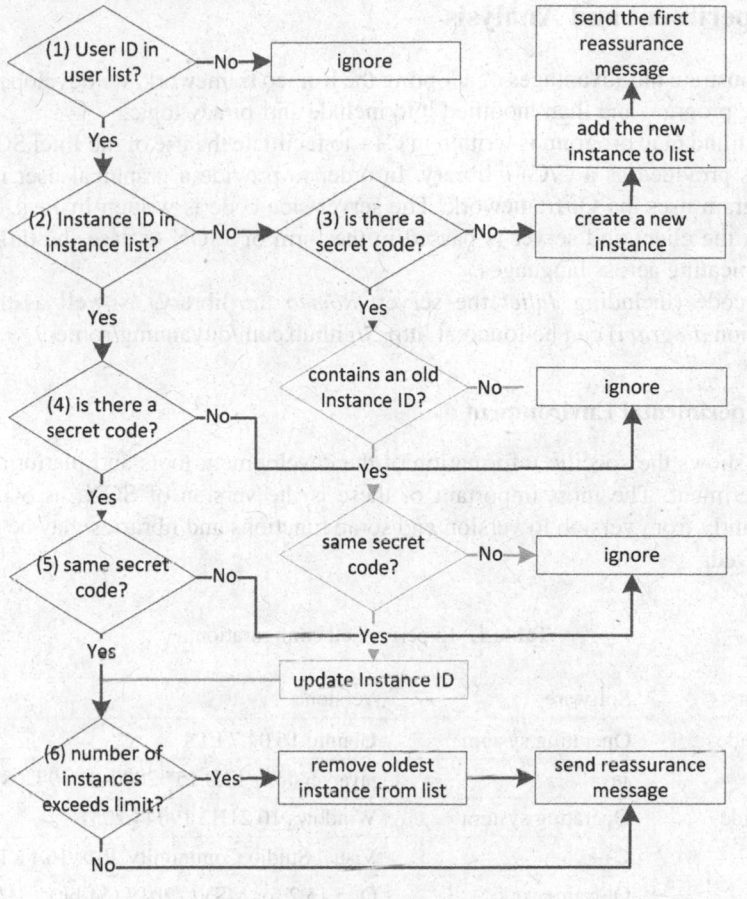

Fig. 3. Server-side workflow.

7. If the code doesn't match, which means you don't even know the secret code, you must be the adversary. Just ignore it.

8. If the secret code is the same, it means that it is a legitimate user and a legitimate instance. At this point, the server will look at the length of the instance list to determine whether the number of active instances exceeds the upper limit of the license.

9. If the upper limit is exceeded, the oldest instances are removed from the instance list. Then the server sends a reassurance message to the client. The reassurance message contains the user ID, a random number from the confession message, and the secret code. This secret code does not change. The reassurance message is encrypted using the server's private key before it is sent to the client as a UDP packet.

5   Experiment and Analysis

To demonstrate the advantages of adopting the Romeo framework, we developed a mind mapping program and then modified it to include anti-piracy logic.

The mind map program is written in C++ to facilitate the use of the Intel SGX SDK, which is provided as a C/C++ library. In order to provide a graphical user interface, the program uses the Qt framework. The server-side code is written in Java. The data between the client and server is passed in the form of JSON to ease the difficulty of communicating across languages.

All code (including *Juliet* the server, *Romeo* the library, as well as the demo application *diagram*) can be found at https://github.com/duyanning/romeo.

5.1   Experimental Environment

Table 1 shows the specific information of the development tools and platform used in the experiment. The most important of these is the version of SGX, as SGX varies significantly from version to version and some functions and libraries may be renamed or removed.

Table 1. Experimental configuration.

Location	Software	Version
Server side	Operating system	Ubuntu 16.04.7 LTS
	Java	java version "11.0.15" 2022-04-19 LTS
Client side	Operating system	Windows 10 21H2 19044.2251
	C++	Visual Studio Community 2019 16.11.18
	Qt framework	Qt 5.15.2 for MSVC 2019 (64-bit)
	Intel SGX	Intel SGX SDK for Windows 2.15.100.4

5.2   Performance Evaluation

The comparison experiment was conducted between the two versions. In one version, a traditional server-centric anti-piracy solution is adopted, in which user-generated mind map files are saved on the server. Although users can export them to local machine, they must be re-imported to the server for viewing and editing. The other version uses our Romeo framework, and the mind map file is saved locally and can be viewed and edited locally.

To compare the performance of the two solutions, we measured the time taken and the amount of data transferred for the five most common mind map operations (*add branch, remove subtree, rename branch, move subtree, relayout*).

In the traditional server-centered solution, any operation on the mind map will trigger the network communication between the client and the server, and the data transmitted is closely related to the business logic of the mind map software itself, and the data amount of this kind of information is large. In a scenario using the Romeo framework, the data transferred has nothing to do with what the client software does. The data transferred is the *confession message* and *reassurance message* used for anti-piracy monitoring, and the amount of data is small. And the manipulation of the mind map only triggers network communication with the server with a certain probability. The client does not send a confession message to the server again when the previous message has not received the corresponding reassurance message.

The *confession messages* are sent in clear text while the *reassurance messages* are sent in encrypted form. The content of the confession message is generated in the enclave, but is delivered by untrusted code located outside the enclave. Decryption and verification of the comfort message must be done in the enclave. Because the amount of data decrypted at a time is very small, and the confession messages are sent as non-blocking UDP datagrams, the Romeo framework's interference with the smooth operation experience of the user of an interactive application is minimal and almost imperceptible.

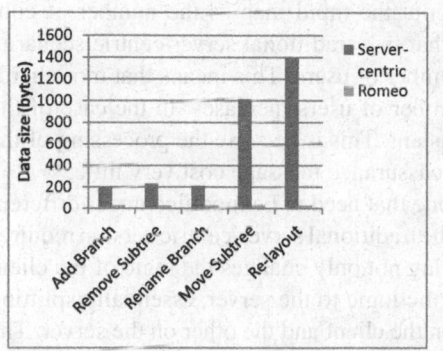

Fig. 4. The amount of data that needs to be transferred to perform a critical operation.

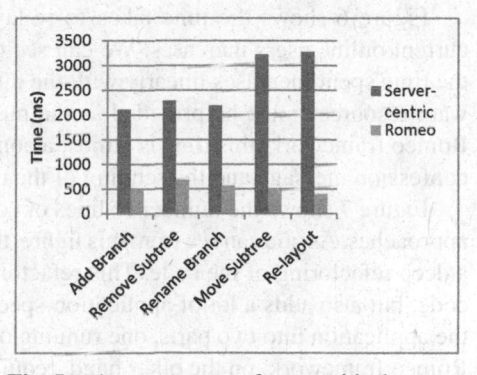

Fig. 5. Time spent to perform a critical operation.

Figure 4 shows the amount of data passed between client and server when various key operations are performed. As you can see, in the version that uses the Romeo framework, the amount of data transferred between the client and server is a constant (which is equal to the size of the confession message plus the reassurance message). In the traditional server-centric version, the amount of data transferred depends on how much different operations change the mind map. Of these, the re-layout operation results in the most staggering amount of data transfer. Also, for layout operations, the amount of data transferred is proportional to the size of the mind map.

Figure 5 shows the time it takes to perform various operations. As you can see, the version with the Romeo framework takes less time. This time is only related to the amount of data changed and the read/write speed of the local disk. In the traditional server-centric version, the time is related to the time spent reading and writing from the server's hard disk, plus the latency associated with network transmission. Also, when the server is serving multiple clients, this time overhead is even greater. And it's not a constant. The busier the server, the longer it takes.

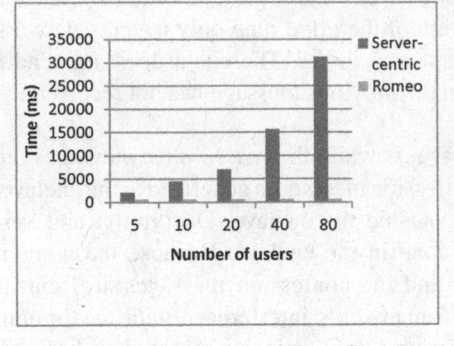

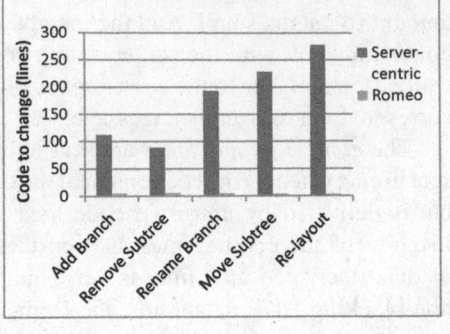

Fig. 6. Scalability as the number of users increases.

Fig. 7. The amount of lines of changes made to the code

Figure 6 shows the time taken to re-layout the mind map as the number of concurrent online users increases. We can see that in a traditional server-centric scenario, the time spent increases linearly with the number of users. This means that more hardware resources must be provided as the number of users increases. In the case of the Romeo framework, this time is almost a constant. This is because the processing of the confession message and the sending of the reassurance message cost very little.

Figure 7 shows the number of lines of code that need to be modified under different approaches. As you can see from this figure, the traditional server-centric version requires a deep refactoring of the code. This refactoring not only changes the logic of the client code, but also adds a lot of application-specific logic to the server, essentially splitting the application into two parts, one running on the client and the other on the server. The Romeo framework, on the other hand, requires very few changes to the code, and these changes are trivial, that is, they do not require substantial changes to the applied logic. And the same server can support multiple software protection.

Table 2 lists potential attacks and how the Romeo framework deals with them. As this table shows, the protection provided by the Romeo framework cannot be breached by every possible attack type we can think of.

Table 2. Potential attacks and corresponding solutions.

Attack	Solution
The adversary creates a cracking environment to breach the strike logic	By placing the strike logic in the enclave along with the core functionality, the adversary cannot bypass the strike logic
The adversary uses a fake server to send a fake reassurance message	Since the fake server does not know the private key of the real server, i.e., Juliet, it cannot mock an reassurance message that can reassure Romeo
By monitoring the network traffic of an instance for a certain period of time, the adversary learns what kind of confession message requires what kind of reassurance message	It is difficult to determine the relationship between the confession message and the reassurance message because the confession message contains a random number, and the random number has a wide range of variation
The confession message sent by the cracked client contains the ID of another user, and this ID will keep changing, but it's always a legitimate ID, so as to rub other users	The user ID of a reassurance message that the cracked client get by sending a confession message containing the ID of another user is different from the user ID that the enclave expects, and the enclave will compare this ID. That is, the cracked client only get reassured by reassurance message that contain its name, and a message that reassure other boy does not help

6 Conclusion

Since crackers can track and analyze the application code, any client-side anti-piracy mechanism will only increase the cost of crackers, but will not be able to stop them in any real sense. The alternative is to put the anti-piracy logic on the server together with the core service of the software. However, this approach will harm the user experience. Intel's SGX technology allows us to put the anti-piracy logic in the client without compromising the user experience. This paper presents an anti-piracy framework based on the SGX extension of new Intel processors, using which applications can easily implement anti-piracy features.

Acknowledgment. This research work is supported by the National Natural Science Founds of China (62072368, U20B2050), Key Research and Development Program of Shaanxi Province (2021ZDLGY05–09, 2022CGKC-09).

References

1. Wójcik, B.: How to make cracker's life harder. Anti piracy protections for programmers. https://www.pelock.com/articles/how-to-make-crackers-life-harder-anti-piracy-protections-for-programmers (2019)
2. Cloosters, T., Rodler, M., Davi, L.: TeeRex: discovery and exploitation of memory corruption vulnerabilities in SGX enclaves. In: 29th USENIX Security Symposium (2020)

3. Wang, W., Liu, W., Chen, H., Wang, X., Tian, H., Lin, D.: Trust beyond border: lightweight, verifiable user isolation for protecting in-enclave services. IEEE Trans. Dependable Secure Comput. **20**, 522–538 (2021)

4. D'Agostino, B., Khan, O.: Seeds of SEED: characterizing enclavelevel parallelism in secure multicore processors. In: 2021 International Symposium on Secure and Private Execution Environment Design (SEED), pp. 203–209 (2021)

5. Youren, S., et al.: Occlum: secure and efficient muvltitasking inside a single enclave of Intel SGX. In: Proceedings of the Twenty-Fifth International Conference on Architectural Support for Programming Languages and Operating Systems (2020)

6. Gu, J.-Y., Li, H., He, Z.-Y.: Unified enclave abstraction and secure enclave migration on heterogeneous security architectures. J. Comput. Sci. Technol. **37**(2), 468–486 (2022)

7. Yavuz, T., Fowze, F., Hernandez, G., Bai, K.Y., Butler, K., Tian, D.J.: ENCIDER: detecting timing and cache side channels in SGX enclaves and cryptographic APIs. IEEE Trans. Dependable Secure Comput. **20**, 1577–1595 (2022)

8. Shweta, S., et al.: Binary compatibility for SGX enclaves. arXiv preprint arXiv:2009.01144 (2020)

9. Intel Software Guard Extensions (Intel SGX) SDK for Windows OS Developer Reference, Rev. 2.14.1 (2021)

10. Fei, S., Yan, Z., Ding, W., Xie, H.: Security vulnerabilities of SGX and countermeasures: a survey. ACM Comput. Surv. (CSUR) **54**(6), 1–36 (2021)

11. Zheng, W., et al.: A survey of Intel SGX and its applications. Front. Comp. Sci. **15**(3), 1–15 (2020). https://doi.org/10.1007/s11704-019-9096-y

12. Zhao, S., Li, M., Zhangyz, Y., Lin, Z.: vSGX: virtualizing SGX enclaves on AMD SEV. In: 2022 IEEE Symposium on Security and Privacy (SP), pp. 321–336. IEEE (2022)

13. Cui, J., Yu, J.Z., Shinde, S., Saxena, P., Cai, Z.: SmashEx: smashing SGX enclaves using exceptions. In: Proceedings of the 2021 ACM SIGSAC Conference on Computer and Communications Security, pp. 779–793 (2021)

14. Randmets, J.: An overview of vulnerabilities and mitigations of Intel SGX applications (2021). https://cyber.ee/research/reports/D-2-116-An-Overview-of-Vulnerabilities-and-Mitigations-of-Inte l-SGX-Applications.pdf

15. Wu, T.Y., Guo, X., Chen, Y.C., Kumari, S., Chen, C.M.: SGXAP: SGX-based authentication protocol in IoV-enabled fog computing. Symmetry **14**(7), 1393 (2022)

16. Chen, Z., Vasilakis, G., Murdock, K., Dean, E., Oswald, D., Garcia, F.D.: VoltPillager: hardware-based fault injection attacks against Intel {SGX} enclaves using the SVID voltage scaling interface. In: 30th USENIX Security Symposium, pp. 699–716 (2021)

17. Wei, W., Wang, J., Yan, Z., Ding, W.: EPMDroid: efficient and privacy-preserving malware detection based on SGX through data fusion. Inf. Fusion **82**, 43–57 (2022)

18. Liu, G., Yan, Z., Feng, W., Jing, X., Chen, Y., Atiquzzaman, M.: SeDID: an SGX-enabled decentralized intrusion detection framework for network trust evaluation. Inf. Fusion **70**, 100–114 (2021)

19. Kogler, A., Gruss, D., Schwarz, M.: Minefield: a software-only protection for SGX enclaves against DVFS attacks. In: USENIX Security Symposium (2022)

20. Kumar, S., Sarangi, S.R.: SecureFS: a secure file system for Intel SGX. In: 24th International Symposium on Research in Attacks, Intrusions and Defenses, pp. 91–102 (2021)

21. Nakano, T., Kourai, K.: Secure offloading of intrusion detection systems from VMs with Intel SGX. In: 2021 IEEE 14th International Conference on Cloud Computing (CLOUD), pp. 297–303. IEEE (2021)

22. Yoon, H., Lee, M.: SGXDump: a repeatable code-reuse attack for extracting SGX enclave memory. Appl. Sci. **12**(15), 7655 (2022)
23. Toffalini, F., Graziano, M., Conti, M., Zhou, J.: SnakeGX: a sneaky attack against SGX enclaves. In: Sako, K., Tippenhauer, N.O. (eds.) ACNS 2021. LNCS, vol. 12726, pp. 333–362. Springer, Cham (2021). https://doi.org/10.1007/978-3-030-78372-3_13

P-TECS: An Energy Balance Algorithm for Opportunistic Networks Integrating Multiple Node Attributes

Gang Xu[1,2(✉)], Xiaoying Yang[1,2], Jingjian Chen[1,2(✉)], and Baoqi Huang[1,2]

[1] College of Computer Science, Inner Mongolia University, Hohhot 010021, China
csxugang@imu.edu.cn, qdsntcjj@163.com
[2] Inner Mongolia A.R. Key Laboratory of Data Mining and Knowledge Engineering,
Inner Mongolia University, Hohhot 010021, China

Abstract. This paper proposes an energy balance opportunistic networks routing algorithm P-TECS. The P-TECS solves the problems of energy consumption of key nodes in existing opportunistic routing algorithms. This paper defines the relay degree of communication between nodes, and designs a P-TECS opportunistic routing algorithm integrating dynamic attributes of multiple nodes. Simulation results show that in resource-constrained opportunistic networks, P-TECS significantly improves the message delivery rate and average remaining energy of nodes, and significantly reduces the routing overhead rate.

Keywords: Opportunistic routing algorithms · resource availability rate · node social engagement · communication relay degree

1 Introduction

Opportunistic network [1] is a new type of Mobile Ad-hoc network [2], which establishes communication by meeting opportunities between nodes. It does not need to form a complete communication link between the source node and the destination node, and the data are forwarded between the nodes in the "storage-carry-forward" manner. Opportunistic networks have irreplaceable advantages in the application of non-fully connected networks due to the characteristics of time-varying topology, node mobility and intermittent connectivity. In recent years, it has been widely used in the Internet of Vehicles, unmanned aerial vehicle, hydrometeorological monitoring, mine safety monitoring, wildlife tracking, mobile edge computing and other fields [3–8].

In opportunistic networks, the node's energy and buffer are consumed when forwarding messages, and attributes of these nodes are different. Existing opportunistic routing algorithms do not integrate energy balance and buffer optimization mechanisms of the node with various node-dynamic-attributes, which leads to the following two main problems in Opportunistic Networks:

ⓒ ICST Institute for Computer Sciences, Social Informatics and Telecommunications Engineering 2023
Published by Springer Nature Switzerland AG 2023. All Rights Reserved
Q. Jiang et al. (Eds.): SPNCE 2022, LNICST 496, pp. 156–166, 2023.
https://doi.org/10.1007/978-3-031-30623-5_11

First, active nodes exit the network due to high energy consumption. The number of available key nodes for network communication is reduced, which leads to a low messages delivery rate.

Second, the nodes with insufficient buffers and infrequent social interactions discard more data in message forwarding, resulting in high routing overhead.

Therefore, this paper comprehensively considers the five dynamic attributes of nodes when selecting relay nodes to forward messages. It effectively solves the above problems and improves the message delivery rate of the whole network.

2 Related Works

Opportunistic routing algorithm based on node information selects relay nodes according to node attributes, which include encounter probability, encounter duration, remaining energy, remaining cache, social relations and so on.

Literature [9] proposed Prophet based on node historical throughput which integrates node historical throughput to calculate node encounter probability, improves message delivery rate, and reduces routing overhead rate and average delay. Prophet based on node cache awareness is proposed in literature [10]. This routing algorithm combines node cumulative contact time and node remaining cache to calculate node encounter probability, which improves message delivery rate and average remaining energy of nodes. Literature [11] proposes an opportunistic routing algorithm based on node energy awareness and node candidate set, which minimizes the number of nodes in the candidate set list of each source node, prolongs the network lifetime and improves the average remaining energy of nodes. Literature [12] proposes Prophet based on node energy awareness and node cache awareness. This routing algorithm combines node remaining energy and node remaining cache to calculate node encounter probability, which improves message delivery rate, prolongs network lifetime, improves average node remaining energy and reduces routing overhead rate. Literature [13] proposed an opportunistic routing algorithm based on node social relations which first extracts node decision attributes according to node social relations, then assigns weights to node decision attributes in combination with information entropy method and feature selection method, and then measures node social relations according to weight allocation results. Finally, relay nodes are selected according to measured node social relations, which improves message delivery rate and reduces routing overhead rate. The opportunistic routing algorithm based on dynamic social relations of nodes is proposed in Literature [14]. This routing algorithm designs a new model to establish dynamic social relations of nodes, and a new method to predict the movement mode and contact time of nodes, which improves the message delivery rate and reduces the average delay, message hop count and network load.

Although the opportunistic routing algorithms mentioned in the above literature improve the network performance to a certain extent, they do not comprehensively analyze the influence of node encounter probability, node cumulative encounter duration, node energy consumption, node cache usage and node social relationship on message forwarding. Therefore, the proposed opportunistic network energy equalization algorithm integrates the above five node attributes to solve the problem of energy consumption caused by excessive computation of key nodes and the problem of important message loss caused by node cache overflow.

3 P-TECS: An Energy Balance Algorithm for Opportunistic Networks Integrating Multiple Node Attributes

The communication relay degree between nodes is composed of five different node-dynamic-attributes (encounter probability, cumulative encounter duration, remaining energy, remaining buffer and social relationship between nodes) according to certain mathematical rules.

3.1   Obtain the Historical Encounter Information Between Nodes

Definition 1. *The encounter probability between nodes. In Opportunistic Networks, the possibility of two nodes encounter in the subsequent time is called the encounter probability between nodes, marked as* $P_{(a,b)}$.

When node a and node b encounter, their number of encounters increase, and in the subsequent time, manifested as their encounter probability increase, as shown in Eq. (1) [15]:

$$P_{(a,b)} = P_{(a,b)old} + (1 - P_{(a,b)old}) \times P_{ini} \tag{1}$$

Among, $P_{(a,b)old}$ is last encounter probability of two nodes, $P_{ini} = 0.75$ [15] is the initial probability.

Definition 2. *The cumulative encounter duration between nodes. In Opportunistic Networks, the sum of each encounter duration between two nodes is called the cumulative encounter duration between nodes, marked as* $T_{(a,b)}$.

When node a and node b encounter for the n-th time, their cumulative encounter duration is the sum of the previous n-1 encounter durations, as shown in Eq. (2):

$$T_{(a,b)} = \sum_{i=1}^{n-1} t_{(a,b)i} \tag{2}$$

Among, $t_{(a,b)i}$ is the i-th time encounter duration of two nodes.

3.2 Obtain the Resource Availability Rate of the Node

Definition 3. *The remaining energy ratio of the node. In Opportunistic Networks, the ratio of the remaining energy of the node to the initial energy of the node is called the remaining energy ratio of the node, marked as R_E.*

After node a forwards message m to node b, its remaining energy is updated, as shown in equation (3) [16]:

$$E_{rem,a} = E_{rem(old),a} - \frac{B_m}{B_{pkt}} \times E_{for} \tag{3}$$

Among, $E_{rem(old),a}$ is the energy before node a forwards message m, B_m is bytes of message m, B_{pkt} is bytes of a data packet, E_{for} is the energy consumed by node a to forwards a data packet to node b.

After node b receives message m forwards by node a and returns acknowledge characters, its remaining energy is updated, as shown in Eq. (4) [16]:

$$E_{rem,b} = E_{rem(old),b} - \frac{B_m}{B_{pkt}} \times E_{rec} \tag{4}$$

Among, $E_{rem(old),b}$ is the energy before node b receives message m, E_{rec} is the energy consumed by node b to receive a data packet forwards by node a.

The remaining energy ratio of the node is the ratio of the remaining energy to the initial energy, as shown in Eq. (5) and Eq. (6):

$$R_E = \frac{E_{rem}}{E_{ini}} \tag{5}$$

Among, E_{rem} is remaining energy after node forwards/receives the message, E_{ini} is the initial energy of the node. The remaining energy ratio of the node reflect the energy consumption degree.

Definition 4. *The remaining buffer ratio of the node. In Opportunistic Networks, the ratio of the remaining buffer of the node to the initial buffer of the node is called the remaining buffer ratio of the node, marked as R_C.*

The remaining buffer ratio of the node as shown in Eq. (5):

$$R_C = 1 - \frac{\sum_{m-1}^{M} N_m \times B_m}{B_{ini}} \tag{6}$$

Among, N_m is the quantity of message m held by nodes, B_m is bytes of message m, B_{ini} is the initial buffer of the node. The remaining buffer ratio of the node reflect the buffer usage degree.

3.3 Obtain the Social Engagement of Nodes

Definition 5. *The social engagement of nodes: When nodes are detected by source nodes as neighbors, the number of network interfaces that they can work is called node social engagement, which reflects the situation that nodes provide network bandwidth. Node mobility may lead to different social engagement of nodes every time, so it is necessary to count the sum of social engagement of nodes every time, that is, the cumulative social engagement of nodes, which reflects the situation that nodes have social relations.*

When a node is detected as a neighbor node for the *n-th* time by the source node, the accumulated social engagement is the sum of the previous *n*-1 social engagement, as shown in Eq. (7):

$$S = \sum_{i=1}^{n-1} s_i \tag{7}$$

Among, s_i is the *i-th* social engagement of the node.

3.4 Calculate the Communication Relay Degree Between Nodes

Definition 6. *The communication relay degree between nodes. In P-TECS, multiple nodes-dynamic-attributes are integrated, and the communication relay degree between nodes is constructed, marked as $P - TECS_{(a,b)}$. The greater the communication relay degree between nodes reflects the rationality of the relay node, that is, the larger the communication relay degree, the more reasonable the messages forwarding between nodes.*

The communication relay degree between nodes as shown in Eq. (8):

$$P - TECS_{(a,b)} = kP_{(a,b)} \times l(1 + \frac{T_{(a,b)}}{100}) \times oR_{E,b} \times pR_{C,b} \times q\frac{S_{a,b}}{10^5} \tag{8}$$

Among, $P_{(a,b)}$ is the encounter probability of node a and node b, $T_{(a,b)}$ is the cumulative encounter duration of a and node b, $R_{E,b}$ is the energy ratio of node b, $R_{C,b}$ is the buffer ratio of node b, and $S_{a,b}$ is the cumulative social engagement of node a and node b. k, l, o, p and q are weights, the experiment shows that when $k = 0.6$, $l = 0.1$, $o = 0.1$, $p = 0.1$, $q = 0.1$, the effect is the best.

3.5 The Pseudo-code of P-TECS

As shown in Algorithm 1, energy-exhausted source nodes will enter the dormant state and no longer forward messages, and remaining source nodes forward messages to destination nodes or relay nodes. The relay node belongs to neighbor nodes of the source node and has the highest communication relay degree with the destination node. After the relay node receives message forwarded by the source node, it becomes the new source node.

Algorithm 1 P-TECS: An Energy Balance Algorithm for Opportunistic Networks Integrating Multiple Node Attributes

---

Input: sn: the source node;

cx: the maximum of the message copies number;

M: the messages collection of the source node;

RN: the relay nodes collection of the source node;

$P - TECS_{(dn,rn)}$: the communication relay degree collection of the destination node and relay nodes collection of the destination node and relay nodes.

Output: rn_{next}: the next hop relay node of the message.

1: **if** $sn.buffer.M ==$ null **then**

2:    exit

3: **end if**

4: **if** $sn.buffer.M \ != $ null **then**

5:    loop:

6:      **for** all $m \in M$ **do**

7:        **for** all $rn \in RN$ **do**

8:          **if** $m.dn ==$ rn **then**

9:            $rn_{next} = rn$

10:            forward m to rn_{next}

11:            delete $m \in M$

12:          **end if**

13:        **end for**

14:        **for** all $rn \in RN$ **do**

15:          add $p - tecs_{(dn,rn)}$ to $P - TECS_{(dn,rn)}$

16:        **end for**

17:        $rn_{next} = rn_{max}$ ▷ The $p - tecs_{(dn,rn)}$ of rn_{max} and dn is the maximum in $P - TECS_{(dn,rn)}$

18:        forward m to rn_{next}

19:        $m.copies = m.copies + 1$

20:        **if** $m.copies == cx$ **then**

21:          delete $m \in M$

22:        **end if**

23:      **end for**

24:      **if** $sn.buffer.M \ != $ null **then**

25:        goto loop

26:      **end if**

27: **end if**

The algorithm flow of P-TECS is as follows:

Step 1: Judge whether M in sn cache is empty. If so, the algorithm ends, otherwise the algorithm continues. This step corresponds to lines 1 through 3 in the P-TECS pseudocode.

Step 2: For m that can be delivered directly to dn, sn directly delivers m to dn, and rn_{next} is dn at this time, and deletes m from M after delivery. This step corresponds to lines 4 through 13 in the P-TECS pseudocode.

Step 3: For m that cannot be directly delivered to dn, sn delivers m to rn_{max}. At this time, rn_{next} is rn_{max}. After delivery, add copies of m from M. If the number of copies of m is greater than cx, delete m from M. This step corresponds to lines 14 to 23 in P-TECS pseudo code.

Step 4: Repeat steps 2 and 3 until M in the sn cache is empty. This step corresponds to lines 24 through 27 in the pseudo code.

4   Simulations and Analyses

4.1   Simulation Settings

This paper uses ONE [17] v1.6.0 as the simulation platform. The data obtained by this platform can be used to calculate the encounter probability, cumulative encounter duration, remaining energy, remaining buffer and social engagement of nodes. Comparing and analyzing the messages delivery rate, routing overhead rate, and average remaining energy of the node of P-TECS with Epidemic, Prophet, and EC-CW [18], the performance improvement of P-TECS to Opportunistic Networks can be evaluated. Both P-TECS and EC-CW contain the energy balance mechanism of the node, that is, nodes consider the impact of the remaining energy of the node on messages forwarding when selecting relay nodes. Simulation settings are shown in Table 1:

4.2   Results Analyses

It can be seen from Fig. 1 that as the initial cache of the node increases, P-TECS overall has the highest messages delivery rate. Epidemic uses the flooding mechanism to forward messages, which makes many nodes unable to receive messages due to energy consumption or cache overflow, and has a low message delivery rate. Prophet only forwards messages to the relay node with the highest probability of meeting the destination node, which reduces the possibility of node energy consumption or node cache overflow, and has a higher message delivery rate than Epidemic. EC-CW only forwards messages to the relay node with the highest communication relay degree with the destination node. The selected relay node has sufficient remaining energy and remaining cache, further reducing the possibility of node energy consumption or node cache overflow, and has a higher message delivery rate than Prophet. P-TECS selects relay nodes according to the communication relay degree of nodes that integrate the cumulative social engagement, which reflects the social relationship of nodes, making the

Table 1. Parameter settings of simulation.

Category	Parameter	Value
Scenario settings	Simulation area size (m)	4500 × 3600
	Simulation time (s)	10000–90000
	Initial energy (mAh)	240000
	Scan energy (mAh)	12
	Transmit energy (mAh)	10
	Scan interval (s)	100
	Pedestrian nodes amount (pcs)	40 × 2
	Pedestrian nodes buffersize (MB)	5–25
	Tram nodes amount (pcs)	2 × 3
	Tram nodes buffersize (MB)	50

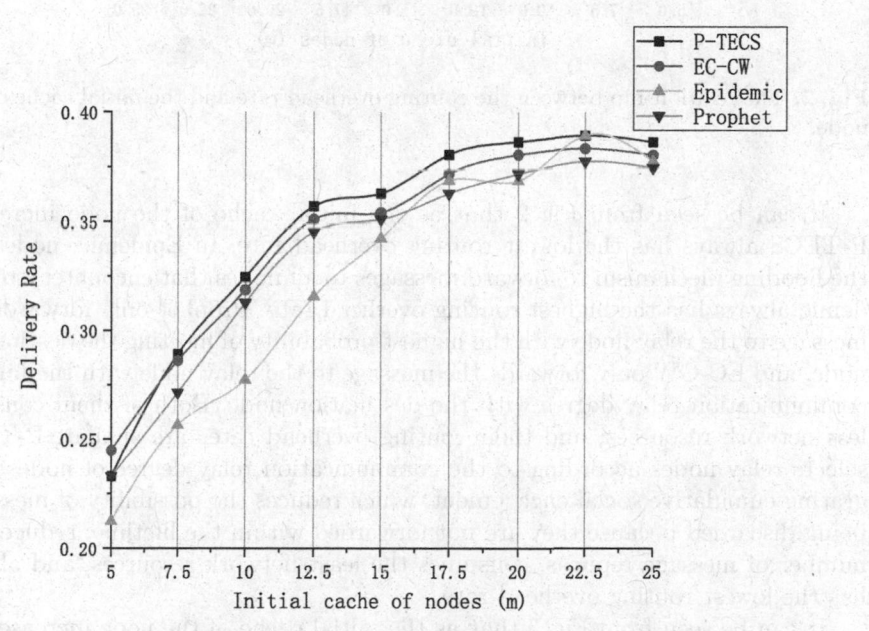

Fig. 1. The relationship between the messages delivery rate and the initial cache of the node.

relay nodes selected by P-TECS more likely to forward messages, reducing the possibility of messages being discarded because they are not forwarded within their lifetime, and having the highest message delivery rate overall.

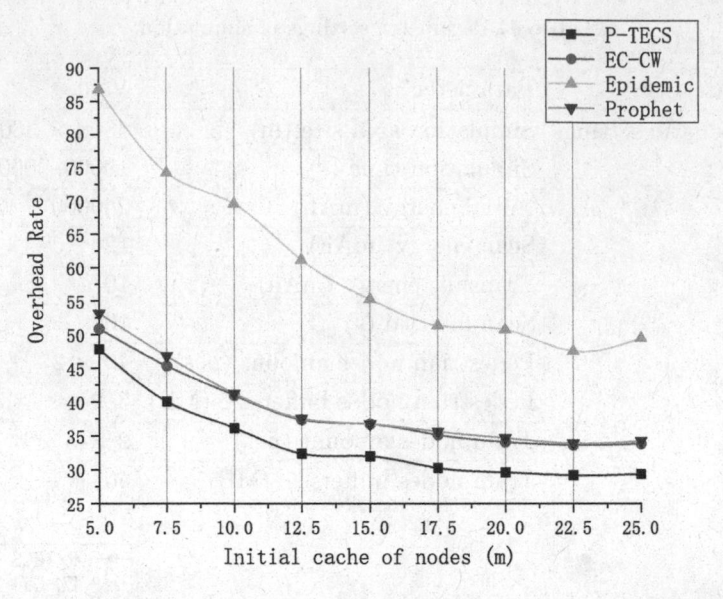

Fig. 2. The relationship between the routing overhead rate and the initial cache of the node.

It can be seen from Fig. 2 that as the initial cache of the node increases, P-TECS always has the lowest routing overhead rate. In Epidemic, nodes use the flooding mechanism to forward messages to all nodes that encounter, so Epidemic always has the highest routing overhead rate. Prophet only forwards the message to the relay node with the highest probability of meeting the destination node, and EC-CW only forwards the message to the relay node with the highest communication relay degree with the destination node. Both of them consume less network resources, and their routing overhead rates are similar. P-TECS selects relay nodes according to the communication relay degree of nodes integrating cumulative social engagement, which reduces the possibility of messages being discarded because they are not forwarded within the lifetime, reduces the number of message replicas, consumes the least network resources, and always has the lowest routing overhead rate.

It can be seen from Fig. 3 that as the initial cache of the node increases, P-TECS always has the highest average remaining energy. Epidemic uses the flooding mechanism to forward messages, which consumes the most energy and always has the lowest average remaining energy of nodes. In this simulation, Prophet uses the node sleep mechanism to make nodes with less remaining energy enter the sleep state and no longer forward messages. EC-CW uses the node energy balance mechanism to reduce the possibility of nodes with less remaining energy becoming relay nodes. Both of them balance the node energy consumption, and the average remaining energy of the two nodes are similar. In addition to using the node energy balance mechanism, P-TECS also reduces the number of mes-

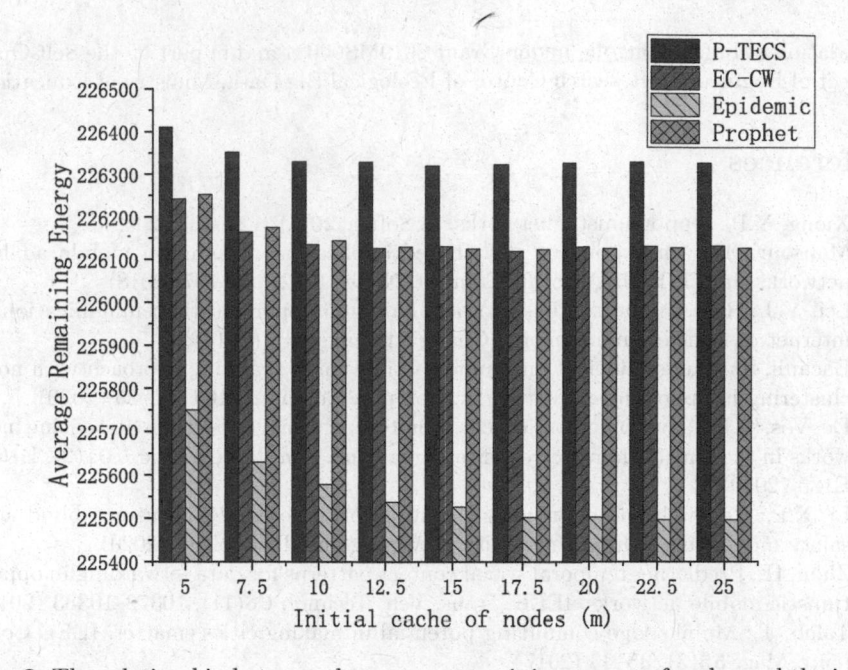

Fig. 3. The relationship between the average remaining energy of nodes and the initial cache of the node.

sage replicas, further reduces the node energy consumption, and has the highest average remaining energy of the node.

5   Conclusion

Existing opportunistic routing algorithms rarely integrate energy balance and buffer optimization mechanisms of the node with various node-dynamic-attributes, which leads to the following two main problems in opportunistic networks: active nodes enter the dead state prematurely due to they consume too much energy; nodes with insufficient buffer and infrequent social interaction discard many messages during the messages forwarding process. To solve the above challenges, this paper defines the communication relay degree between nodes based on the encounter probability, cumulative encounter duration, remaining energy, remaining buffer and social relationship between nodes, and then P-TECS: an energy balance algorithm for opportunistic networks integrating multiple node attributes is proposed. The simulation results show that in resource-constrained Opportunistic Networks, P-TECS significantly improves the messages delivery rate and the average remaining energy of nodes, and significantly reduces the routing overhead rate.

Acknowledgment. This work was supported by the National Natural Science Foundation of China under Grants 62061036, 61841109, and 62077032; Natural Science

Foundation of Inner Mongolia under Grant 2019MS06031 and in part by the Self-Open Project of Engineering Research Center of Ecological Big Data, Ministry of Education.

References

1. Xiong, Y.P.: Opportunistic networks. J. Softw. **20**(1), 124–137 (2009)
2. Mansouri, H.: Checkpointing distributed application running on mobile ad hoc networks. Int. J. High Perform. Comput. Netw. **11**(2), 95–107 (2018)
3. Lei, Y.J.: Research on routing protocol based on opportunistic communication in internet of vehicles environment. Chang'an University (2018)
4. Bacanli, S.: Energy-efficient unmanned aerial vehicle scanning approach with node clustering in opportunistic networks. Comput. Commun. **161**, 76–85 (2020)
5. De Vos, L.D.: Hydrometeorological monitoring using opportunistic sensing networks in the Amsterdam metropolitan area. Bull. Am. Meteor. Soc. **101**(2), E167–E185 (2019)
6. Li, X.P.: Research on opportunistic routing for mine wireless coverage blind area safety monitoring. China University of Mining and Technology (2020)
7. Zhou, H.: Predicting temporal social contact patterns for data forwarding in opportunistic mobile networks. IEEE Trans. Veh. Technol. **66**(11), 10372–10383 (2017)
8. Taleb, T.: Mobile edge computing potential in making cities smarter. IEEE Commun. Mag. **55**(3), 38–43 (2017)
9. Ma, H.: Application of throughput rate-based Prophet routing in DTN. Comput. Technol. Dev. **28**(7), 187–191 (2018)
10. Zhang, F.: The ProPHET routing algorithm. Comput. Eng. Design **36**(5), 1145–1149 (2015)
11. Fradj, H.B., Anane, R., Bouallegue, R.: Energy consumption for opportunistic routing algorithms in WSN. In: 2018 IEEE 32nd International Conference on Advanced Information Networking and Applications, pp. 259–265. IEEE, Krakow (2018)
12. Bista, B.B., Rawat, D.B.: EA-PRoPHET: an energy aware PRoPHET-based routing protocol for delay tolerant networks. In: 2017 IEEE 31st International Conference on Advanced Information Networking and Applications, pp. 670–677. IEEE, Taipei (2017)
13. Chen, Z.G.: Social relationship-based data transmission mechanisms in opportunistic social networks. J. Huazhong Univ. Sci. Technol. (Nat. Sci. Edn.) **49**(2), 79–84 (2021)
14. Xu, G., Xu, Z.D., He, Y.: Opportunistic networks routing algorithm based on the uncertain social relationship. In: 2018 IEEE 22nd International Conference on Computer Supported Cooperative Work in Design, pp. 301–306. IEEE, Nanjing (2018)
15. Lindgren, A.: Probabilistic routing in intermittently connected networks. Serv. Assur. Partial Intermittent Resour. **7**(3), 19–20 (2013)
16. Chen, Z.G.: Energy balanced routing algorithm for opportunistic network based on message importance. J. Commun. **39**(12), 91–101 (2018)
17. Wang, Z.: Research on opportunistic network simulator ONE and its extension. Appl. Res. Comput. **29**(1), 272–277 (2012)
18. Chen, J.J., Xu, G., Wu, X.R., Wei, F.Q., He, L.Q.: Energy balance and cache optimization routing algorithm based on communication willingness. In: 2021 IEEE Wireless Communications and Networking Conference, pp. 1–6. IEEE, Nanjing (2021)

Network Situation Awareness Model Based on Incomplete Information Game

Hongbin Zhang[1,2], Yan Yin[1], Dongmei Zhao[2(✉)], Bin Liu[3,4], Yanxia Wang[5], and Zhen Liu[1]

[1] School of Information Science and Engineering, Hebei University of Science and Technology, Shijiazhuang 050000, China
[2] Hebei Key Laboratory of Network and Information Security, Hebei Normal University, Shijiazhuang 050024, Hebei, China
zhaodongmei666@126.com
[3] School of Economics and Management, Hebei University of Science and Technology, Shijiazhuang 050000, China
[4] Research Center of Big Data and Social Computing, Hebei University of Science and Technology, Shijiazhuang 050000, China
[5] Hebei Geological Workers' University, Shijiazhuang 050081, China

Abstract. Game theory has been widely used in network security situational awareness. However, most of the currently proposed game based offensive and defensive situational awareness methods are for traffic data, and there are fewer models or methods for analysis using vulnerability data. To overcome these issues, this paper proposes collecting periodic security vulnerability information in the network and utilizing the change in vulnerability status to achieve network security situational awareness. At this time, a network attack and defense game model based on incomplete information is proposed, which uses the state changes of the vulnerability life cycle to model the attack and defense behavior, calculates the benefits of both attack and defense through the evaluation of the exploitability of the vulnerability, and then quantifies the security situation value. We carried out the experiments using the vulnerability dataset, which was obtained by scanning the IP addresses of several enterprises in Hebei Province, China. The experimental results show that the approach of using network security vulnerabilities to assess network security status is feasible.

Keywords: Situation awareness · incomplete information · attack-defense game · vulnerability lifecycle · state transition matrix

1 Introduction

Nowadays, the network is moving towards large scale, big data, and multiple levels. At the same time, the types and number of attacks have increased dramatically. The number of security vulnerabilities released by the China National Vulnerability Database (CNVD) in 2021 was as high as 26,562, an increase of 24.2% compared with the previous year.

Q. Jiang et al. (Eds.): SPNCE 2022, LNICST 496, pp. 167–178, 2023.
https://doi.org/10.1007/978-3-031-30623-5_12

Due to the untimely discovery and patching of vulnerability information, users continue to suffer from attacks, resulting in the network status being unpromising. To address the many potential risks in the network, network security situational awareness (NSSA) has been created.

Network situation awareness was defined as the acquisition, understanding, and display of security elements that can bring about the network situation changes in a large-scale network environment, as well as the prediction of network development trends [1]. By extracting and comprehensively understanding many network security risk elements, situational awareness can evaluate the network security status and predict the impact of risks [2 3, 4, 5]. Therefore, using situational awareness to discover potential threats and respond has become a research priority in network security [6–8].

In 1999, game theory model theory gradually emerged in the field of network security and was applied to the assessment of network security status [9]. Game theory is the theory of strategy selection and confrontation between different game parties, and the process of network attack and defense is to use the limited resources in the network to select the appropriate strategy for confrontation, and the process is in line with the idea of game [10]. The literature [11] uses stochastic games to assess the network security posture and constructs an assessment model. In order to solve the problem that the power IoT is vulnerable to security threats due to the weak distributed open structure, the literature [12] proposes to construct a differential game model to model the interaction behavior of power IoT smart terminals and attackers, and gives the optimal defense strategy for the system by solving for the equilibrium value. In addition to this, network attack and defense games are combined with attack graphs [13, 14], Markov theory [15], and Bayesian networks [16] for situational awareness of the network.

In local area networks or small-scale networks, network security situational aware-ness is primarily based on the analysis of attack traffic data [17, 18]. However, in the context of large-scale networks, the amount of traffic data is huge and the workload on data processing is high. As a result, NSSA becomes more difficult and accuracy is greatly reduced. To overcome these issues, this paper collects information on security vulnerabilities by probing the network assets, analyses the state of the vulnerabilities, and then builds an attack-defense game model based on incomplete information accord-ing to the transfer of each state in the vulnerability lifecycle. Drawing on the Common Vulnerability Scoring System (CVSS) to evaluate the exploitability of vulnerabilities, this paper achieves a quantitative assessment of the network situation.

In summary, considering the characteristics of large-scale networks with complex topology, numerous network nodes, and difficulty in processing traffic information. The main contributions of this paper are divided into two points: 1) According to the peri-odic changes of vulnerabilities in the network, the vulnerability state transition matrix is determined. Combined with the attacker's ability, vulnerability availability, and the expected probability of vulnerability repair, the matrix is revised to improve the accuracy of the state transition matrix. 2) An incomplete information attack-defense game model is constructed, which uses CVSS to evaluate the exploitability of vulnerabilities, and quantifies the network security situation value.

2 State Transfer for Vulnerability

2.1 Vulnerability Lifecycle and State Transition Matrix

Vulnerabilities are flaws or errors in the specific implementation of hardware, software, protocols, or the customization of system security policies, which may be exploited intentionally or unintentionally, allowing outsiders to gain unauthorized access or destroy the system. The vulnerability lifecycle describes the entire process of a vulnerability from creation to remediation, and it is divided into 5 stages, as shown in Fig. 1.

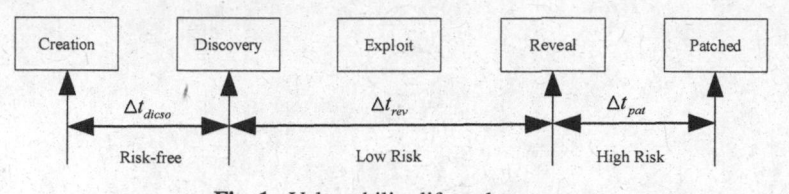

Fig. 1. Vulnerability lifecycle stages

2.2 State Transition Matrix

2.2.1 Determination of State Transition Matrix

As the life cycle of a vulnerability has different status characteristics at different times, this paper divides the life cycle status of the vulnerability into two categories: vulnerability disclosure and vulnerability undisclosed, and analyzes the life cycle of the vulnerability respectively.

- *Vulnerability disclosure*

After the vulnerability is disclosed, the vulnerability database records most of the information about the vulnerability such as the type, discovery time, collection time, and patch program. The life cycle is complete, and the state transition model is shown in Fig. 2. At this time, the vulnerability state transition matrix is given in Eq. (1).

$$Q_1 = \begin{bmatrix} P_{CC} & P_{CD} & 0 & 0 \\ 0 & P_{DD} & P_{DR} & P_{DE} \\ 0 & 0 & P_{RR} & P_{RE} \\ 0 & 0 & 0 & 1 \end{bmatrix} \tag{1}$$

In the formula, $State_a$ ($a = Cre, Dis, Rev, Exp$) is a tuple representation of each state of the vulnerability lifecycle. P_{ab} denotes the probability of a vulnerability moving from $State_a$ to $State_b$ in one step. The sum of the probabilities of transitioning from one state to another is 1.

The transition probability of each state is calculated as follows:

$$P_{CD} = \sum_{k=1}^{x} \left(\frac{NumAdd(State_{Cre \to Dis})_k}{Num(State_{Cre \to Dis})_{k-1}} \right) \Big/ x \tag{2}$$

$$P_{CC} = 1 - P_{CD} \tag{3}$$

Among: $NumAdd(State_{Cre \to Dis})_k$ represents the number of state transfers from $State_{Cre}$ to $State_{Dis}$, after the result of the kth scan. $Num(State_{Cre \to Dis})_{k-1}$ represents the number of identical state transfers, after the result of the $k\text{-}1th$ scan. By analogy, other vulnerability state transfer probabilities are calculated. $P_{DR} \sim P_{EE}$ can be calculated using the same method.

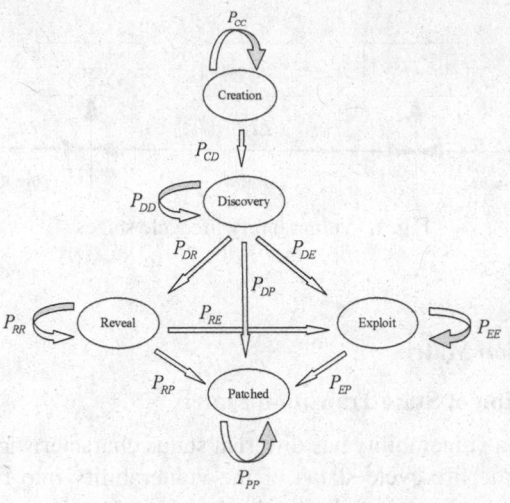

Fig. 2. State transition model

- *Vulnerability undisclosed*

When a vulnerability is not publicly disclosed, the exploitation of the vulnerability and the availability of patches have not yet been determined. Figure 3 illustrates the state transition model when the vulnerability is undisclosed.

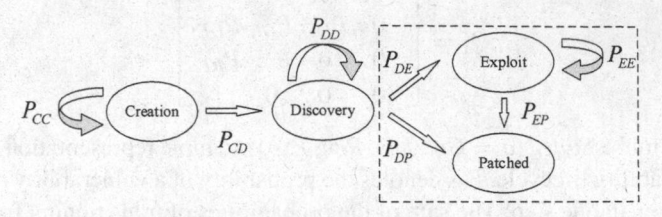

Fig. 3. State transition model when the vulnerability is undisclosed

The state transition matrix Q_2 is divided into 4 cases, namely, the vulnerability is not exploited and the security vendor has not provided a patch, the vulnerability is not exploited but the patch has been provided, the vulnerability is exploited but the patch has not been provided, the vulnerability is exploited and the patch has been provided. Therefore, Q_2 is:

$$Q_{21} = \begin{bmatrix} P_{CC} & P_{CD} \\ 0 & 1 \end{bmatrix} Q_{22} = \begin{bmatrix} P_{CC} & P_{CD} & 0 \\ 0 & P_{DD} & P_{DE} \\ 0 & 0 & 1 \end{bmatrix} Q_{23} = \begin{bmatrix} P_{CC} & P_{CD} & 0 & 0 \\ 0 & P_{DD} & P_{DE} & P_{DP} \\ 0 & 0 & P_{DE} & P_{DP} \\ 0 & 0 & 0 & 1 \end{bmatrix} Q_{24} = \begin{bmatrix} P_{CC} & P_{CD} & 0 \\ 0 & P_{DD} & P_{DP} \\ 0 & 0 & 1 \end{bmatrix}$$

2.2.2 Correction of State Transition Matrix

The state transition probability of vulnerability is also related to the attacker's ability, the exploitability of the vulnerability, and the repair of the vulnerability. Therefore, define the correction function ρ of the vulnerability state transition matrix as Eq. (4).

$$\rho = \left(\sum_{\alpha=1}^{3} AB(\alpha) \cdot EA \cdot EP(Vuln) \right) \Big/ 3 \tag{4}$$

AB represents the ability of the attacker. According to the ability of the attacker, the attacker is divided into 3 levels: junior attacker, skilled attacker, and professional. The probability is set as 4/5, 4/25, and 1/25. EA represents the availability of vulnerabilities. According to the CVSS3.0, Table 1 lists the relevant indicators, description information, classification, and impact score of the vulnerability exploits. According to CVSS3.0, the calculation formula for EA is Eq. (5).

$$EA = 8.22 \times AV \times AC \times PR \times UI \tag{5}$$

Table 1. Vulnerability availability indicator score

Indicator	Classification	Score
Attack Vector (AV)	Network/Adjacent/Local/Physical	0.85/0.62/0.55/0.2
Attack Complexity (AC)	Low/High	0.77/0.44
Permission Requirement (PR)	None/Low/High	0.85/0.62/0.27
User Interaction (UI)	None/Require	0.85/0.62

$EP(Vlun)$ is the expected probability of vulnerability repair.

$$EP(Vuln) = \sum_{k=1}^{x} \left(k_{Dis \to Pat} \, k_{Rev \to Pat} \, k_{Exp \to Pat} \right) \begin{bmatrix} P_{DP} \\ P_{RP} \\ P_{EP} \end{bmatrix} \tag{6}$$

According to ρ, the correct result of the state transition matrix is $Q' = \rho \times Q$. When the probability of vulnerability transferring to Patched is greater than the probability of vulnerability transferring to Exploit, the network is in a safe state; otherwise, it is in a dangerous state.

3   Attack-Defense Game Based on Incomplete Information

1) Model Definition

Definition 1. The Incomplete Information Attack-defense Game Model (IIADGM) describes the network attack and defense behavior in the incomplete information scenario. $IIADGM = (N, T, S, P, U)$, the meaning of each element is as follows:

N: The participants in the game.

T: $T = (T_A, T_D)$ represents the set of types of players.

S: $S_A = (S_A^1, S_A^2, \cdots, S_A^i),$, $(1 \leq i \leq n)$ denotes the set of attack strategies; the set of defense strategies is $S_D = (S_D^1, S_D^2, \cdots, S_D^j),$, $(1 \leq j \leq m)$.

P: It denotes the set of a priori beliefs of the players.

U: $U = (U_A, U_D)$ is the set of the utility function.

2) Situation Quantification

The quantification of the benefits of both sides of the game is the basis of game analysis and the key to network situation assessment.

(1) Attack Reward (AR) AR is related to the probability that the vulnerability life cycle is in Exploit (P_{Exp}) and the impact of the vulnerability on the network (IS).

$$AR = P_{Exp} \times IS \tag{7}$$

Among: IS is related to Confidentiality (C), Integrity (I), and Availability (A). (C,I,A) are divided into 3 categories, namely None, Low, and High. The corresponding scores are 0, 0.22, and 0.56. P_{Exp} and IS are calculated as follows:

$$P_{Exp} = \sum_a P(State_{a \to Exp}), a = Cre, Dis, Rev, Exp \tag{8}$$

$$IS = 10.41 \times [1 - (1 - C) \times (1 - I) \times (1 - A)] \tag{9}$$

(2) Attack Cost (AC) The cost of launching an attack varies depending on the maturity of the attacker's exploitation of the code (Pro). The more proficient the code exploitation, the fewer resources and time it consumes. Pro is divided into 4 levels: Unproven that exploit exists, Proof of concept code, Functional exploit exists, and High, corresponding to the values of 0.91, 0.94, 0.97, and 1.

In addition, AC is also related to the perfection of the patch released by the vendor (Pre). The more complete the patch release, the higher the difficulty level for an attacker to exploit the vulnerability and the higher the cost required. Pre is also divided into 4 levels: Unavailable, Workaround, Temporary fix, and Official fix, corresponding to the values of 0.91, 0.94, 0.97, and 1. So

$$AC = Roundup(EA \times Pro \times Pre) \tag{10}$$

(3) Defense Reward (*DR*) The defender takes certain defensive measures that result in the attacker not getting the expected reward. Therefore, *DR* is numerically equal to the impact on the network if the attack is successful. So $DR = AR$.

(4) Defense Cost (*DC*) The cost incurred by a defender in employing some defensive measures to repel an attack. As real-life vulnerability remediation scenarios and techniques vary, costs are not easy to quantify. This paper considers that the cost of fixing a vulnerability is related to the base score of the vulnerability and the probability of the vulnerability being patched (P_{Pat}). The equation is shown below:

$$BaseScore = Roundup(IS + EA) \tag{11}$$

$$P_{Pat} = \sum_a P(State_{a \to Pat}), a = Cre, Dis, Rev, Exp, Pat \tag{12}$$

$$DC = BaseScore \times P_{Pat} \tag{13}$$

(5) Attack Success Rate (θ) It reflects the probability that the attacker successfully exploits the vulnerability and has an impact, and is determined by the probability λ of the attack being detected and the probability β of the defense being successful.

Therefore, when the attacking and defending sides take strategies (S_A^i, S_D^j) to fight, the attack utility U_A and the defense utility U_D are:

$$U_A = \sum_{i=1}^{n} \sum_{j=1}^{m} \left\{ \left[1 - \lambda(S_D^j)\beta(S_D^j) \right] AR(S_A^i) - AC(S_A^i) \right\} \tag{14}$$

$$U_D = \sum_{j=1}^{m} \sum_{i=1}^{n} \left\{ \lambda(S_D^j)\beta(S_D^j) AR(S_A^i) - DC(S_D^j) \right\} \tag{15}$$

According to the utility value, the security situation of the target network is defined as $S = U_D - U_A$. When $S > 0$, the network is in a safe state. The larger the $|S|$, the more secure the network is. Instead, the network is in a dangerous state.

4 Experiments and Analyses

1) State Transition Matrix

To determine the state transfer matrix, this paper performs vulnerability scans on the IP addresses of the websites of over 100 enterprises in Hebei Province. Since each round of vulnerability scanning takes a long time, this paper has conducted vulnerability scanning on a 7-day cycle. The scan started on January 25, 2021, and ended on January 19, 2022, going through 52 rounds of vulnerability scanning, with a total of 587 vulnerabilities scanned. These vulnerabilities are divided into 10 types. The vulnerability types and quantity statistics are shown in Table 2.

Table 2. Vulnerability type and number statistics

Type	Quantity	Type	Quantity
HTTP Request Smuggling	5	Command Injection	8
SQL Injection	5	Directory Traversal	34
SSRF	47	Arbitrary File Deletion	47
Safe Mode Bypass	79	Unauthorized Access	13
Command Execute	73	File Upload	29

As the time of the creation of a vulnerability is not recorded in vulnerability database, the time of discovery of a vulnerability is the time of exploitation of the vulnerability. Therefore, in the experiment, this paper only discusses the transition between the 3 states of Discovery, Exploit, and Patched.

Code execution vulnerabilities were selected for state transition analysis and the probability of state occurrence for this type of vulnerability in different vulnerability scanning cycles was calculated. As code execution vulnerabilities are not continuous throughout the scanning phase, this paper extracts three scanning cycles of $k = 1-7$, $k = 19-28$, and $k = 36-46$ to calculate the probability of state occurrence. The probability change curves are shown in Fig. 4.

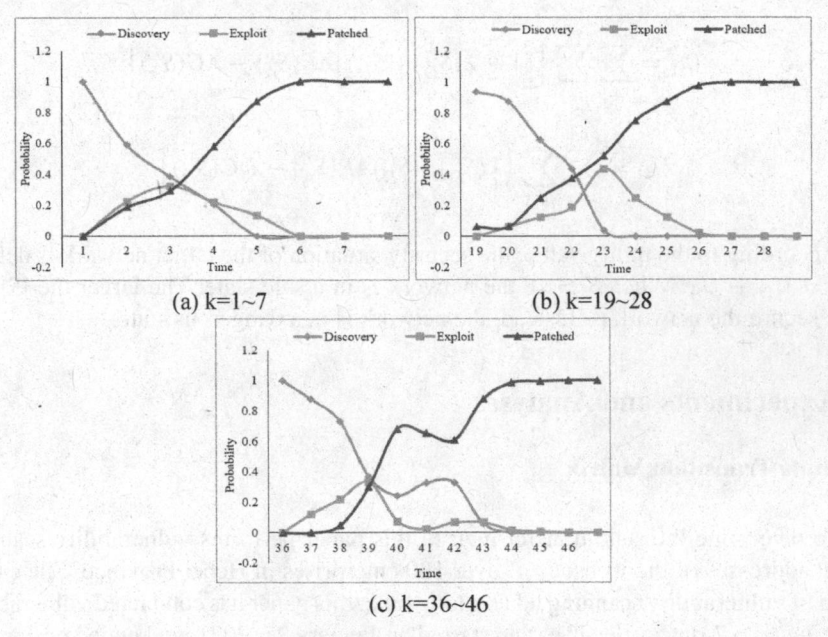

(a) k=1~7   (b) k=19~28

(c) k=36~46

Fig. 4. Probability curve

It can be seen from the Fig. 4 that: 1) In Discovery: When a vulnerability is first discovered, its probability value is 1. Over time, the vulnerability state gradually moves to the Exploit and Patched. 2) In Exploit: The Exploit state starts with a probability of 0. As the vulnerability is published and exploited, the probability of the Exploit state occurring increases and reaches the maximum value. However, after security vendors released vulnerability patches, the probability of Exploit gradually decreased. 3) In Patched: The initial probability is also 0. As the vulnerability was discovered, they began to be fixed. Over time, the probability of the Patched continues to increase, and eventually reaches a stable level.

To verify the accuracy of the state transfer method proposed in this paper, a comparative analysis with the single vulnerability state transition probability [19] method was performed. The comparison results are shown in Fig. 5.

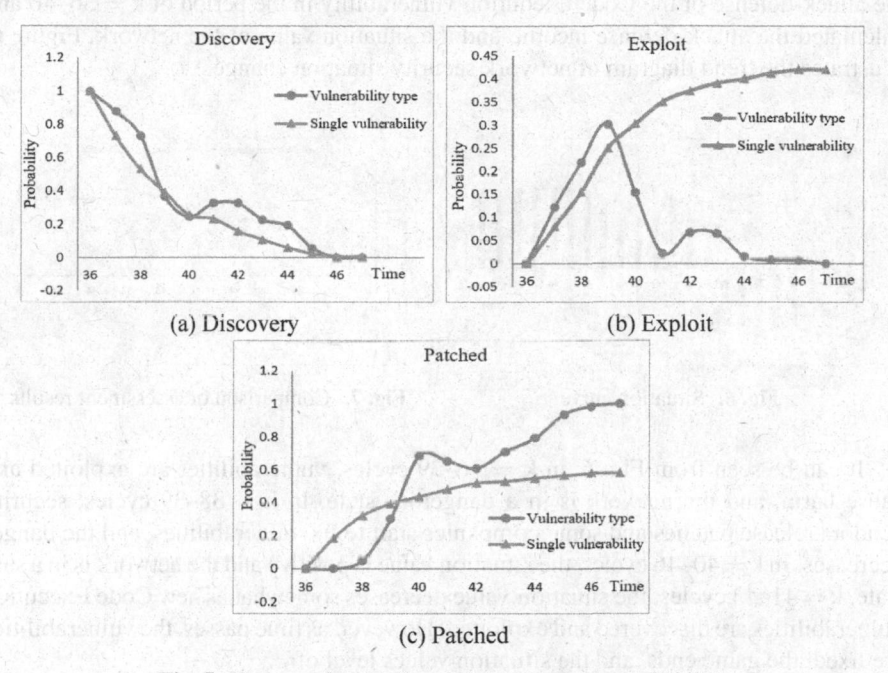

(a) Discovery   (b) Exploit

(c) Patched

Fig. 5. Comparative graphs of state occurrence probability

Figure 5 illustrates that the life cycle state transition method has 2 improvements compared to the state transition of a single vulnerability: 1) The method in this paper has a certain degree of recoverability. For example, the probability of Discovery appears to decrease, and then increase. This is because vulnerability patches are targeted, the same vulnerability patch does not fix all vulnerabilities of the same type, so vulnerabilities of that type may still be found in the next scan cycle. However, the state transition probabilities based on single vulnerabilities do not discuss this situation. 2) During the process of vulnerability state transfer, as the vulnerability is discovered and submitted, the probability of being in the Exploit increases. However, as patches are released and vulnerabilities are gradually fixed, the probability of Exploit decreases, and the probability of Patched increases. However, based on the state transition process of single vulnerabilities, the probability of the Exploit keeps rising and eventually remains unchanged, ignoring the possibility of the above situation.

The modified state transfer matrix Q' is:

$$Q' = \rho \times Q = 0.9 \times \begin{bmatrix} 0.2858 & 0.1428 & 0.5714 \\ 0 & 0.0437 & 0.9563 \\ 0 & 0 & 1 \end{bmatrix} = \begin{bmatrix} 0.2572 & 0.1285 & 0.5143 \\ 0 & 0.0393 & 0.8607 \\ 0 & 0 & 0.9 \end{bmatrix}$$

2) Situation Assessment

Combined with the state transition matrix, this paper analyzed the game process of the attack-defense of the Code Execution vulnerability in the period of k = 36–46 and calculated the attack-defense income and the situation value of the network. Figure 6. Illustrates the trend diagram of network security situation change.

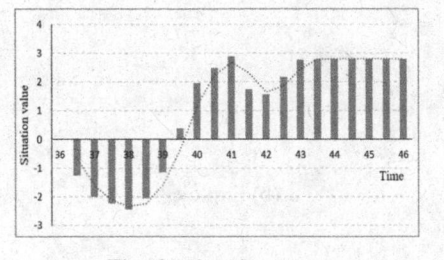
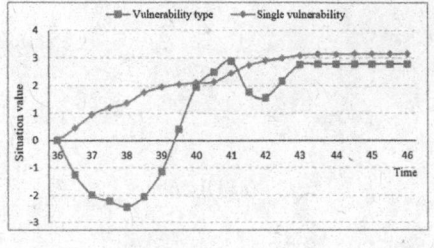

Fig. 6. Situation curve   **Fig. 7.** Comparison of assessment results

It can be seen from Fig. 6: in k = 36–39 cycles, vulnerabilities are exploited and cause harm, and the network is in a dangerous state. In k = 38–39 cycles, security vendors release patches and some companies start to fix vulnerabilities, and the danger decreases. In k = 40–46 cycles, the situation value is positive and the network is in a safe state. k = 41–43 cycles, the situation value decreases somewhat as new Code Execution vulnerabilities are discovered and exploited. However, as time passes, the vulnerabilities are fixed, the game ends, and the situation values level off.

Figure 7 compares the assessment methods based on a single vulnerability and type of vulnerability. The single-vulnerability situational assessment method only considers the risk value of the vulnerability and does not consider the reduction of the risk value after the vulnerability has been fixed. This method cannot reflect the changes in the network situation in the long term, so the vulnerability type-based situational assessment method proposed is more in line with reality.

5 Conclusions

This paper proposes to use the transition of a vulnerability state to study the network security situation. In the time dimension, the security state of the network is analyzed according to the state transition matrix of the vulnerability. Based on the process of vulnerability exploitation and repair, an incomplete information game model is constructed to assess the changes in the network situation. Through experimental analysis, the vulnerability type-based posture assessment method can provide an effective assessment of the network situation, and the assessment results are more realistic. The next work is to implement the prediction part of situational awareness and make accurate and reasonable prediction about unknown threats in the network.

References

1. Husák, M., Komárková, J., Harb, E.B., Čeleda, P.: Survey of attack projection, prediction, and forecasting in cyber security. IEEE Commun. Surv. Tutorials **21**(1), 640–660 (2018)
2. Park, M., Oh, H., Lee, K.: Security risk measurement for information leakage in IoT-based smart homes from a situational awareness perspective. Sensors **19**(9), 2148 (2019)
3. Zhang, H.B., Yi, Y.Z., Wang, J.S., Cao, N., Duan, Q.: Network security situation awareness framework based on threat intelligence. Comput. Mater. Continua **56**(3), 381–399 (2018)
4. Gong, J., Zang, X.D., Su, Q., Hu, X.Y., Xu, J.: Survey of network security situation awareness. J. Softw. **28**(4), 1010–1026 (2017)
5. Li, Y., Huang, G.-Q., Wang, C., Li, Y.-C.: Analysis framework of network security situational awareness and comparison of implementation methods. EURASIP J. Wirel. Commun. Netw. **2019**(1), 1–32 (2019). https://doi.org/10.1186/s13638-019-1506-1
6. Kou, G., Wang, S., Tang, G.: Research on key technologies of network security situational awareness for attack tracking prediction. Comput. Netw. Commun. **28**(1), 162–171 (2019)
7. Han, W.H., Tian, Z.H., Huang, Z.Z., Zhong, L., Jia, Y.: System architecture and key technologies of network security situation awareness system YHSAS. Comput. Mater. Continua **59**(1), 167–180 (2019)
8. Zhao, D., Liu, J.: Study on network security situation awareness based on particle swarm optimization algorithm. Comput. Ind. Eng. **2018**(125), 764–775 (2018)
9. Burke, D.A.: Towards a game theory model of information warfare. Airforce Institute of Technology (1999)
10. He, F.F., Zhang, Y.Q., Liu, H.Z., Zhou, W.: SCPN-based game model for security situational awareness in the internet of things. In: 2018 IEEE Conference on Communications and Network Security (CNS), pp. 1–5. IEEE, Beijing (2018)
11. Li, T.F., Li, Q., Yu, X., Wu, D.Y.: A topological vulnerability analysis-based network security situational awareness model. J. Comput. Sci. **38**(S2), 157–163+169 (2018)
12. Li, Z., Liu, Y.Z., Liu, D., Zhang, N., Lu, D.W., Huang, X.G.: A security defense model for ubiquitous electric internet of things based on game theory. In: 2020 IEEE 4th Conference on Energy Internet and Energy System Integration (EI2), pp. 3125–3128. IEEE, Wuhan (2020)
13. Jin, Z.G., Wang, J.X., Li, G., Yue, M.S.: A network defense policy generation method incorporating attack graphs and game models. Inf. Netw. Secur. **21**(01), 1–9 (2021)
14. J. Liu, Y. C. Zhang, H. Hu, J. L. Tan, Q. Len and C. W. Zhang: Efficient Defense Decision-Making Approach for Multistep Attacks Based on the Attack Graph and Game Theory. Mathematical Problems in Engineering (2020)
15. Li, X., Lu, Y., Liu, S., Nie, W.: Network security situation assessment method based on Markov game model. KSII Trans. Internet Inf. Syst. (TIIS) **12**(5), 2414–2428 (2018)
16. Hu, H., Liu, Y.L., Zhang, H.Q., Pan, R.X.: Optimal network defense strategy selection based on incomplete information evolutionary game. IEEE Access **6**, 29806–29821 (2018)
17. Liao, Y.W., Zhao, G., Wang, J., Li, S.: Network security situation assessment model based on extended hidden Markov. Math. Probl. Eng. 2020 (2020)

18. Shang, L., Zhao, W., Zhang, J., Fu, Q., Zhao, Q., Yang, Y.: Network security situation prediction based on long short-term memory network. In: 2019 20th Asia-Pacific Network Operations and Management Symposium (APNOMS), pp. 1–4. IEEE,Matsue (2019)
19. Hu, H., Ye, R.G., Zhang, H.Q., Chang, D.X., Liu, Y.L., Yang, Y.J.: Vulnerability life cycle oriented security risk metric method. J. Softw. **29**(5), 1213–1229 (2018)

Author Index

Printed in the United States
by Baker & Taylor Publisher Services

Printed in the United States
by Baker & Taylor Publisher Services